The Politics of Memory in the Italian Populist Radical Right

The Politics of Memory in the Italian Populist Radical Right examines the role of colonial memory in the contemporary Italian populist radical right, which includes the Lega and Fratelli d'Italia (FdI).

The book originally adopts postcolonialism as an analytical framework to critically examine which roles colonial memory plays in the Italian populist radical right. Considering the timeframe between 2013 and 2021, this book suggests that the contemporary Italian populist radical right selectively shaped its memory of the colonial past, expunging the most difficult aspects from it. The fact that the Italian populist radical right parties examined do not fully acknowledge the controversial aspects of Italy's colonial past, which are bracketed off discourse, may contribute to the deployment of colonial discourse by these same parties when discussing immigration. From this Italian case study, broader implications can be drawn regarding the role of colonial memory in political discourse, which is a topical matter across Europe.

The book will be of interest to those studying populism, the radical right, Italian politics and history, colonialism, and the politics of memory.

Marianna Griffini is a Lecturer in International Political Economy at the Department of European and International Studies at King's College London, UK.

Routledge Studies in Fascism and the Far Right
Series editors

Nigel Copsey, Teesside University, UK and Graham Macklin, Center for Research on Extremism (C-REX), University of Oslo, Norway.

This book series focuses upon national, transnational and global manifestations of fascist, far right and right-wing politics primarily within a historical context but also drawing on insights and approaches from other disciplinary perspectives. Its scope also includes anti-fascism, radical-right populism, extreme-right violence and terrorism, cultural manifestations of the far right, and points of convergence and exchange with the mainstream and traditional right.

Titles include:

Histories of Fascism and Anti-Fascism in Australia
Edited by Evan Smith, Jayne Persian and Vashti Jane Fox

Foreign Fighters in Ukraine
The Brown–Red Cocktail
Kacper Rękawek

The Nazi Party and the German Communities Abroad
The Latin American Case
João Fábio Bertonha and Rafael Athaides

Nazi Occultism
Between the SS and Esotericism
Stéphane François

The Rise of the Radical Right in the Global South
Edited by Rosana Pinheiro-Machado and Tatiana Vargas-Maia

Global Identitarianism
Edited by José Pedro Zúquete and Riccardo Marchi

The Politics of Memory in the Italian Populist Radical Right
From Mare Nostrum to Mare Vostrum
Marianna Griffini

For more information about this series, please visit: www.routledge.com/ Routledge-Studies-in-Fascism-and-the-Far-Right/book-series/FFR

The Politics of Memory in the Italian Populist Radical Right
From Mare Nostrum to Mare Vostrum

Marianna Griffini

LONDON AND NEW YORK

First published 2023
by Routledge
4 Park Square, Milton Park, Abingdon, Oxon OX14 4RN

and by Routledge
605 Third Avenue, New York, NY 10158

Routledge is an imprint of the Taylor & Francis Group, an informa business

© 2023 Marianna Griffini

The right of Marianna Griffini to be identified as author of this work has been asserted in accordance with sections 77 and 78 of the Copyright, Designs and Patents Act 1988.

All rights reserved. No part of this book may be reprinted or reproduced or utilised in any form or by any electronic, mechanical, or other means, now known or hereafter invented, including photocopying and recording, or in any information storage or retrieval system, without permission in writing from the publishers.

Trademark notice: Product or corporate names may be trademarks or registered trademarks, and are used only for identification and explanation without intent to infringe.

British Library Cataloguing-in-Publication Data
A catalogue record for this book is available from the British Library

ISBN: 978-1-032-17200-2 (hbk)
ISBN: 978-1-032-18043-4 (pbk)
ISBN: 978-1-003-25259-7 (ebk)

DOI: 10.4324/9781003252597

Typeset in Times New Roman
by Deanta Global Publishing Services, Chennai, India

Contents

Preface viii
Acknowledgements ix

Introduction 1

1 The Italian Populist Radical Right: Debates and the Missing Link with Memory 10

1.1 Introduction 10
1.2 Self-Definition v. Academic Definitions of the Populist Radical Right 11
1.3 The Ideational Approach: The Populist Radical Right Ideology Unpacked 11
1.4 Who Belongs to the Italian Populist Radical Right? Taxonomy and Historical Development of the Lega and FdI 13
1.5 The Co-optation of the Populist Radical Right 14
1.6 The Populist Radical Right and Colonialism: A Gap to Fill 15
1.7 Conclusion 18
Notes 19
References 19

2 Nation and Race: The Theoretical Roots of Nativism 23

2.1 Introduction 23
2.2 The Janus-Faced Nation 24
2.3 Nationalism + Racism = Nativism 25
2.4 Italy's Presumed Immunity to Racism 26
2.5 Nativism beyond the Populist Radical Right Confines 28
2.6 Conclusion 30
Notes 31
References 31

| 3 | **Research Design** | 35 |

References   37

| 4 | **"Italians First": The Ethno-cultural Nation with Civic Undertones** | 39 |

4.1 Introduction   39
4.2 The Ethno-cultural Nation   40
4.3 The Civic Nation   43
4.4 The Anathema of Multiculturalism   43
4.5 Who Belongs to the Italian Nation?   45
4.6 Conclusion   47
Notes   48
References   48

| 5 | **"I am not racist, but ...": Problematisation, Differentiation, and Othering of Immigration** | 50 |

5.1 Introduction   50
5.2 Problematisation of Immigration   51
5.3 Differentiation of Immigration   57
5.4 Othering of Immigration   61
5.5 Conclusion   69
Notes   70
References   71

| 6 | **Echoes from Colonialism: Criminalisation, Inferiorisation, and Abjectification of Immigration** | 75 |

6.1 Introduction   75
6.2 Criminalisation of Immigration   75
6.3 Inferiorisation of Immigration   89
6.4 Abjectification of Immigration   94
6.5 Conclusion   96
Notes   100
References   100

| 7 | **Memory and Forgetting: The Colonial Past in the Italian Populist Radical Right** | 106 |

7.1 Introduction   106
7.2 The Rejection of the Link between Colonialism and Immigration   107
7.3 Selective Colonial Memory: What is Remembered   109

    7.4 Selective Colonial Memory: What is Forgotten   113
    7.5 Conclusion   120
    Notes   122
    References   122

8 Memory and Forgetting: The Fascist Past in the Italian Populist Radical Right   126

    8.1 Introduction   126
    8.2 Fascist Residues in the Italian Right?   127
    8.3 Selective Fascist Memory: What Causes Discomfort and What Is Forgotten   128
    8.4 Selective Fascist Memory: What Is Celebrated and What Is Remembered   129
    8.5 Of Mixed Assessments of Fascism   131
    8.6 Reasons for Selective Memory   132
    8.7 The Politics of Memory: Bringing Together the Strands of the Argument   134
    8.8 Conclusion   136
    Notes   138
    References   138

Conclusion   141
Contemporary Significance of the Research and Research Puzzle   141
The Argument of the Book   142
Contribution to the Literature   143
Key Takeaways from the Book   156
Note   156
References   156

Postscript   159
Primary Sources   165
Appendix 1 Rationale for Interview Questions   167
Index   171

Preface

The Italian populist radical right, anti-immigrant sentiment, and colonial memory are profoundly linked. The connection between the former two concepts is straightforward, since hostility to immigration is an ideological staple of populist radical right parties. Conversely, the nexus interconnecting the Italian populist radical right and anti-immigrant sentiment with colonial memory is less apparent. Unsurprisingly, a number of disciplines, ranging from Political Science, to Sociology, History, and Discourse Studies, have grappled with the ideology of the populist radical right, but comparatively fewer studies have analysed the nexus between the anti-immigrant ideology of these parties and the memory of the colonial past they construct. However, such nexus deserves scholarly attention, as hostility against immigrants coming to Italy through the Mediterranean route is underpinned by a specific articulation of colonial memory on the part of Fratelli d'Italia (FdI) and the Lega.

In order to investigate this significant and complex relationship, the aim of this book is to offer a fresh reading of the populist radical right's anti-immigrant discourse through a postcolonial perspective. The analysis will be primarily focused on colonial memory, while being mindful of the inextricability of colonialism and fascism, since fascism represented the most prosperous phase of colonialism. The central argument is that the Italian populist radical right has articulated immigration by reiterating colonial discourse, peppered with fascist tropes. In doing so, it has engaged in the transfiguration of the Mediterranean from a *Mare Nostrum* (a space through which fascist Italy extended its natural and necessary *spazio vitale*) to what I define as a "Mare Vostrum" (a space that is a source of danger as it washes up seemingly "undesired immigrants" onto Italian shores).

Acknowledgements

Speaking about racism, fascism, and colonialism in Italy is an arduous undertaking, as it probes topics that have long been deemed divisive and uncomfortable to discuss. This onerous task was made possible thanks to the generous financial support provided by the Fondazione Einaudi (Turin) and the UK Economic and Social Research Council, as well as several travel grants offered by the Centre for Doctoral Studies at King's College London and the School of Social Policy and Politics at King's College London. In the PhD phase of the project, I was guided by apt supervisors. Dr Jim Wolfreys, Professor John Foot, and Professor Derek Duncan provided food for thought with their numerous comments. Dr Roberto Roccu provided insightful comments on different chapters and constant encouragement and support, well beyond the lifespan of the PhD project. Professor Marcello Carmagnani, from Fondazione Einaudi, infused me with courage to proudly and openly challenge the view that the Italian populist radical right is immune to racism and residual fascism.

Dr Manuel Anselmi, Dr Andrea Mammone, Professor Carlo Ruzza, and Professor Michele Sorice became invaluable far-sighted, generous, and sensitive mentors, helping me wade through the murky waters of the end of my PhD and my first years as an early career researcher. Last, but not least, the completion of this book has greatly benefitted from the professional and diligent help of Maria Chiara Aquilino and Laura Montecchio, who have assisted my research at different times in the project, and of Laura Fano, who has been of invaluable help in the final phase of manuscript writing.

Several academics generously shared their precious insights on the topic and provided thought-provoking comments and materials: thanks are owed to Professor Daniele Albertazzi, Dr Marco Antonsich, Professor Charles Burdett, Alessandra Ferrini, Dr Gaia Giuliani, Dr Humeira Iqtidar, Dr Gianmarco Mancosu, Dr Elizabeth Morrow, Dr Fiorenza Pedrabissi, Dr Amanda Sciampacone, Dr Simon Sleight, and Dr Stijn van Kessel. Gabriele Zagni kindly and enthusiastically shared sharp insights on the topic from his journalistic background. The interviews involved long spells of fieldwork spent in Italy: this experience was made hugely enjoyable and lively by the disarming beauty and humanity that every corner of Italy exudes. Presenting my research at several conferences further contributed to the shaping of this project; thanks go to the institutions, media, and individuals who honoured me with their invitation to present my work.

Finally, this project is the result of 13 years of an educational and professional journey around the world, which moulded my academic interests and personality. The Washington DC years were made bearable and enriching by the small Italian community in DC: Pino Cicala and Professor Lynn Westwater were my Italian roots abroad. The London years were made interesting and fun by solid friendships from around the world. The College Hall group breathed new life into my then precarious enthusiasm to live abroad; in particular, Mercedes always offered a helping hand from the other side of the ocean. The King's gang provided thought-provoking discussions, reinvigorating fun, and delicate understanding; in particular, the support of Cristina, Margherita, Matilde and Malte has been heart-warming, comforting, and encouraging. These colleagues, and, foremost, friends gave me roots when I felt rootless. They proved an unbreakable rock of understanding during a constant series of challenges, when my personal and professional lives became shaken by the COVID-19 pandemic, and the last push towards the finishing line of the PhD was an immense challenge for myself. I am thankful to Stella, for our professional exchanges and fun company in our London explorations. I am also grateful to Matia, for his patient professional guidance and unwavering encouragement during the final and eventful stretch of my PhD journey, and the rocky start of my academic career. Special gratitude is due to Talitha, who appeared later in the PhD process: our daily "press reviews" provided great stimulus for my academic development; but foremost, our friendship provided a source of heart-warming, relentless, and empathetic support.

As the last 13 years were spent straddling two continents and three countries, there are countless people to thank in Italy for their genuine sympathy and unenvious support. Especially the ones who showed utmost sensitivity and closeness in helping me gain stability: rain or shine, they were there, physically and symbolically, at my doorstep. Lastly, thanks are owed to my family, who endured the experience of a 19-year-old daughter and sister living an eventful existence on the other side of the world, when phones did not have Internet and distances were extended.

Introduction

Giorgia Meloni, Fratelli d'Italia's (FdI's) leader, has been crowned as "the opinion polls Emperor, prisoner of her own past," by the Italian newspaper *la Repubblica* in an article published in June 2022 (De Gregorio 2022). The characterisation of Meloni, the leader of FdI, as an emperor uncannily evokes the Italian past as a colonial empire, and as the cradle of fascism. The memory of the Italian past is a thorny issue, resurfacing, with different degrees of explicitness, in the discourse of the Italian populist radical right, composed of FdI and the Lega. The appropriation of the Italian past is subtly bound up with the polarisation of the debate over immigration: the Italian populist radical right occupies the right end of the polarised immigration debate, with a conspicuous anti-immigrant sentiment towards immigrants coming to Italy through the Mediterranean route.

The Mediterranean has been the deathbed of immigrants attempting to reach Italian shores. Inscribed in public memory is, especially, the 3 October 2013 shipwreck, when 368 migrants lost their lives off the coast of Lampedusa (Gatti 2017). They came mainly from Eritrea, Somalia, and Ghana (Spica 2014), but their hopes of escaping political and economic turmoil drowned in the Mediterranean. Their corpses were hastily buried in anonymous Sicilian cemeteries, while the state, in an odd twist of fate, organised official funerals with a delegation from the Eritrean government that some of the migrants were escaping from (F.Q. Redazione 2013). Later that month, the Italian government launched Operation *Mare Nostrum*, a search and rescue operation, which saved 100,000 migrants off the Italian coastline, until it was phased out at the end of 2014, due to the financial burden it was allegedly imposing on Italy, and replaced by the EU-coordinated Operation Triton, which was more limited in funds, equipment, and scope (Eduati 2016). Operation *Mare Nostrum* bears an uncanny resemblance to the name colonialism first, and fascist colonialism later, used to define the Mediterranean, at the time a much sought-after space of conquest. Nowadays, however, the Mediterranean is perceived as a space of immigration, far off from the well-desired *Mare Nostrum*.

The number of immigrants arriving in Italy through the Mediterranean route has been increasing since 2013, with a peak in 2016 with 181,436 migrant arrivals through sea crossings. After a short decline due to the COVID-19 pandemic, with 34,154 migrant arrivals registered in 2020, the numbers rose again quickly

DOI: 10.4324/9781003252597-1

to 67,040 in 2021 (Ministero dell'Interno 2022). The year 2013 was a meaningful year for Italian politics, not only as it signalled the start of an upward turn in immigrant arrivals, but also for two fateful events: Matteo Salvini arose as the Lega's leader and Giorgia Meloni, FdI's leader, contested the first national elections, after the foundation of her party the year before, recreated from the ashes of the defunct Alleanza Nazionale (AN). Since 2013, Salvini and Meloni have been dominating the Italian populist radical right arena and have deployed a nativist discourse, composed of nationalist and racist connotations.

Immigration and the Italian populist radical right are strictly intertwined: while the rise and success of the Italian populist radical right is not due to the ideological appeal of these parties' backlash against immigration, the latter plays a prominent role in these parties' ideology. The Italian populist radical right's anti-immigrant sentiment is also tightly interwoven with issues of race, colonialism, and fascism. Nativism is not a fringe phenomenon in Italy: especially, it dominates the Italian populist radical right's discourse, which reveals a particular relationship between anti-immigrant racism, and colonial and fascist memory. As the following chapters will examine, this relationship is characterised by a selective memory of colonialism and fascism. Moreover, the relationship between the Italian populist radical right's nativism[1] and colonial memory is an under-developed topic in academic literature. Colonial memory has been tied to the nationalist component of nativism, as well as to the racist one, which is the primary focus of this book.

In the literature, the examination of the link between wider Italian society's attitudes to Italy's colonial past, and Italy's stance towards immigrants is limited to the realm of Italian culture, but does not concentrate on political parties, including populist radical right ones. Populist radical right parties in Italy are the focus of existing scholarly investigation on their relationship with fascist memory. No scholarly attention has been devoted, to date, to their interaction with colonial memory. For instance, Giuliani (2018) deals extensively with the memory of colonialism in Italian culture and with nativism but does not dwell specifically on political parties. Traverso (2017) provides an insightful analysis of residual fascism in the populist radical right but does not consider the role of colonial memory on the populist radical right in Italy.

Nativism in the Italian populist radical right has attracted the attention of a copious amount of literature, since the early 1990s, when immigration started to be profiled as an issue Italy was coming to grips with, after its shift from being a country of emigration to a country of immigration (King 1993: 283). Immigration, thus, began to be politicised and anti-immigrant sentiment became prominent (Perlmutter 1996). The Italian populist radical right itself is a "complex galaxy" (Tateo 2005), composed of parties with different historical trajectories and ideologies. While acknowledging the definitional and taxonomical issues surrounding the study of the populist radical right, this book adopts the concise definition of populist radical right as a party family ideologically characterised by a call for a strong state, populism, and nativism, which bifurcates itself into nationalism and racism (Mudde 2007). Indeed, against perceived imminent social and political decay, the Italian populist radical right advocates a strict state, and promotes the will of the people as opposed to the elites, while championing a view of the nation mainly demarcated along ethno-cultural lines, which excludes the immigrant out-group.

The Italian populist radical right, since the fateful year 2013, has been dominated by the Lega and FdI. While FdI was created in 2012, the Lega took shape in the early 1990s, which was a time characterised by the corruption scandal of *Tangentopoli*[2] that badly damaged the reputation of the main parties existing at the beginning of the 1990s (Newell 2000: 475). The emergence of the Lega was also facilitated by the introduction of voting grounded in opinion rather than in clientelism, by a new mixed majoritarian and proportional electoral system (Newell 2000: 477), and by the increased salience of immigration (Caiani, Della Porta, and Wagemann 2012: 44), although initially the Lega was more markedly anti-southern than anti-immigrant (Albertazzi and Vampa 2021).

The hallmark of the Italian populist radical right, nativism, is not limited to this party family, but is also co-opted by mainstream parties (Carvalho 2014), such as the centre-right Forza Italia (FI), as well as the centre-left Partito Democratico (PD), and the Movimento Cinque Stelle (M5S), a populist party escaping classification on the left-right political spectrum (Mosca and Tronconi 2019). Nativism is also tangible in the wider population (see, for instance, Andrisani and Naletto 2009; Rivera 2020), aided by the adoption of anti-immigrant racism by competing parties, by the media (see, for instance, Barretta 2020) that propagate racist prejudice, and by the educational system, which does not encourage a critical analysis of race and racism (Caravita, Valente, and Castellani 2014). As the OHCHR 2019 report suggests, Italian school textbooks often miss accounts of Italian colonial history and are frequently inoculating racist stereotypes within children. Therefore, the OHCHR recommends that

> Italy [must] ensure that (…) its colonial past be included in the school curriculum to convey the impact of racially discriminatory policies. The Committee also recommended that Italy ensure that Roma, Sinti and Caminanti children can access quality education (…) where they suffer no segregation or negative treatment by staff or students.
>
> (2019)

The motivations underlying the populist radical right's nativism are multifaceted, ranging from an unfavourable economic situation (see, for instance, Arzheimer 2009; Anelli, Colantone, and Stanig 2019), social change (see, for instance, Knigge 1998; Zaslove 2004; Inglehart and Norris 2019), and ethnic competition theory (Gijsberts, Hagendoorn, and Scheepers 2004). The economic justifications for the populist radical right's nativism are predicated on the supposition that, at times of economic crisis, immigrants deprive the national in-group of jobs and welfare resources. This is a controversial assumption, as immigrants may not take away jobs from the in-group (Fusaro and Lopez-Bazo 2018). Moreover, historically not all countries experiencing economic crises have witnessed the rise of populist radical right's nativism, for example Spain and Portugal, and, during

4 *Introduction*

the 2008 recession, populist radical right's nativism also emerged in European countries that did not undergo an economic crisis, such as Austria and Switzerland (Hopkin 2020). The socio-demographic explanation for the populist radical right's nativism (see, for instance, Knigge 1998; Zaslove 2004), positing that immigration precipitates a loss of sense of community, is equally flawed, as immigration may also trigger tolerance of the Other (Fysh and Wolfreys 2003; Perrineau 1985). Finally, ethnic competition theory, drawing on both economic and social justifications for the populist radical right's nativism, offers a more comprehensive explanation, by supposing that at times of economic scarcity, the in-group tends to attack the out-group in order to safeguard its economic and social status (Gijsberts, Hagendoorn, and Scheepers 2004). Yet, this political psychological justification mistakenly assumes that individuals' natural tendency to scapegoat the out-group automatically results in nativist attitudes against such out-groups. Instead, first of all, both in-group and out-group are constructed and not inherently ascribed by nature. Second, while human beings by nature tend to identify themselves positively with the in-group and adopt a sceptical view of the out-group, this does not necessarily make xenophobia an intrinsic human condition.

Interesting research shows a connection between nativism and the memory of colonialism and fascism, (see, for instance, Andall and Duncan 2005; De Cesari 2012; Giuliani 2018; Ponzanesi 2005; Proglio 2019; Siddi 2020). However, to date no attention has been paid to the link between the Italian populist radical right's nativism and its stance towards its colonial past, particularly under fascism. Indeed, attention to this topic is deserved. In fact, the Italian populist radical right's nativism towards trans-Mediterranean immigration testifies to the same racism that drove the fascist belief in the superiority of the Italian ethnic nation, fuelling the fascist colonisation of territories across the Mediterranean. Therefore, it is interesting to interrogate the relationship between the Italian populist radical right and the Italian fascist colonial past, marked by continuity in nationalist and racist discourse and discontinuity in the perception of the Mediterranean.

Studies developed in different geographical contexts are useful to investigate this relationship. Indeed, Gilroy's notion of postcolonial melancholia links British nativism to a lack of mourning of the colonial past, of which immigrants are constant reminders (2005). Additionally, Mols and Jetten's study of nostalgia for a golden age similarly blames nativism on the longing for the return to an idealised past (2014). Finally, various studies have highlighted that Italians are generally reluctant to come to terms with their uncomfortable colonial, fascist, and especially fascist colonial past (see, for instance, Andall and Duncan 2005; De Cesari 2012; Foot 2009; Giuliani 2018; Manucci 2020; Ponzanesi 2005; Proglio 2019; Siddi 2020), which remains hidden on the fringes of memory.

Through the Critical Discourse Analysis (CDA) of two rounds of in-depth elite interviews with Italian populist radical right party representatives and intellectuals, conducted between 2016 and 2018, and in 2021, and of party manifestos from 2013 to 2018,[3] this monograph will uncover a correlation between the Italian populist radical right's attitudes towards Italy's colonial past, including colonialism under fascism, and its position on immigration. This project will contribute to our understanding of the role played by immigration in the discourse of the Italian populist radical right, focusing in particular on the relationship between racism against immigrants, and colonial and fascist memory. Crucially, the analysis of the politics of memory of the Italian populist radical right points to a discursive shift from the colonial and fascist representation of the Mediterranean as a treasured *Mare Nostrum,* to the Italian populist radical right's representation of the Mediterranean as a dangerous "Mare Vostrum."

The book is structured in the following way. Chapter 1 will chart the historical background of the Italian populist radical right, its taxonomy, ideology, and terminological debates surrounding it. It will make the case for the use of the term *populist radical right*, vis-à-vis the broader category of the *far right*. Chapter 1 will highlight the underappreciated missing link between nativism and colonial memory in the populist radical right. Chapter 2 will zoom onto two ideological pillars of the populist radical right's ideology: nationalism and racism, which, combined, result in nativism. Chapter 2 will make a theoretical foray into the construction of the notion of nation and race from a historical and conceptual viewpoint. In doing so, this chapter foregrounds the necessity to advance a comprehensive contextual understanding of Italy's nativism, which has its roots in Italy's colonial past, especially in its fascist stage. This chapter will lay the theoretical framework constituting an innovative take on the nativism animating the populist radical right. Chapter 3 will provide methodological considerations, justifying the use of the CDA of two rounds of in-depth elite interviews (2016–2018; 2021) and of party manifestos at times of national elections (2013–2018). This chapter will argue that the benefits of capturing nuance and complexity afforded by these data collection and data analysis methods definitely outweigh the disadvantage of subjectivity inherent to qualitative methods.

Departing from the solid theoretical foundations developed in Chapters 1 and 2, Chapters 4, 5, 6, 7, 8, and 9 will provide empirical substantiation to the main strands of the argument inherent to this book, namely the complexity of the entanglements of civic and ethno-cultural nationalism in the predominantly ethno-cultural interpretation of the nation; the intertwinement of the Italian populist radical right's notion of the nation with racist tones, which forms the nativist ideology that is a signature trait of the populist radical right; the colonial echoes surfacing in the racist discourse on immigration, which are aptly blunted by civic and more moderate traits; the selective colonial, and fascist, memory underpinning contemporary nativism.

Chapter 4 dramatises the multicoloured picture of the nation in the Lega and in FdI, by using rich interview material. What emerges challenges the monolithic view of the nation as solely ethno-cultural, and, instead, complicates the picture by highlighting strands of civic nationalism. Chapter 4 makes an attempt to painstakingly outline and explain the dilemma posed by the predominance of ethno-cultural nationalism in the Italian populist radical right, sitting uncomfortably with the discursive and symbolic opening up of the nation to regular immigrants. This move is in line with apparently antithetical goals: on the one hand, the attempt of the populist radical right to mainstream itself, by appearing more moderate and permeated by civic values; on the other hand, the attempt to further scapegoat irregular immigrants, whose exclusion from the symbolic body of the nation becomes further underlined by juxtaposing them to regular immigrants welcomed into the symbolic body of the nation.

The civic discourse becomes even more apparent in the analysis of the Lega's and FdI's otherwise racist discourse on immigration analysed in Chapters 5 and 6. These chapters are theoretically sustained by the concept of civic discourse, as well as by the reiteration of colonial rhetoric highlighted by a postcolonial analytical framework. Chapter 5 will offer insights into the Italian populist radical right's ideological elements that are linked to its nativism, in order to offer a comprehensive picture of the parties under scrutiny. This chapter will flesh out the inextricability of nativism with the call for law and order, with a sharp criticism of the multifarious category of the "elite," and with a prevailingly ethno-cultural understanding of the Italian nation. The analysis of nativism is complemented by the original detailed analysis of racism unfolding in Chapter 5 and Chapter 6. Chapter 5 will delve in depth into the Italian populist radical right's racism, in particular its problematisation, differentiation, and Othering of immigration. Chapter 6 integrates Chapter 5 with a focus on the criminalisation, inferiorisation, and abjectification[4] of immigration inherent to the racist component of nativism. Chapters 5 and 6 show the reiteration of colonial rhetoric, mixed with "civic" undertones, in the anti-immigrant discourse of the Lega and FdI.

The materialisation of colonial echoes in the racist discourse on immigration is complemented by the dematerialisation of some elements of colonial memory, when the Lega and FdI are called to reflect on immigration as well as on Italy's colonial past. This is the main argument put forward by Chapters 7 and 8. These chapters are theoretically built on the concept of the politics of memory, which is foregrounded in Chapter 1. More in detail, Chapter 7 will provide an in-depth analysis of the colonial memory held by the parties analysed. This chapter will argue that the Lega and FdI engage in a politics of memory, consciously and unconsciously constructing a selective memory of Italy's colonial past. Chapter 8 will demonstrate that a similar line of reasoning may be applied to fascist memory, which selectively picks elements of the fascist past, dooming other elements to oblivion. Dwelling on fascist memory is not coincidental or does not deflect attention away from the main focus of the book on colonial memory, because fascism constituted the most prosperous stage of Italian colonialism. Possible explanations for such selective memory are suggested.

Finally, the Conclusion will offer reflections on the relationship between the Italian populist radical right's anti-immigrant nativism, and colonial and fascist memory. Then, it will extrapolate lessons applicable to the European political context, as well as suggesting useful avenues of future research on this fascinating and incredibly complex and thorny topic.

Notes

1 Mudde (2007) uses the term *nativism*, which this project breaks down into nationalism and racism for clarity's sake. Moreover, this project deems *strong state* more appropriate to the Italian populist radical right ideology, rather than *authoritarianism*, which Mudde (2007) privileges.

2 Literally "bribe city," *Tangentopoli* was the scandal that exposed fraudulent deals between politicians and businesses.
3 The last national election contested before this book went into press took place in 2018.
4 I coined the term *abjectification* by merging the root *abject* (meaning cast off), deployed by the literature on race (see, for instance, Kristeva 1982; Gandesha 2003), with the suffix *-ification* signifying the action of casting off somebody.

References

Albertazzi, D. & Vampa, D. (2021) *Populism and New Patterns of Political Competition in Western Europe*, London: Routledge.

Andall, J. & Duncan, D. (eds) (2005) *Italian Colonialism: Legacy and Memory*, Oxford, Bern: Peter Lang.

Andrisani, P. & Naletto, G. (2009) "Cronache di ordinario razzismo", in *Rapporto sul razzismo in Italia*, Naletto, G. & Andrisani, P. (eds), Manifestolibri, Rome: Lunaria, pp. 146–152.

Anelli, M., Stanig, P. & Colantone, I. (2019) "We were the robots: Automation in manufacturing and voting behavior in Western Europe", *CreAM Discussion Paper Series, no. 1917*.

Arzheimer, K. (2009) "Contextual factors and the extreme right vote in Western Europe, 1980–2002", *American Journal of Political Science*, vol. 53, no. 2, pp. 259–275.

Barretta, P. (2020) "Luci e ombre dell'informazione mediatica sul razzismo", in *Cronache di ordinario razzismo*, Lunaria (ed.), Rome: Lunaria, pp. 30–39.

Caiani, M., Della Porta, D. & Wagemann, C. (2012) *Mobilizing on the Extreme Right Germany, Italy, and the United States*, Oxford: Oxford University Press.

Caravita, S., Castellani, T. & Valente, A. (2014) "Rappresentazione dei migranti nei libri di testo italiani di storia e geografia", *National Research Council, Institute for Research on Population and Social Policies working paper, no. 59*.

Carvalho, J., (2014) *Impact of Extreme Right Parties on Immigration Policy: Comparing Britain, France and Italy*, London: Routledge.

De Cesari, C. (2012) "The paradoxes of colonial reparation: Foreclosing memory and the 2008 Italy–Libya Friendship Treaty", *Memory Studies*, vol. 5, no. 3, pp. 316–326.

De Gregorio, C. (2022) "Meloni, l'imperatrice dei sondaggi prigioniera del suo passato", *Repubblica*. 28 June 2022. Available: https://www.repubblica.it/cronaca/2022/06/27/news/meloni_limperatrice_dei_sondaggi_prigioniera_del_suo_passato-355705268/ [20 February 2023].

Eduati, L. (2016) "'Il fuoco dentro' di Riccardo Nencini, scritti inediti di Oriana Fallaci: 'Firenze matrigna con i suoi figli migliori'", *Huffington Post*. 21 March 2016. Available: https://www.huffingtonpost.it/2016/03/21/riccardo-nencini-oriana-fallaci_n_9515600.html [November 2019].

F.Q. Redazione (2013) "Naufragio Lampedusa, i funerali celebrati senza i superstiti. Alfano contestato", *Il Fatto Quotidiano*. 21 October 2013. Available: https://www.ilfattoquotidiano.it/2013/10/21/naufragio-lampedusa-commemorazione-ad-agrigento-perche-non-sullisola/751350/ [21 May 2018].

Foot, J. (2009) *Italy's Divided Memory*, New York: Palgrave Macmillan.

Fusaro, S. & López-Bazo, E. (2018) "The impact of immigration on native employment: Evidence from Italy", *Research Institute of Applied Economics working paper, no. 22*.

Fysh, P. & Wolfreys, J. (2003) *The Politics of Racism in France*, Basingstoke: Palgrave Macmillan.

Gandesha, S. (2003) "The political semiosis of populism", *The Semiotic Review of Books*, vol. 13, no. 3, pp. 1–12.

Gatti, F. (2017) "Il naufragio di bambini strage senza colpevoli", *Repubblica*. 13 May 2017. Available: https://www.repubblica.it/cronaca/2017/05/13/news/il_naufragio_dei_bambini_strage_senza_colpevoli-165309112/?refresh_ce [21 November 2018].

Gijsberts, M., Hagendoorn, A. & Scheepers, P.L.H. (2004) *Nationalism and Exclusion of Migrants: Cross-national Comparisons*, Aldershot: Ashgate.

Gilroy, P. (2005) *Postcolonial Melancholia*, New York: Columbia University Press.

Giuliani, G. (2018) *Race, Nation and Gender in Modern Italy: Intersectional Representations in Visual Culture*, London: Palgrave Macmillan.

Hopkin, J. (2020) *Anti-System Politics: The Crisis of Market Liberalism in Rich Democracies*, Oxford: Oxford University Press.

Inglehart, R. & Norris, P. (2019) *Cultural Backlash. Trump, Brexit, and Authoritarian Populism*, New York: Cambridge University Press.

King, R. (1993) "Recent immigration to Italy: Character, causes and consequences", *GeoJournal*, vol. 30, no. 3, pp. 283–292.

Knigge, P. (1998) "The ecological correlates of right-wing extremism in Western Europe", *European Journal of Political Research*, vol. 34, no. 2, pp. 249–279.

Kristeva, J. (1982) *Powers of Horror. An Essay on Abjection*, New York: Columbia University Press.

Manucci, L. (2020) *Populism and Collective Memory: Comparing Fascist Legacies in Western Europe*, London: Routledge.

Ministero dell'Interno (2022) *Cruscotto Immigrazione*. Available: http://www.libertaciviliimmigrazione.dlci.interno.gov.it/it/documentazione/statistica/cruscotto-statistico-giornaliero [30 September 2022].

Mols, F. & Jetten, J. (2014) "No guts, no glory: How framing the collective past paves the way for anti-immigrant sentiments", *International Journal of Intercultural Relations*, vol. 43, pp. 74–86.

Mosca, L. & Tronconi, F. (2019) "Beyond left and right: The Eclectic populism of the Five Star Movement", *West European Politics*, vol. 42, no. 6, pp. 1258–1283.

Mudde, C. (2007) *Populist Radical Right Parties in Europe*, Cambridge, UK: Cambridge University Press.

Newell, J.L. (2000) "Coming in from the cold: The extreme right in Italy", *Parliamentary Affairs*, vol. 53, no. 3, pp. 369–485.

Perlmutter, T. (1996) "Immigration politics Italian style: The paradoxical behaviour of mainstream and populist parties", *South European Society and Politics*, vol. 1, no. 2, pp. 229–252.

Perrineau, P. (1985) "Le Front National: Un électorat autoritaire", *Revue Politique et Parlamentaire*, vol. 87, no. 918, pp. 24–31.

Ponzanesi, S. (2005) "Beyond the Black Venus: Colonial sexual politics and contemporary visual practices", in *Italian Colonialism: Legacy and Memory*, Andall, J. & Duncan, D. (eds), London: Peter Lang, pp. 165–190.

Proglio, G. (2019) "The Mediterranean as a mirror and ghost of the colonial past: The role of cultural memory in the production of populist narratives in Italy", in *European Memory in Populism: Representations of Self and Other*, De Cesari, C. & Kaya, A. (eds), London: Routledge, pp. 112–128.

Rivera, A. (2020) "Un decennio d'infamie razziste, fino all'estremo", in *Cronache di ordinario razzismo*, Lunaria (ed.), Rome: Lunaria, pp. 9–18.

Siddi, M. (2020) "Silencing history: Forgetting Italy's past during the refugee crisis in Europe", *International Politics*, vol. 57, no. 6, pp. 1030–1046.

Spica, G. (2014) "Lampedusa, le immagini in esclusiva del naufragio all'Isola dei Conigli", *Repubblica*. 14 May 2014. Available: https://video.repubblica.it/edizione/palermo/lampedusa-le-immagini-in-esclusiva-del-naufragio-all-isola-dei-conigli/165876/164365 [21 May 2021].

Tateo, L. (2005) "The Italian extreme right on-line network: An exploratory study using an Integrated Social Network Analysis and Content Analysis approach", *Journal of Computer-Mediated Communication*, vol. 10, no. 2.

Traverso, E. (2017) "Mutations of fascism: An interview with Enzo Traverso", Verso. 28 February 2017. Available: https://www.versobooks.com/blogs/3112-mutations-of-fascism-an-interview-with-enzo-traverso [28 February 2017].

Zaslove, A. (2004) "Closing the door? The ideology and impact of radical right populism on immigration policy in Austria and Italy", *Journal of Political Ideologies*, vol. 9, no. 1, pp. 99–118.

1 The Italian Populist Radical Right
Debates and the Missing Link with Memory

1.1 Introduction

From the 1990s onwards, the phenomenon of immigration into Italy started to be described as an issue, and academic interest in the Italian populist radical right's stance on immigration blossomed.

While immigration into Italy had begun in the 1970s, prompting Italy's shift from being a country of emigration to a country of immigration, it boomed in the 1990s, only to further burgeon in the 2000s. Before the 1990s, immigrants in Italy were not present in great numbers and Italy did not perceive itself as included in the major migration routes (Giuliani 2018: 198). By 1991, Italy's regular immigrant population was 860,000, increasing to 1 million including irregular migrants (King 1993: 283). Immigration became a political issue, featuring in policy debates, electoral campaigns, and the media (Perlmutter 1996: 229, 233). In particular, the murder of Jerry Masslo, a South African political refugee and activist working in Villa Literno, in August 1989, galvanised political attention around immigration (Perlmutter 1996: 234). This murder brought immigration under the spotlight, since it stimulated news coverage, and public and academic debate around it. The murder also cast light on anti-immigrant nativism, in response to which unions, religious and voluntary associations organised a protest march in Rome attracting 200,000 people (Perlmutter 1996: 234).

The landing of the *Vlora* from Albania in the port of Bari in 1991 further put immigration into Italy under the spotlight. As Giuliani argues, the mass landing of Albanians made Italians aware of Italy's place as a destination country for immigrants (2018: 198) and triggered the criminalisation of Albanians, perceived as criminals, linked to banditry, and at the same time stripped of any "human semblance" (Dal Lago 1999).

This chapter deals with thorny theoretical issues surrounding definitional, ideological, and taxonomical debates related to the populist radical right. In order to lay solid theoretical foundations for the subsequent investigation of the populist radical right's nativism, which uncovers colonial and fascist memories expedient to transmit political messages against immigrants, the chapter first takes issue with alternative definitions of the populist radical right and justifies the use of the latter label. It then argues in favour of the ideational approach to populism,

DOI: 10.4324/9781003252597-2

over the stylistic and strategic approaches to the study of populism. The debate on the approaches to the populist radical right leads to the analysis of its main ideological features, including the call for a strong state, populism, and nationalism coupled with racism. This ideological couple makes up nativism, which is the ideological element that Chapter 2 will unpack theoretically. This chapter ends by charting the taxonomy and development of the Italian populist radical right, which is complicated by the fluidity of its parties' platforms.

1.2 Self-Definition v. Academic Definitions of the Populist Radical Right

The Italian populist radical right's party representatives and intellectuals reject their classification within this party family, to which they tend to prefer the category of "centre-right." Despite the Italian populist radical right's self-representation, this project considers the label *populist radical right* more appropriate to denote such a varied party family and its ambiguity towards fascism. Indeed, the populist radical right does not include clearly fascist and anti-democratic parties, but includes parties that operate within democracy and are devoid of clear fascist references. Cavalieri and Froio (2021) believe that populism is not antithetical to democracy per se, but disfigures some elements of liberal democracy, since right-wing populism outwardly opposes the democratic principle of pluralism (Moffitt 2020: 97), through its hostility against the national out-group. Additionally, the category of *neo-fascist right* does not correctly portray the Italian populist radical right's protean ideology, which *populist radical right* captures better, through its emphasis on populist, nationalist and racist parties, promoting a strong state, and maintaining an ambiguous link with fascism. Nevertheless, this project takes the term *populist radical right* only as a starting point to identify the parties to be analysed, but avoids considering this category as a straitjacket defined by immutable ideological elements.

1.3 The Ideational Approach: The Populist Radical Right Ideology Unpacked

While being cognisant of the array of approaches to populism focusing on style (see, for instance, Bobba and Seddone 2019) and strategy (see, for instance, Weyland 2001), this book adopts the ideational approach to populism grounding its analysis on ideology (spearheaded by Mudde 2019). The ideational approach to populism goes beyond a focus on a stylistic analysis of discourse, and strategic considerations about policies, leadership, and relationship with the people, and has a two-fold advantage. First, it allows to capture the "thin ideology" (see, for instance, Freeden 2017) of populism revolving mainly around the juxtaposition between the Self vis-à-vis dangerous Others (such as elites and migrants). Second, the ideational approach to populism illuminates the thick side of populist ideology, through more in-depth ideological elements typical of the radical right (nationalism and racism, as well as a focus on a strong state).

Indeed, the Italian populist radical right calls for a strong state, characterised by rigid laws and strict policing, but does not advocate measures characterising authoritarian states, such as the suspension of free and fair elections and democratic freedoms (Finchelstein and Urbinati 2018: 16). The fact that this party family abandoned their initial call for the death penalty highlights how the Italian populist radical right is not a static category, but rather a dynamic phenomenon that evolves according to context. In this case, the shift away from outright authoritarianism may be part of the Italian populist radical right's mainstreaming strategy, in order to improve its electoral results. Nevertheless, the mainstreaming trajectory of the Italian populist radical right appeared to deviate as soon as the Lega was elected to a coalition government with the catch-all populist party M5S in March 2018.

The M5S is hard to encase within left-wing or right-wing populism: it is a unique case of a populist party escaping any consensual classification. On the one hand, the M5S and the Lega share antagonism against the elites, embodied, among others, by political parties, the media, and the EU. On the other hand, the M5S does not share with the Lega economic beliefs and immigration-related stances, since it blends redistributionist policies with a socialist flavour, such as a universal basic income, with opacity on the notion of the nation and on whether immigration is unwelcome or should be restricted. Before its experience in government, the M5S held an elusive immigration policy and did not display any nativist discourse. In government with the Lega, the M5S acted ambivalently: a few M5S representatives condemned the Lega's nativist policies, while the majority of M5S representatives favoured nativist policies and employed anti-immigrant discourse. In the absence of a mainstream party as coalition partner acting in the interest of counterbalancing the radical traits of the Lega, the latter was left unfettered to radicalise its anti-immigrant discourse and pass restrictive Security Decrees targeting immigration. The current radicalisation of the Italian populist radical right is to be considered against the background of the radicalisation of the mainstream. In fact, as I will explore later, the centre-right and even the centre-left have co-opted strands of the populist radical right's ideology.

Populism is a further ideological component of the Italian radical right, which pits the pure people against the supposedly corrupt elites, embodied by the state, the government, other political parties, the EU, the media, Germany, the US, and global phenomena, such as capitalism and globalisation. These targets of the Italian populist radical right are inextricable from immigration, as it is their management of, and connections to, immigration that are harshly criticised by the Lega and FdI. Hence, the people that the populist radical right claims to speak for excludes not only the elites, but also the out-group, thus aligning with the Italian populist radical right's predominantly ethno-cultural view of the nation, also featuring rare civic undertones. Not only populism and nationalism, but also the call for a strong state is articulated against immigration, evident in the Italian populist radical right's reactionary hostility towards multiculturalism and in its demand for a strict state against immigration-related crime.

The Italian Populist Radical Right 13

The hostility towards immigration comes through very evidently in the Italian populist radical right's construction of nativism, which this project groups into six categories: problematisation, differentiation, Othering, criminalisation, inferiorisation, and abjectification of immigration. In fact, the Italian populist radical right frames immigration as a problem of insurmountable proportions, differentiates between supposedly welcome and deserving refugees and regular immigrants, and allegedly unwelcome and undeserving economic migrants and irregular immigrants, and depicts immigrants as inherently *Other*, posing social and economic threats. Moreover, the Italian populist radical right associates immigrants with crime, especially with a holy war waged by Muslim immigrants against the West, and depicts immigrants as inferior human beings, devoid of respect for women's rights, human rights, and reciprocity.

Islamophobia predominates in the Italian populist radical right's criminalisation and inferiorisation of Muslim immigrants, which are related to terrorism, to an invasion, to the lack of respect for human rights in general, and for women's rights in particular. Indeed, after the end of the Cold War and the demise of the Eastern bloc, Islam became the enemy of the West. This reconfiguration was exacerbated by 9/11 and became pivotal to the war Western countries, including Italy, pursued against Islamic terrorism. "Eurabianist" racist conspirationist arguments forecasting a merger of European and Arab countries have further stoked the fires of Islamophobia. As the interviews reveal, the Roma are an example of another ethnicity that is criminalised and inferiorised by the Italian populist radical right. Various authors (see, for instance, Giuliani 2018; Sigona 2003; Woodcock 2010) document anti-Roma racism in Italy at large, where the Roma are constructed as dirty and as beasts, inferior to the Italian Self, and as prone to stealing, raping, and lying. However, the focus of this research is on sentiment against immigrants coming from Africa and the Middle East through the Mediterranean to Italy. Finally, the Italian populist radical right connects immigrants to diseases that were once eradicated from Italy, and to lack of hygiene. Nevertheless, as part of the "civic turn" of the populist radical right (Halikiopoulou, Mock, and Vasilopoulou 2013), the Italian populist radical right cloaks its nativist discourse under a façade of civic values, which is indicative of the Italian populist radical right's attempt at mainstreaming, in order to appear legitimate, credible, and palatable to a larger electorate.

1.4 Who Belongs to the Italian Populist Radical Right? Taxonomy and Historical Development of the Lega and FdI

The Italian populist radical right is a "complex galaxy" (Tateo 2005), constituted by parties with a different lifespan and entwisted through ideological convergencies and divergencies. FdI, born in 2013, is the resuscitation of the defunct Alleanza Nazionale (AN), the post-fascist political party dominating the Italian political scene from 1994 to 2012. The genealogy of FdI is more than an anecdote: FdI, as hinted at in the Introduction, has not yet receded completely from its post-fascist matrix. At the time of writing, the fascist heritage of FdI has become

14 *The Italian Populist Radical Right*

a cumbersome legacy the FdI leader Meloni is trying to brush off in the run-up to the 25 September 2022 Italian national elections (Berizzi 2022). Remarkably, FdI adopted the Movimento Sociale Italiano (MSI) symbol of the tricolour flame (Alemanno 2014: 68), as AN did (Eatwell and Mudde 2003: 25), thus staking a claim to being the heir to the post-war populist radical right party. Despite heated debates, the tricolour flame is still alive and well on the FdI logo (Berizzi 2022).

The political humus where AN sprouted was the same in which the Lega grew its own roots. In 1992, two years earlier than AN, the Lega (originally called *Lega Nord*) emerged on the political scene, against the backdrop of *Tangentopoli*, a corruption scandal that shattered the existing *partitocrazia*, i.e., a party system where, given the forced absence of left and right extremes from the government, party elites were the principal basis of rule and operated through clientelism (Newell 2000: 475). *Tangentopoli* threw into disarray the long-standing parties, such as the Democrazia Cristiana (DC), the Partito Comunista Italiano (PCI), and the Partito Socialista Italiano (PSI), and left a window of opportunity open for the emergence of political parties which portrayed themselves as uncontaminated by the corruption scandal.[1] The success of AN and the Lega is also attributable to a change in voting patterns. Due to the disaffection with the pre-*Tangentopoli* political system, and the loosening of traditional party loyalties, the *voto d'opinione*[2] replaced the *voto d'appartenenza*[3] (Newell 2000: 472; Perlmutter 1996: 242).

1.5 The Co-optation of the Populist Radical Right

While the anti-immigrant component of nativism is owned as a salient issue by the populist radical right, it has not kept within the confines of this party family. This is not uncommon: populist radical right parties entering into competition with mainstream parties may be treated as pariahs, antagonised, or even accommodated. Using Albertazzi and Vampa's (2021) typology of party competition, it is possible to argue that populist parties may be dismissed as irrelevant by mainstream parties; may be actively opposed, marginalised, or co-opted by mainstream parties; may cooperate or merge with mainstream parties. The Italian populist radical right discourse and policies have often been co-opted by mainstream parties.

Apart from the wholly populist Lega-M5S government (2018–2019), Italy has already experienced three government coalitions formed, under Silvio Berlusconi's aegis, by the populist radical right Lega, the former AN, and the centre-right FI (1994; 2001–2006; 2008–2011). During this time, the Lega influenced FI's agenda-setting and policy-making, evident in the adoption of anti-immigrant and race-conscious discourse and policies (Curran 2004: 37). The incorporation of traditionally populist radical right discursive constructions of immigration and immigration policies was made possible by the process of co-optation, whereby a political party aims at improving its standing and increasing its votes, by integrating policy proposals supported by a challenger party into its policy-making process (Carvalho 2014). As emerges from Carvalho's (2014) comparative analysis of immigration policies in Italy, France, and the UK, co-optation is a proficuous strategy: co-opting parties can regain the votes lost to challenger parties and neutralise the latter (Carvalho 2014: 1).

Indeed, the strategy of co-optation paid off in the three Berlusconi-led coalition governments that saw the participation of the Lega and AN. Berlusconi managed to attract populist radical right voters through the creation of coalitions with AN and the Lega. First, the Lega and FI joined forces in the 1994 elections through the Polo delle Libertà coalition; the government lasted only one year, due to internal skirmishes between Umberto Bossi and Berlusconi. Second, a coalition branded Casa delle Libertà saw, among others, AN and the Lega governing from 2001 to 2006. Third, a new political party built from the merger of AN and FI made its first appearance on the political scene in 2008, and started a new government in 2009. The Popolo della Libertà's (PdL's) life in government was brief, as it lasted only until 2011, before the technocratic government led by Mario Monti was established. However, the electoral success of FI's co-optation of the populist radical right did not last long: at the elections disputed in 2018, the Lega polled more votes than FI, leading the ballot with 17.35% versus FI's 14%. After a slump in polls, FI has been involved in an upswinging trajectory: the 2022 opinion polls report that FI now garners 8% of votes. FdI is now leading opinion polls with 23.8%, while the Lega's performance in opinion polls is constantly precipitating, polling at 12.5%. In particular, the candidature of Berlusconi at the end of 2021 for the post of President of the Republic (who then lost in favour of Sergio Mattarella), has given Berlusconi and FI increased media resonance (Balduzzi 2022).

1.6 The Populist Radical Right and Colonialism: A Gap to Fill

The existing literature on the populist radical right and on colonialism in Italy ignores the investigation of the connection between the Italian populist radical right's anti-immigrant nativism on one side, and the Italian populist radical right's attitudes towards its colonial past on the other. This constitutes a glaring omission, which this book aims to rectify. Indeed, this book hypothesises a connection between the current nativism against immigrants and the selective colonial memory at work among the populist radical right in Italy. The hypothesis of the above-mentioned link is grounded in two correlations: first, the generic correlation articulated by the extant literature between the memory of colonialism in society at large and in political parties in former colonising countries, and the stance towards immigration articulated by society and political parties; second, the correlation between Italian colonialism and the populist radical right's nativism, based on their continuity in racism. In fact, it is racism against the colonised Other that underpins a certain kind of colonial memory, and it is racism against the immigrant Other that underpins nativism.

Regarding the Italian case, De Donno and Srivastava claim that immigration has encouraged Italy to reconsider its colonial history (2006: 378). Indeed, through immigration, the former colonised Other re-encountered the former coloniser in the colonial motherland. Such encounters may result in different outcomes: on the one hand, it may encourage mutual understanding, tolerance, and Italy's critical assessment of its colonial past. On the other hand, such encounters may lead to hostility, and the lack of a critical appraisal of Italy's colonial deeds. This line of reasoning also applies to immigrants who do not come from former Italian colonies: as Andall and Duncan state, Italy's colonial past influences issues related to immigrants even if they are not originally from former Italian colonies (2005: 21). In fact, immigrants from Ethiopia, Eritrea, Somalia, and Libya, do not represent the majority of immigrant nationalities. In the late 1970s, Ethiopians and Eritreans were the second largest group of non-European immigrants (ECAP-CGIL 1979) in Italy. In the 1990s, a significant number of immigrants came from former Italian colonies, although they did not play the lion's share (Andall 2005: 194): in 1991, Ethiopia, Eritrea, and Somalia were among the 30 largest foreign groups in Italy (Caritas di Roma 1992). In 2018, Eritreans constituted the second largest nationality among immigrant arrivals in Italy (Ministero dell'Interno 2018). By June 2022, data have changed: the majority of immigrants landed in Italy come from Bangladesh, followed by Egypt and Tunisia (Ministero dell'Interno 2022).

Labanca (2002) argues that colonial attitudes in Italy, underpinned by racism, remained latent due to the lack of a colonial debate in the decades following the end of Italian colonialism, but have been reactivated by immigration. Similarly, Galeazzo opines that Italian public opinion was not prepared for the arrival of immigrant workers due to a lack of discussion about colonialism (1994: 15). Moreover, De Cesari asserts that the short-circuits affecting Italy's colonial memory led to violations of human rights against immigrants (2012: 316). Finally, Chambers claims that contemporary nativism is associated with the unwillingness to deal with the colonial past (2008: 7), and Ponzanesi argues that in Italy the representations of the immigrant Other produced by populist radical right parties crystallise stereotypes that fuelled colonialism (2005: 185). As Fogu asserts, the representation of the Mediterranean, once a treasured living space to project Italy's potence, shifted from being a *Mare Nostrum* in Roman and fascist times, to being a *Mare Aliorum* at present (2010: 1). The conceptualisation of the Mediterranean as a *Mare Aliorum*, belonging to other countries, and vehicle of unwelcome immigration, finds resonance within Italian society at large where anti-immigrant nativism is widespread, and with the Italian populist radical right, as the following chapters will explore more in depth.

In order to remedy the conspicuous omission in the study of the connection between populist radical right's nativism, and colonial memory in the Italian populist radical right, this book adopts postcolonialism as an analytical framework. Postcolonialism refers to the period following colonialism (Labanca 2005: 16) and highlights the continuity between the latter and its legacy today (Lombardi-Diop and Romeo 2012: 2). Mols and Jetten's study of Dutch, French, and Belgian populist right-wing parties sheds light on the nostalgic narrative that political actors deploy to emphasise the success of their collective past, to fuel collective fear, and to legitimise their tough treatment of immigrants (2014: 74). Indeed, by appealing to a magnificent past and marking its difference from the bleak present and future, populist radical right parties in the countries at stake frame the in-group's identity as under threat, in order to induce a sense of anxiety over the present (Mols and Jetten 2014: 74–75). Melancholia is directed towards a remote past (Cheng et al. 2010) and strategically serves the purpose of crystallising the in-group's social identity against the immigrants' threat (Liu and Khan 2014). Transposing this analysis onto the Italian scenario, it is possible to advance the hypothesis that the Italian populist radical right exploits a melancholic narrative, carrying alarmist overtones, to mark the difference between a gloomy present and a glorious past and thereby justifying its anti-immigrant nativism. Italy being a comparatively recent nation state, its glorious past can be traced to the alleged splendour of its colonial age, especially under fascism.

A key contribution to the study of postcolonial melancholia is provided by Gilroy, who, in the British context, sheds light on the buried and disavowed colonial past, which actually emerges only in the service of nostalgia and melancholia (2005). Indeed, the UK, according to Gilroy's (2005) argument, is drenched in postcolonial melancholia, as it is unable to deal with the loss of imperial prestige and the changes ensuing from the loss of the Empire. This inability to mourn is entwined with preoccupations over political and economic crises, the arrival of postcolonial migrants, and the resulting anxiety over the perceived loss of a distinctive binding national culture (Gilroy 2005). Therefore, the Empire in the British imagery becomes a source of shame and discomfort. Consequently, the disturbing colonial history has been forgotten and postcolonial migrants have been represented as "unwanted alien intruders" allegedly without any connections to the life of the British (Gilroy 2005: 81), and feared as bearers of the colonial past (Gilroy 2005: 89). Hence, Gilroy's argument identifies racism as driven by "guilt-ridden loathing and depression" (2005: 81), rooted in the uncomfortable relationship with the colonial past, which is wilfully set aside (2005: 82). Gilroy draws the term *melancholia* from Alexander and Margarete Mitscherlich's understanding of post-war Germany's social, political, and psychological attitude (1975), imbued with melancholia about Hitler's death, whose mourning was avoided, while Nazi history was denied (Gilroy 2005: 88).

The concept of the lack of mourning, predicated upon the idealisation of the colonial era, is particularly useful to this project, as it not only relates to melancholia, but also to the connected notion of the lack of elaboration of in-group war violence (Leone and Mastrovito 2014). In fact, when atrocities, such as Italian colonial crimes, are committed by the in-group, they imply the loss of the abstract sense of an ideal social identity (Leone and Mastrovito 2014: 16). The ensuing process of mourning is lengthy and complex and entails the painstaking elaboration of the violence perpetrated. If the issue of violence is no longer avoided or postponed, the enemy stops being the scapegoat to blame for the suffering triggered by war crimes (Leone and Mastrovito 2014: 17). The enemy's image thus becomes marginalised in the in-group's construction of their social identity, and a socio-emotional reconciliation process follows (Leone and Mastrovito 2014: 17). Reconciliation signals the beginning of a critical analysis of the past (Leone and Mastrovito 2014: 13), geared towards the necessity to protect self-esteem

18 *The Italian Populist Radical Right*

and self-integrity (Pratto and Glasford 2008), and the end of the obstinate need to defend the in-group's identity (Leone and Mastrovito 2014: 12).

Although Gilroy mentions that Italy's behaviour with regards to colonialism and immigration is similar to Britain's (2005: 89), the Italian case is different from the British colonial and postcolonial paradigms. Indeed, Italy was a latecomer in the colonial arena and Italian colonies did not undergo a decolonising process involving struggles against Italy, as decolonisation was a consequence of Italy's defeat in the Second World War and of the Great Powers' decisions. Despite these differences, Andall and Duncan recognise that post-war Italy nurtured nostalgia for its colonies, due to the abrupt dispossession it underwent at the hands of the Allies (2005: 18). Triulzi adds that "waves of ambiguous nostalgia" concerning its colonial past have pervaded Italy (2005: 157), and Lombardi-Diop claims that colonial nostalgia is an essential element of Italian literature and popular culture (2012: 176). Moreover, Pinkus argues that Italy nurtures a nostalgic link with Africa (1997: 152). Therefore, this project, by applying Mols and Jetten's notion of nostalgia for an idealised past (2014) and Gilroy's theory of postcolonial melancholia (2005), along with Leone and Mastrovito's concept of the lack of elaboration of war crimes (2014), to the present Italian context, advances the hypothesis that the nativism imbuing the Italian populist radical right since the 1990s is due to the nostalgia these parties nurture towards Italy's former colonial past, which is linked to the reluctance to elaborate colonial violence.

1.7 Conclusion

Against the backdrop of the increasing success of the Italian populist radical right's nativist discourse, this chapter first traced the development of this party family, which emerged in the early 1990s aided by the *Tangentopoli* corruption scandal signalling the end of established mainstream parties and opening a window of opportunity for parties challenging the traditional *partitocrazia* and the *pentapartito*.[4] Although the Lega was involved to a certain extent in *Tangentopoli*, it did still frame itself as a challenger of the old party system. The consequent loosening of political affiliations to traditional parties caused a shift in the way of voting, which facilitated the rise of the Lega and AN, which benefited from the incipient salience of issues such as immigration and security. FdI, the heir to AN, was born more recently, in 2012, from the ashes of its parent party.

This party family has been in constant evolution. The Lega has gradually replaced its regionalism with nativism against the immigrant Other. FdI, like its forefather AN did for the whole duration of its life, is walking a tightrope between covertly maintaining its allegiance to its post-fascist predecessor AN and taking its distance from it, in its quest for normalisation within the Italian party system. The Lega's and the FdI's 2018 electoral campaign as part of the so-called "centre-right" coalition is a recent example of the dynamism of these parties, which strategically formed a coalition with the mainstream right FI, in order to pool votes. At the time of writing, another fateful election is about to take place on 25 September 2022, and the Lega, FdI, and FI are set to form a coalition, with Meloni likely to become Italy's first female (and ambivalently post-fascist) Prime Minister.

Therefore, the Italian populist radical right is a complex and multifaceted party family. Despite the incongruence between parties' self-representation and academic labels, the term *populist radical right* is adequate to capture the dynamic phenomenon of the parties studied in this project, and it is still preferable to competing labels, such as *neo-fascism* and the generic *far right*. These two terms are inaccurate, as they depict only a part of the populist radical right's ideology and can be applied to a broad range of parties different from the ones at stake. Instead, *populist radical right* captures the ambivalence of the Lega and FdI regarding fascism (explained in depth in Chapter 6), without encasing them rigidly within the *far right*.

The Italian populist radical right's ideology, which I will analyse in depth in Chapters 4, 5, and 6, using interviews with intellectuals, party representatives and manifestos, is constantly evolving according to the changing context. However, a few ideological features recur in these parties throughout time: the call for a strong state, populism, nationalism, and nativism. The latter taps into a nativist sentiment that is widespread at a popular level. The existing literature on the causes behind the populist radical right's nativism offers a bewildering array of possible explanations encompassing the economic, the socio-demographic, and the political psychological, which have a real or presumed crisis as a common denominator. The assumption underpinning these explanations is that the populist radical right's political elites adopt nativism responding to popular grievances, in order to gain support.

Notes

1 The Lega's involvement in *Tangentopoli* is subject to debate. While some scholars, such as Heinisch (2003) and Spruce (2007), claim that the Lega was not involved in *Tangentopoli*, the Lega was embroiled in the corruption scandal, since its treasurer had admitted to having accepted bribes from the CEO of Montedison, an investment firm (see, for instance, Colaprico and Fazzo 1993). Nonetheless, the Lega portrayed itself as a viable and valuable alternative to the *partitocrazia*, by offering bitter criticism of the DC and the so-called *pentapartito*, i.e., the coalition the DC belonged to composed of the PSI, the PCI, the Partito Socialista Democratico Italiano (PSDI), and the Partito Repubblicano Italiano (PRI) (Passarelli 2013: 55).
2 Vote based on opinion.
3 Vote based on belonging to a political party.
4 The coalition the DC belonged to composed of the PSI, the PCI, the Partito Socialista Democratico Italiano (PSDI), and the Partito Repubblicano Italiano (PRI).

References

Albertazzi, D. & Vampa, D. (2021) *Populism and New Patterns of Political Competition in Western Europe*, London: Routledge.
Alemanno, G. (2014) *Il Partito della nazione*, Rome: I libri del Borghese.

Andall, J. & Duncan, D. (eds) (2005) *Italian Colonialism: Legacy and Memory*, Oxford, Bern: Peter Lang.

Balduzzi, G. (2022) "Sondaggi elettorali Swg, giù la Lega, cresce Forza Italia", *SWG*. 25 January 2022. Available: https://www.termometropolitico.it/1599627_sondaggi-elettorali-swg-forza-italia-quirinale.html [25 January 2022].

Berizzi, P. (2022) "Fondazione An, scrigno di Meloni tra business e 'radici'", *La Repubblica*. 03 August 2022. Available: https://www.repubblica.it/politica/2022/08/03/news/meloni_fondazione_an-360197404/ [3 August 2022].

Bobba, G. & Seddone, A. (2019) "Between the ideological and communicative approaches: Hard and soft populism in France and Italy", *Journal of Representative Democracy*, vol. 58, no. 1, pp. 46–66.

Carvalho, J. (2014) *Impact of Extreme Right Parties on Immigration Policy: Comparing Britain, France and Italy*, London: Routledge.

Caritas di Roma (1992) *Immigrazione. Dossier Statistico 1992*, Rome: Sinnos editrice.

Cavalieri, A. & Froio, C. (2021) "The behaviour of populist parties in parliament. The policy agendas of populist and other political parties in the Italian question time", *Italian Political Science Review/Rivista Italiana di Scienza Politica*, vol. 52, no. 3, pp. 1–14.

Chambers, I. (2008) *Mediterranean Crossings: The Politics of an Interrupted Modernity*, Durham, NC: Duke University Press.

Cheng, S.Y., Chao, M.M., Kwong, J., Peng, S., Chen, X., Kashima, Y. & Chiu, C. (2010) "The good old days and a better tomorrow: Historical representations and future imaginations of China during the 2008 Olympic Games", *Asian Journal of Social Psychology*, vol. 13, no. 2, pp. 118–127.

Colaprico, P. & Fazzo, L. (1993) "È il turno della Lega", *Repubblica*. 08 December 1993. Available: https://ricerca.repubblica.it/repubblica/archivio/repubblica/1993/12/08/il-turno-della-lega.html [10 November 2019].

Curran, G. (2004) "Mainstreaming populist discourse: The race-conscious legacy of neo-populist parties in Australia and Italy", *Patterns of Prejudice*, vol. 38, no. 1, pp. 37–55.

Dal Lago, A. (1999) *Non-persone: L'esclusione dei migranti in una società globale*, Milano: Feltrinelli.

De Cesari, C. (2012) "The paradoxes of colonial reparation: Foreclosing memory and the 2008 Italy–Libya Friendship Treaty", *Memory Studies*, vol. 5, no. 3, pp. 316–326.

De Donno, F. & Srivastava, N. (2006) "Colonial and postcolonial Italy", *Interventions; International Journal of Postcolonial Studies*, vol. 8, no. 3, pp. 371–379.

Eatwell, R. & Mudde, C. (eds) (2003) *Western Democracies and the New Extreme Right Challenge*, London: Routledge.

Finchelstein, F. & Urbinati, N. (2018) "On populism and democracy", *Populism*, vol. 1, no. 1, pp. 15–37.

Fogu, C. (2010) "From *Mare Nostrum* to *Mare Aliorum*: Mediterranean theory and Mediterraneism in contemporary Italian thought", *California Italian Studies*, vol. 1, no. 1, pp. 1–23.

Freeden, M. (2017) "After the Brexit referendum: Revisiting populism as an ideology", *Journal of Political Ideologies*, vol. 22, no. 1, pp. 1–11.

Galeazzo, P. (1994) "La nuova immigrazione a Milano. Il caso dell'Eritrea", in *Tra due rive. La nuova immigrazione a Milano*, Barile, G., Dal Lago, A., Marchetti, A. & Galeazzo, P. (eds), Milan: Franco Angeli, pp. 367–412.

Gilroy, P. (2005) *Postcolonial Melancholia*, New York: Columbia University Press.

Giuliani, G. (2018) *Race, Nation and Gender in Modern Italy: Intersectional Representations in Visual Culture*, London: Palgrave Macmillan.

Halikiopoulou, D., Mock, S. & Vasilopoulou, S. (2013) "The civic zeitgeist: Nationalism and liberal values in the European radical right", *Nations and Nationalism*, vol. 19, no. 1, pp. 107–127.

Heinisch, R. (2003) "Success in opposition: Failure in government: Explaining the performance of right-wing populist parties in public office", *West European Politics*, vol. 26, no. 3, pp. 91–130.

King, R. (1993) "Recent immigration to Italy: Character, causes and consequences", *GeoJournal*, vol. 30, no. 3, pp. 283–292.

Labanca, N. (2005) "History and memory of Italian colonialism today", in *Italian Colonialism: Legacy and Memory*, Andall, J. & Duncan, D. (eds), Oxford, Bern: Peter Lang, pp. 29–46.

Leone, G. & Mastrovito, T. (2014) "Learning about our shameful past: A socio-psychological analysis of present-day historical narratives of Italian colonial wars", *International Journal of Conflict and Violence*, vol. 4, no. 1, pp. 11–27.

Liu, J.H. & Khan, S.S. (2014) "Nation building through historical narratives in preindependence India: Gandhi, Nehru, Savarkar, and Golwarkar as entrepreneurs of identity", in *Warring with Words: Narrative and Metaphor in Domestic and International Politics*, Hanne, M. (ed.), New York: Psychology Press, pp. 211–237.

Lombardi-Diop, C. & Romeo, C. (eds) (2012) *Postcolonial Italy: Challenging National Homogeneity*, New York: Palgrave Macmillan.

Ministero dell'Interno (2018) *Cruscotto statistico giornaliero*. Available: http://www.interno.gov.it/sites/default/files/cruscotto_statistico_giornaliero_12-11-2018.pdf [12 November 2018].

Ministero dell'Interno (2022) *Cruscotto statistic giornaliero*. Available: https://www.interno.gov.it/sites/default/files/2022-07/cruscotto_statistico_giornaliero_15-07-2022.pdf [15 July 2022].

Mitscherlich, A. (1975) *The Inability to Mourn*, New York: Grove Press.

Moffitt, B. (2020) *Populism*, Cambridge, UK: Polity Press.

Mols, F. & Jetten, J. (2014) "No guts, no glory: How framing the collective past paves the way for anti-immigrant sentiments", *International Journal of Intercultural Relations*, vol. 43, part A, pp. 74–86.

Mudde, C. (2019) *The Far Right Today*, Cambridge, UK: Polity Press.

Passarelli, G. (2013) "Extreme right parties in Western Europe: The case of the Italian Northern League", *Journal of Modern Italian Studies*, vol. 18, no. 1, pp. 53–71.

Perlmutter, T. (2015) "A narrowing gyre? The Lega Nord and the shifting balance of Italian immigration policy", *Ethnic and Racial Studies*, vol. 38, no. 8, pp. 1339–1346.

Pinkus, K. (1997) "Shades of black in advertising and popular culture", in *Revisioning Italy: National Identity and Global Culture*, Allen, B. & Russo, M.J. (eds), Minneapolis: University of Minnesota Press, pp. 134–155.

Ponzanesi, S. (2005) "Beyond the Black Venus: Colonial sexual politics and contemporary visual practices", in *Italian Colonialism: Legacy and Memory*, Andall, J. & Duncan, D. (eds), Oxford, Bern: Peter Lang, pp. 165–190.

Pratto, F. & Glasford, D.E. (2008) "How needs can motivate intergroup reconciliation in the face of intergroup conflict", in *The Social Psychology of Intergroup Reconciliation*, Nadler, A., Malloy, T.E. & Fisher, J.D. (eds), Oxford: Oxford University Press, pp. 117–144.

Sigona, N. (2003) "How can a 'nomad' be a 'refugee'?: Kosovo Roma and labelling policy in Italy", *Sociology*, vol. 37, no. 1, pp. 69–79.

Spruce, D. (2007) "Empire and counter-empire in the Italian far right: Conflicting nationalisms and the split between the Lega Nord and Alleanza Nazionale on immigration", *Theory Culture & Society*, vol. 24, no. 5, pp. 99–126.

Tateo, L. (2005) "The Italian extreme right on-line network: An exploratory study using an Integrated Social Network Analysis and Content Analysis approach", *Journal of Computer-Mediated Communication*, vol. 10, no. 2.

Triulzi, A. (2005) "Adwa: From monument to document", in *Italian Colonialism: Legacy and Memory*, Andall, J. & Duncan, D. (eds), Oxford, Bern: Peter Lang, pp. 23–40.

Weyland, K. (2001) "Clarifying a contested concept: Populism in the study of Latin American politics", *Comparative Politics*, vol. 34, no. 1, pp. 1–22.

Woodcock, S. (2010) "Gender as catalyst for violence against Roma in contemporary Italy", *Patterns of Prejudice*, vol. 44, no. 5, pp. 469–488.

2 Nation and Race
The Theoretical Roots of Nativism

2.1 Introduction

As Chapter 1 has outlined, nationalism and racism are the components of nativism as a concept. Nativism is, in turn, an essential ideological component of the Italian populist radical right. Before delving into the discursive constructions of the pivotal concepts of nation and race, this chapter sheds light on the entanglement of the theoretical articulations of nation and race in the Italian populist radical right against the backdrop of Italy's colonial and fascist past, and of the more recent immigration inflow.

The nation, and nationalism, as well as racism, are highly contested topics, hence unanimity on their definition is impossible to achieve. This chapter, however, aims at providing conceptual clarity on these concepts, which are two pillars of the theoretical framework of this book, alongside memory and postcolonialism. The end goal is to furnish, with sound theoretical foundations, the subsequent empirical analysis of the role of colonial, and fascist, memory in the populist radical right.

Starting with the nation and nationalism, this chapter outlines the definitions adopted by this book, which capture the protean notion of the nation, and the nature of nationalism within the context of contemporary political circumstances marked by immigration, and in the context of the historical Italian past. The major contribution of this chapter is to go beyond the neat dichotomy civic v. ethno-cultural nation (and, by extension, nationalism), and to characterise the nation envisaged by the populist radical right as Janus-faced. Indeed, the Lega and FdI's nationalism are built both around ethno-cultural views of the nation emphasising its history, and ethno-cultural plus civic views of the nation that these parties aim to achieve. The populist radical right, thus, becomes the custodian of the past and traditions, as well as the saviour of the nation's future. The ethno-cultural cum civic blend of the empirical manifestations of the Lega's and FdI's nationalism will be the focus of Chapter 4.

Chapter 2, then, moves on to explain how the above-mentioned notion of the nation becomes interwoven with racism, in order to form nativism. Therefore, a working definition of racism, stressing its elasticity and contextuality, is provided, along with the examination of the ambiguity surrounding Italy's presumed

DOI: 10.4324/9781003252597-3

immunity from racism. This belief will be challenged and dismantled from a theoretical viewpoint in this chapter, and from an empirical perspective in Chapters 5 and 6. Chapter 2 will conclude with the contextualisation of nativism within Italy's larger political and social milieu. Clearly, nativism is not the exclusive domain of the populist radical right, although it is one of their essential selling points.

2.2 The Janus-Faced Nation

Nationalism is one of the two key pillars of nativism. Before treading the murky waters of the notion of the Italian nation and nationalism, it is imperative to delineate these two concepts. Regardless of the ethno-cultural v. civic divide delineated below, nationalism is the belief in the preservation of unity, autonomy, and identity of the nation (Smith 1991). The nation is understood in this book as a modern construct, which is not primordially given, being moulded by political parties for political purposes.[1]

In the populist radical right, nationalism is Janus-faced:[2] it harks back to the past of Italian national history, decries the alleged contemporary decline of the Italian nation, while projecting itself into the future as the saviour of the nation. The characterisation of nationalism as Janus-faced brings together the two branches of the ethno-cultural v. civic dichotomous classification of nationalism: ethno-cultural nationalism, which is exclusive, ascriptive, and anchored in a community of birth, in national history, culture, language; and civic nationalism, which is inclusive, voluntary, and grounded on common laws and institutions (see, for instance, Renan 1996; Smith 1991). The mechanisms determining membership to the nation diverge depending on whether nationalism is ethno-cultural or civic. In the former case, membership of the nation is deterministically defined (Hearn 2006), while in the latter it is voluntarily acquired (Renan 1996).

The populist radical right has been traditionally associated with ethno-cultural nationalism (Curran 2004: 48; Tarchi 2003: 146; Rydgren 2007), though Gomez-Reino Cachafeiro traces within the Lega some civic elements associated with the north, such as democracy, good government, and hard work, mixed with the predominantly ethno-cultural nationalism grounded in shared culture, language, and ethnicity (2002: 100–102). In fact, FdI usually identifies culture, language, religion, customs, ethnicity, and history (Alemanno 2014: 53) as the hallmarks of its ethno-cultural nationalism. Despite Ciampi's and Napolitano's efforts to foster a civic constitutional nationalism (Nevola 2011), Italian nationalism as a whole has been traditionally classified as belonging to the ethno-cultural genus, since the ethnic nation and culture in Italy predated the establishment of a state with its related civic culture (Martinelli 2013).

Dichotomous categories carry the burden of stifling variety and simplifying classification. Indeed, the die-hard dichotomy that has reigned over the field of nationalism studies for decades juxtaposing ethno-cultural nations to civic nations has been under fire for years. This is due mainly to two reasons. First, in the scholarly field, the dichotomy between civic and ethno-cultural nations (Kohn 1945) has been criticised for ossifying debate (Zimmer 2003), as classifying a nation either within the civic or the ethno-cultural camp seems reductive. Second, more recent studies have questioned the monolithic interpretation of Italian nationalism as unequivocally ethno-cultural, by identifying both civic and ethno-cultural traits (Antonsich 2016; Vidali 2011:44). Third, the interviews demonstrate that the Italian populist radical right blurs a neat border between ethno-cultural and civic notions of the *patria*, i.e. the nation.

In the populist radical right's discourse, despite civic undertones, the goal of nationalism is to achieve and preserve the purity and homogeneity of the ethno-cultural nation. This results in the exclusion of those not belonging to the national in-group, i.e., the out-group embodied by the Other as diametrically opposed to the national Self, which translates into an aversion to immigration and the transnational systems correlated with it, such as globalisation, multiculturalism, and the EU (Hainsworth 2008: 12). Hence, in the populist radical right's discourse, the conceptualisation of the *people* populism speaks to and on behalf of has largely shifted from *demos*[3] to *ethnos*[4] (Curran 2004: 19).

The Italian populist radical right's call for a stronger national identity departs from the assumption that the Italian sense of national identity is weak. Italy has been traditionally defined as having a problematic notion of national identity, coupled with high levels of political alienation (Almond and Verba 1963: 402–403). For instance, Dickie (2001) argues that Italian national history has been characterised by internal diversity and lack of unity, which have impaired the creation of one notion of Italian national identity. The Italian state that took shape in 1861 did not have a historical precedent and the population was not culturally and socially cohesive, which hindered the formation of a sense of Italian national identity (Dickie 2001: 26). The causes of a weak national identity lie in a nation-building process (Allen and Russo 1997: 8) that occurred later than in other European countries, such as France and the UK, and that unified a linguistically and socially diverse population (Dickie 2001: 26). Another factor that allegedly contributed to the weakness in national identity is the fragmentation of the nation along a north v. south divide, whereby the south becomes an internal Other (Verdicchio 1997: 194). Despite capturing only one aspect of national identity, a EURISPES 2022 survey confirms a certain weakness in the Italian sense of national identity: only 47% of Italians feel proud of their nation when it comes to international recognition in the political sphere.

2.3 Nationalism + Racism = Nativism

In spite of the traditional characterisation of Italian national identity as weak, the Lega and FdI strive to revive Italian national identity through ardent nationalism. Nationalism intertwines with racism, which together form nativism. The relationship between nationalism and racism is straightforward: if the populist radical right espouses a predominantly ethno-cultural kind of nationalism, it believes that the nation should be inhabited only by natives, and perceives the immigrant Other as a threat to national identity.

Following Hall's definition of racism as relational and contextual (1997), this book argues that racism is the ideology, constructed by contextual factors and social relations, which holds that human groups have essential differences, legitimating stigmatisation, discrimination, and exclusion of the Other (Rivera 2007). Hall recognised that, by the 1990s, biological racism had become obsolete, and differences between human groups were instead predicated upon culture, religion, and ethnicity (1992). Contextualising Hall's definition of racism within the historical conjuncture characterised by an intense flow of immigrants into the Italian nation, it is possible to note that the populist radical right holds a racist and ethnocultural nationalist view of the immigrant as inherently belonging to a different and threatening national out-group. The Manichean distinction between in-group and out-group, corresponding to the Self versus Other dichotomy of colonial reminiscence, is contingent upon ethnicity, religion, and culture, as the following chapters will explore. Therefore, nativism lies at the foundations of the Italian populist radical right's ideology, since it draws the borders between the in-group and the out-group (both delineated in nationalist and racist terms), consolidates the identity of the in-group, while debasing the identity of the out-group (Balibar 1991).

2.4 Italy's Presumed Immunity to Racism

The connection between nationalism and racism, in their intertwined formation of nativism, is logically straightforward. However, in Italy racism has long been a taboo question, and the country still has a vexed relationship with racism, despite it being a widespread phenomenon. Indeed, despite the self-absolving mythology of Italy's immunity from racism (Burgio 2000), Conelli argues that racism is deeply rooted in the Italian nation (2014: 151).

Italian national and racial identity have been imbricated with each other since the liberal era. In the racism of early twentieth-century Italy, the Other was represented by the Italian southerner, seen as alien and different from the northerner, due to their supposed Arabic (Semitic) or African (Hamitic) racial background (Giuliani 2014: 575). The southerner was framed as degenerate, criminal, irrational, inferior, insubordinate, inclined to alcoholism, filth, and sexual disease (Giuliani 2010: 37, 135), in need to be homogenised and tamed, through the civilising mission of Italy's north towards the south (Giuliani 2018: 32). Fascism consolidated the imbrication of Italian national and racial identity; however, it enacted a shift from the liberal era construction of racial and national identity in opposition to southern Italians, to the articulation of racial and national identity in opposition to the colonised Africans.

Therefore, fascism represented a turning point in the conceptualisation of national and racial identity in Italy: it unified the fragmented Italian national and racial identity of the liberal era, by incorporating and whitening the southern Italian, who had been the main Other against which Italy had defined its identity since unification (Giuliani 2018: 27). Indeed, the southern Italian came to symbolise the new model citizen: fertile, rural, loyal to the family, the church, the nation, and fascism (Giuliani 2018: 27). Hence, the negative qualities previously attached to the southerner started to be transposed onto the colonised Other. Moreover, it was fascist colonialism that adopted violence as a widespread colonial practice (Finaldi 2019). Fascist Italian national identity was thus refashioned to encompass both the north and south of Italy, knitted together by the fascist values of virility, patriarchy, obedience, and anti-urbanism. In an interesting twist of fate, the values connoting fascist national and racial identity were exemplified by the southerner, as opposed to the colonised African Other (Giuliani 2014: 573, 577), deemed to be inferior, weak, unruly, and prone to crime.

The racist representation of the colonised Other served a nationalist purpose. By depicting colonised people as uncivilised, the Italian state was able to shift the figure of the Other from southern Italians to the colonised, thus escaping its division between an allegedly superior north and a supposedly inferior, poor, and backward south. This was an instrumental move aimed at strengthening the cohesiveness of the Italian nation (Poidimani 2014: 215) and reducing its internal Otherness (Nani 2006). The internal Otherness that affected Italy was caused by its feeling inferior to Europe's Great Powers, due to its fragmentation between the north and south, which stunted political and economic development (King 1992: 154). This perception was exacerbated by the defeat of Italy's expansionist goals at the end of the First World War and worked as a propeller for Mussolini's aggrandisement plans.[5]

The analysis of the entanglement of national and racial identity during fascism serves as a theoretical background to grasp the complexity, contextuality, and historical roots of today's nativism. Indeed, Italy's lack of immunity to racism becomes patent in its late and sometimes failed attempts at multiculturalism (Agustoni, Ailetti, and Mantovan 2015). Although multiculturalism has failed in practice in some contexts, it is here to stay as a concept (Johansson 2022). Conceptually, multiculturalism consists of the co-existence of different ethno-cultural groups, through recognising and prizing religious, racial, and cultural diversity, along with fostering inclusion (Fowers and Richardson 1996). Hierarchies between different ethnic groups within a multicultural society may affect the ethnic groups' attitudes to multiculturalism, as the ethnic majority may conceive the latter as a threat to its economic and social rights (Sidanius and Pratto 2001), and to the uniqueness of its culture (Huntington 1996: 318). Indeed, as Werbner and Modood posit, multiculturalism does not necessarily have a positive value, as it can also be defined as the political outcome of continuous negotiations of cultural, ethnic, and racial differences (1997: vii). Such a definition throws into sharp relief the multiple, fluid and contested, and elastic nature of multiculturalism (Johansson 2022), which finds itself "between the Scylla of homogenising nationalism and the Charybdis of nativist cultural nationalism" (Werbner and Modood 1997: 262).

Multiculturalism is, in particular, the target of the populist radical right's nativist crusade, which is clearly blind to the changed international context (Veugelers 2000: 28–29): as Werbner and Modood maintain, multiculturalism is the paradigm of the postmodern global age (1997: 240). In fact, migration is a defining feature of contemporary international politics, due to dynamics and phenomena that are hard to reverse, such as climate change, wars, political and economic instability, and the economic exploitation of developing countries. Therefore, multiculturalism nowadays is not just ephemeral, but rather a long-lasting reality. The current multicultural reality the populist radical right is facing is well encapsulated in Hall's words on the multicultural question:

> And what that is, for me, is this: how are people from different cultures, different backgrounds, with different languages, different religious beliefs, produced by different and highly uneven histories, but who find themselves either directly connected because they've got to make a life together in the same place, or digitally connected because they occupy the same symbolic worlds – how are they to make some sort of common life together without retreating into warring tribes, eating one another, or insisting that other people must look exactly like you, behave exactly like you, think exactly like you – that is to say cultural assimilation?
>
> (Hall 2007: 150)

2.5 Nativism beyond the Populist Radical Right Confines

To treat the Italian populist radical right's racism as exclusive to these political parties is misleading. Nativism is not limited to the Italian populist radical right or to mainstream political parties co-opting the populist radical right, as it is also widespread at popular level due to a vicious circle: the nativist rhetoric of political elites, especially monopolised by the Italian populist radical right, deploys stereotypes linked to immigration, which are then reproduced by the media that shape social representations of immigrants (Bruno 2015: 63) and have an impact on public opinion (Rivera 2009: 13). Since the 1990s, the Italian media have deployed simplifications, exaggerations, and omissions in the processes of Othering, inferiorisation, and criminalisation of immigrants.

The media have generally represented immigrants as public enemies, criminals, and inferior Others, opposed to the idealised respectable Italian national. Moreover, the Italian media use a kind of linguistic inferiorisation, as they employ a specific lexicon to describe the immigrant Other, such as "clandestine," "invisible," "suspects," "violent," and "strangers" (Naletto 2011: 99). The linguistic inferiorisation of immigrants is further demonstrated by their denomination as *vu' cumpra'*, a term which has become common currency in the Italian language, a disparaging stereotypical adaptation of a southern Italian phrase to designate immigrants (Herzfeld 2007: 264). Similarly, the denomination of immigrants as *vu' lava'* mocks the immigrants' mispronunciation of the Italian *vuoi lavare*, which recalls the abjectifying stereotype of immigrants as unclean (Parati 1997: 171).

As Gerbaudo argues, there is an affinity between populist parties (such as the Lega and FdI) and social media, which provide a channel for the people (that populist parties claim to represent and speak to) to express their voices and coalesce by forming "online partisan crowds" (2018). Twitter, in particular, provides populist radical right leaders with a platform to perform their own charismatic persona (Kissas 2020). They cast themselves as authentic and, at the same time, they directly appeal to "the people" they claim to speak to and speak for (Kissas 2020). Therefore, social media turn into an instrument of political campaigning and renegotiation of power relations, thus increasing support for the populist parties that rely on them (Kissas 2020). Indeed, social media allow the propagation of messages in a direct, immediate, and interactive way, which suits a populist communication that is based on an unmediated and personalised relationship between the leader and the people (Bobba 2018; Viviani 2017). Social media are not just sites accessible to a wide number of people where individuals can initiate anti-immigrant discourse, but also act as an echo chamber for it. An echo chamber can, in fact, foster in-group communication (thus in-group cohesion), opposed to out-group demonisation (Lorenzetti 2020: 68).

Within the realm of nativism, Islamophobia is particularly deep-seated in Italian public opinion beyond the populist radical right. In the Italian multicultural setting, opposition to immigrants has frequently conflated with opposition to Islam (Caponio 2012). Most Italians have only a superficial knowledge of Islam, which is simplified and reduced to fundamentalism, caricaturised, Othered, inferiorised, and criminalised (Russo Spena 2009: 38–44). Especially in the aftermath of the 2015 terror attacks in Paris, the Muslim is represented as the dangerous and debased Other (Rivera 2017: 20). In 2010, *Corriere della Sera*, one of Italy's most widely read centrist newspapers, reported a commentary by political scientist Giovanni Sartori, who claimed that the integration of Muslims in Italy was impossible because of their supposed incompatibility with Italians (Rivera 2011: 11). Moreover, according to the thorough analyses of racism carried out by the research group *Cronache di Ordinario Razzismo*, Muslims, along with the Roma, are most vulnerable to racist attacks (Russo Spena 2014), carried out offline and online, especially on social media platforms such as Twitter, Facebook, YouTube and, more recently, TikTok (Andrisani 2020).

Islamophobia crystallises multiple tropes inherent to the discourse constructed by the West after the Cold War: the reconfiguration of the West's enemy from communism to Islam (Sciolino 1996); the conceptualisation, triggered by 9/11 and the war on terror, of Muslims as intrinsically dangerous (Hirschkind and Mahmood 2012); and the myth of Eurabia, namely a racist conspiracy theory foreseeing the unification of Europe and Arab countries (Carr 2006). While undeniably widespread in the West, these Islamophobic themes became a particularly attractive topic to the Italian populist radical right, because they resonated with these parties' call for increased security within a strong state, with their idealised promotion of an ethnically and culturally homogenous national community untainted by multiculturalism, and with their framing of the immigrant as Other.

It is not only the media that spread nativism, normalising it; school textbooks perform the same function. As education is coordinated by the state, it provides interesting insights into the message that the state intends to convey to its citizens. As Tabet acutely observes, a number of school textbooks in Italy have contributed to spread racism against immigrants (1997: 262). The literature does not offer abundant surveys of the presence and extent of racism in school textbooks. Valente, Caravita, and Castellani's survey of the representations of immigrants in Italian history and geography textbooks sheds light on how immigrants are depicted in a simplistic way, by falling prey to biological determinism and sexism (2014: 2). Despite the predominant historical role of Italy as an emigration country in the twentieth century and as an immigration country since the 1990s, the school curriculum does not contemplate the study of immigration as a topic, which hence becomes fragmented into different topics (Valente, Caravita, and Castellani 2014: 6, 9).

Among the textbooks examined by the authors, 4.6% of geography textbooks and only 1.6% of history textbooks deal with immigration (Valente, Caravita, and Castellani 2014: 6). Moreover, some aspects of migration are not adequately covered, such as the link between internal migration and immigration coming from abroad, the entrepreneurial projects established by immigrants and the massive employment of immigrant women in the welfare system (Valente, Caravita, and Castellani 2014: 10, 12). The images accompanying the texts mainly represent men, thus showing a gender imbalance in how immigration is portrayed in the Italian educational system (Valente, Caravita, and Castellani 2014: 12). Terminological confusion over terms such as *extracomunitari* and *clandestini* (Valente, Caravita, and Castellani 2014: 11) compounds the problem of lack of clarity and completeness. A further issue is the informative style being predominant in texts on immigration, while there is little persuasive style and almost no participatory style; thus, these texts do not persuade students or involve them in the discussion of this topic (Valente, Caravita, and Castellani 2014: 25). The fact that this survey was conducted in 2014 constitutes a limitation for its current applicability. Despite this limitation, it can be suggested that school textbooks have become vehicles of the discourse on immigration in Italy, whereby the immigrant Other takes the place of the colonial Other.

2.6 Conclusion

This chapter has set the theoretical foundations for the empirical analysis of the populist radical right discourse on immigration, which ensues in Chapters 4, 5, and 6. Nativism appears as the trait of the multidimensional ideology of the radical right that is more expedient to grasp the intricacies of the discourse on immigration. Nativism is composed of nationalism and racism. The nationalist belief that the nation (understood as an ethno-cultural construct) is to be inhabited solely by the native, i.e., those belonging to the nation, is inextricably connected with racism. Drawing on Hall's notion of racism as a discursive, dynamic, relational, and floating signifier whose meaning is strongly bound to context (1997), this chapter has critically considered Italian racism against the background of the Italian historical context, marked by fascism and colonialism.

Despite a supposedly weak Italian national identity, and the self-absolving mythology of Italian nation-building that considers Italy as exempt from racism (Burgio 2000), nationalism is a prime feature of the populist radical right, and racism is profoundly embedded in the Italian nation at large (Conelli 2014: 151; Giuliani 2018). Under fascism, the southern Other against which Italy defined its own national and racial identity was resignified by the colonised African (Conelli 2014: 151; Giuliani 2018: 26). Therefore, Italian racism is deeply rooted in the fracture of the peninsula between north and south and in Italian colonialism, especially in its fascist phase, which advanced and revived the colonial enterprise.

Notes

1 For an in-depth discussion of the debate between primordialist and modernist notions of the nation, see Ozkirimli (2010).
2 The Janus-faced representation of nationalism is drawn from Nairn (1975) and adapted to the context of the Italian populist radical right. In its original connotation, the Janus-faced figure of nationalism indicated both its inclusive and progressive force, and its reactionary and regressive force.
3 From Ancient Greek, meaning "the people intended as a civic community."
4 From Ancient Greek, meaning "the people intended as an ethno-cultural community."
5 Racism against southerners and against the colonial Other are not the only strands of racism present in Italian history after Italian unification: anti-Gipsyism and anti-Semitism were deep-seated as well (Giuliani 2018: 25).

References

Agustoni, A., Alietti, A. & Mantovan, C. (2015) *Territori e pratiche di convivenza interetnica*, Milan: Franco Angeli.
Alemanno, G. (2014) *Il Partito della nazione*, Rome: I libri del Borghese.
Allen, B. & Russo, M.J. (eds) (1997) *Revisioning Italy: National Identity and Global Culture*, Minneapolis: University of Minnesota Press.
Almond, G. & Verba, S. (1963) *The Civic Culture*, Princeton: Princeton University Press.
Andrisani, P. (2020) "Discorrendo d'odio. Un decennio di retoriche violente e razziste online e non solo", in *Cronache di ordinario razzismo. Quinto libro bianco sul razzismo in Italia*, Lunaria (eds), Rome: Lunaria, pp. 39–50
Antonsich, M. (2016) "International migration and the rise of the 'civil' nation", *Journal of Ethnic and Migration Studies*, vol. 42, no. 11, pp. 1790–1807.
Antonsich, M. (2016) "The neoliberal culturalist nation: Voices from Italy", *Transactions of the Institute of British Geographers*, vol. 41, no. 4, pp. 490–502.
Balibar, E. (1991) "Racism and nationalism", in *Race, nation, class: Ambiguous identities*, Balibar, E. & Wallerstein, I.M. (eds), London: Verso, pp. 37–68.
Bobba, G. (2018) "Social media populism: Features and "likeability" of Lega Nord communication on Facebook", *European Political Science*, vol. 18, pp. 11–23.
Bruno, M. (2015) "The journalistic construction of 'Emergenza Lampedusa': The 'Arab Spring' and the 'Landings' issue in media representations of migration", in *Destination Italy: Representing Migration in Contemporary Media and Narrative*, Bonsaver, G., Bond, E. & Faloppa, F. (eds), Oxford: Peter Lang.
Burgio, A. (2000) *Nel nome della razza. Il razzismo nella storia d'Italia, 1870–1945*, Bologna: Il Mulino.
Caponio, T. (2012) "Multiculturalism Italian Style: Soft or Weak Recognition?", in *Challenging Multiculturalism*, Taras, E. (ed.), Edinburgh: Edinburgh University Press. pp. 216–235.

Caravita, S., Castellani, T. & Valente, A. (2014) "Rappresentazione dei migranti nei libri di testo italiani di storia e geografia", *National Research Council, Institute for Research on Population and Social Policies working paper, no. 59*.

Carr, M. (2006) "You are now entering Eurabia", *Race and Class*, vol. 48, no. 1, pp. 1–22.

Conelli, C. (2014) "Razza, colonialità, nazione", in *Quel che resta dell'impero: La cultura coloniale degli italiani*, Deplano, V. & Pes, A. (eds), Milan: Mimesis, pp. 149–168.

Curran, G. (2004) "Mainstreaming populist discourse: The race-conscious legacy of neo-populist parties in Australia and Italy", *Patterns of Prejudice*, vol. 38, no. 1, pp. 37–55.

Dickie, J. (2001) "The notion of Italy", in *The Cambridge Companion to Modern Italian Culture*, Barański G.Z. & West R.J. (eds), Cambridge, UK: Cambridge University Press, pp. 17–34.

EURISPES (2022) *Italy Report 2022 Findings. 34th Italy Report – For a "Good Society"*. Available: https://eurispes.eu/en/news/italy-report-2022-findings/ [26 May 2022].

Finaldi, G. (2019) "Fascism, violence, and Italian colonialism", *The Journal of Holocaust Research*, vol. 33, no.1, pp. 22–42.

Fowers, B.J. & Richardson, F.C. (1996) "Why is multiculturalism good?", *American Psychologist*, vol. 51, no. 6, pp. 609–621.

Giuliani, G. (2010) "Whose whiteness? Cultural dis/locations between Italy and Australia", in *Transmediterranean: Diasporas, Histories, Geopolitical Spaces*, Pugliese, J. (ed.), Peter Lang, Brussels, pp. 125–138.

Giuliani, G. (2014) "L'Italiano Negro: The politics of colour in early twentieth-century Italy", *Interventions; International Journal of Postcolonial Studies*, vol. 16, no. 4, pp. 572–587.

Giuliani, G. (2018) *Race, Nation and Gender in Modern Italy: Intersectional Representations in Visual Culture*, London: Palgrave Macmillan.

Gomez-Reino Cachafeiro, M. (2002) *Ethnicity and Nationalism in Italian Politics: Inventing the Padania: Lega Nord and the Northern Question*, London: Routledge.

Hainsworth, P. (2008) *The Extreme right in Western Europe*, London, New York: Routledge.

Hall, S. (1992) "Race, culture, and communications. Looking backward and forward at cultural studies", *Rethinking Marxism*, vol. 5, no. 1, pp. 10–18.

Hall, S. (1997) "Race, the floating signifier featuring Stuart Hall transcript", The Media Education Foundation.

Hall, S. (2007) "Living with difference: Stuart Hall in conversation with Bill Schwarz", *Soundings*, vol. 37, pp. 148.

Hearn, J. (2006) *Rethinking Nationalism: A Critical Introduction*, New York: Palgrave Macmillan.

Herzfeld, M. (2007) "Small-mindedness writ large: On the migrations and manners of prejudice", *Journal of Ethnic and Migration Studies*, vol. 33, no. 2, pp. 255–274.

Hirschkind, C. & Mahmood, S. (2012) "Feminism, the Taliban, and politics of counter-insurgency", *Anthropological Quarterly*, vol. 75, no. 2, pp. 339–354.

Huntington, S.P. (1996) *The Clash of Civilizations and the Remaking of World Order*, New York: Simon & Schuster.

Huntington, S.P. et al. (1996) *The Clash of Civilizations?: The Debate*. New York: Council on Foreign Relations.

Johansson, T.R. (2022) "In defence of multiculturalism – Theoretical challenges", *International Review of Sociology*.

King, R. (1992) "Italy: from sick man to rich man of Europe", *Geography*, vol. 77, no. 2, pp. 153–169.

Kissas, A. (2020) "Performative and ideological populism: The case of charismatic leaders on Twitter", *Discourse & Society*, vol. 31, no.3, pp. 268–284.
Kohn, H. (1945) *The Idea of Nationalism: A Study in its Origins and Background*, London: The MacMillan Company.
Lorenzetti, M.I. (2020) "Right-wing populism and the representation of immigrants on social media. A critical multimodal analysis", *Iperstoria*, no. 15, pp. 59–95.
Martinelli, A. (2013) *Mal di nazione: Contro la deriva populista*, Milan: EGEA.
Nairn, T. (1975) "The modern Janus", *New Left Review*, vol. 1, no. 94, pp. 3–29.
Naletto, G. (2011) "Il razzismo istituzionale e il welfare", in *Cronache di ordinario razzismo*, Lunaria (eds), Rome: Edizioni dell'asino, pp. 25–30.
Nani, M. (2006) *Ai confini della nazione. Stampa e razzismo nell'Italia di fine Ottocento*, Bologna: Carocci.
Nevola, G. (2011) "A constitutional patriotism for Italian democracy: The contribution of president Napolitano", *Bulletin of Italian Politics*, vol. 3, no. 1, pp. 159–184.
Ozkirimli, U. (2010) *Theories of Nationalism: A Critical Introduction*, 2nd Revised and Extended Edition, Basingstoke: Palgrave Macmillan.
Parati, G. (1997) "Strangers in paradise: Foreigners and shadows in Italian literature", in *Revisioning Italy: National Identity and Global Culture*, Allen, B. & Russo, M.J. (eds), Minneapolis: University of Minnesota Press, pp. 169–190.
Poidimani, N. (2014) "Ius Sanguinis. Una Prospettiva di genere su razzismo e costruzione dell'italianità tra colonie e madrepatria", in *Quel che resta dell'impero. La cultura coloniale degli italiani*, Deplano, V. & Pes, A. (eds), Milan: Mimesis, pp. 209–234.
Renan, E. (1996) "What is a nation?", in *Becoming National: A Reader*, Eley, G. & R.G. Suny (eds), Oxford: Oxford University Press, pp. 42–56.
Rivera, A. (2007) "Razzismo", in *Diritti umani. Cultura dei diritti e dignità della persona nell'epoca della globalizzazione*, Turin: ed. UTET.
Rivera, A. (2009) "Il circolo vizioso del razzismo", in *Rapporto sul razzismo in Italia*, Naletto, G. & Andrisani, P. (eds), Rome: Manifestolibri; Lunaria, pp. 11–19.
Rivera, A. (2011) "Due anni di scena razzista in Italia. Protagonisti e comprimari, vittime e ribelli", in *Cronache di ordinario razzismo*, Lunaria (eds), Rome: Edizioni dell'asino, pp. 6–30.
Rivera, A. (2017) "Dalle politiche migranticide dell'Unione Europea alle comunità del rancore", in *Cronache di ordinario razzismo*, Lunaria (eds), Rome: Lunaria, pp. 10–22.
Russo Spena M. (2014) "L'Islam 'migrante' in casa. Tra processi di 'inclusione differenziale integrazione normativa' e aperta criminalizzazione", in *Cronache di ordinario razzismo*, Lunaria (eds), Rome: Lunaria, pp. 49–64.
Rydgren, J. (2007) "The sociology of the radical right", *Annual Review of Sociology*, vol. 33, no.1, pp. 241–262.
Sciolino, E. (1996) "Seeing green; The red menace is gone. But here's Islam", *The New York Times*. 21 January 1996. Available: https://www.nytimes.com/1996/01/21/weekinreview/seeing-green-the-red-menace-is-gone-but-here-s-islam.html [21 May 2018].
Sidanius, J. & Pratto, F. (2001) *Social Dominance: An Intergroup Theory of Social Hierarchy and Oppression*, Cambridge: Cambridge University Press.
Smith, A.D. (1991), *National Identity*, London: Penguin Books.
Tabet, P. (1997) *La Pelle giusta*, Turin: Einaudi.
Tarchi, M. (2003) "The political culture of the Alleanza Nazionale: An analysis of the party's programmatic documents (1995–2002)", *Journal of Modern Italian Studies*, vol. 8, no. 2, pp. 135–181.

Verdicchio, P. (1997) "Discourse in Southern Italy", in *Revisioning Italy: National Identity and Global Culture*, Allen, B. & Russo, M.J. (eds), Minneapolis: University of Minnesota Press, pp. 191–212.

Veugelers, J.W. (2000) "Right-wing extremism in contemporary France: A 'Silent Counterrevolution'?", *The Sociological Quarterly*, vol. 41, no. 1, pp. 19–40.

Vidali, Z. (2011) "The socio-political and ideological-cultural elements of the Italian nation and the national minority question in Italy", *Journal of Ethnic Studies*, vol. 65, pp. 36–59.

Viviani, L. (2017) "A Political Sociology of Populism and Leadership", *Società Mutamento Politica*, vol. 8, no. 15, pp. 279–303.

Werbner, P. & Modood, T. (1997) *The Politics of Multiculturalism in the New Europe: Racism, Identity and Community*, London: Zed Books.

Zimmer, O. (2003) *Nationalism in Europe, 1890–1940*, Basingstoke: Palgrave Macmillan.

3 Research Design

The research aim of this book is to investigate the role of colonial and fascist memory in the Italian populist radical right. In order to do so, this book analyses a unique set of 46 in-depth interviews, complemented with an analysis of manifestos. Quantitative methods have been fruitfully employed to analyse political discourse: for instance, Cavalieri and Froio (2021) offer a quantitative analysis of parliamentary questions from 1996 to 2019 in Italy, to measure the level of attention given to a set of 21 topics. They demonstrate that populist parties in office do not behave radically, given institutional constraints and the desire to present themselves as responsible (Cavalieri and Froio 2021). Ruzza and Fella (2011) provide a frame analysis of the discourse of the populist radical right extracted from party programmes, before proceeding with a quantitative analysis to identify the ideological frames prevailing in party official communication to the electorate. However, purely qualitative approaches to the topic are comparatively much less frequent. For example, Berti (2021) deploys a qualitative content analysis of Salvini's Facebook posts concerning the *Sea-Watch 3* case, to identify the discursive features of the criminalisation of NGOs in the Lega. Especially, a CDA of interviews and manifestos applied to the research aim at hand is missing to date. Therefore, this book makes the original move of using a CDA of 46 in-depth interviews with populist radical right representatives and intellectuals, enriched with manifesto analysis for contextualisation.

In general, qualitative methods have the commendable ability to generate data that are sensitive to the social context and allow the researcher to capture depth, complexity, and nuances of data (Mason 2002: 64). In particular, interviews with the members of Italian populist radical right parties and with Italian populist radical right intellectuals allow to elicit their perspectives on immigration and on colonial and fascist memory, which would not otherwise emerge through official documents, such as parliamentary debates, party manifestos, surveys, and press releases. Indeed, semi-structured interviews offer flexibility to the researcher in terms of questions to ask, which can be tailored to the research participant, in order to gauge the information sought after. An additional advantage afforded by semi-structured interviews is that open-ended questions enable the respondents to articulate their answers spontaneously, openly, and fully (Harrison and Bruter 2011: 56–57). A set of targeted standardised interview questions, though, were selected

DOI: 10.4324/9781003252597-4

to ensure the comparability of interviews and consistency in the data gathered (Harrison and Bruter 2011: 57). Interview questions were created based on the existing literature on the populist radical right, the Italian historical and political context, and the memory of colonialism and fascism. Contemporary news related to current events were crucial to make sure the interviews would be relevant to the political, economic, and social current situation in Italy and across the world. The detailed rationale behind interview questions is explained in Appendix 1.

Interviews carry inevitable drawbacks. As Mason points out, objectivity is difficult to achieve, and it is impossible to completely eradicate bias (2002: 65). In any case, the validity of a research method does not hinge on the achievement of complete neutrality and on the eradication of the political stance of researchers (Heller et al. 2017). However, to mitigate the risk of subjectivity, the researcher adheres to a scrupulous analysis that proceeds both deductively, based on categories drawn from the literature on nativism, populism, and memory; and inductively, generating categories grounded in the data gathered. Furthermore, the researcher is aware of multiple perspectives in interpreting data, and, through the concept of reflexivity, acknowledges that their unique position influences the interview and the production of knowledge (Heller et al. 2017). As Perrino (2019) notes, the interviewer and the interviewee engage in the process of co-production of discourse, and, in turn, of knowledge.

Another potential shortcoming is scarce representativeness that may endanger the validity of interview data (Dierickx 1996). To mitigate this risk, inherent to small-N qualitative studies, this study selected a sample of party representatives based on their party membership (16 Lega; 24 FdI) and of intellectuals related to the populist radical right (6); level of involvement within the chosen political parties (6 parliamentarians, 11 regional councillors, 23 local councillors), and geographical area (24 north, 11 centre, 5 south of Italy). The interviewees represent a wide range of regions: Lombardy, Friuli-Venezia Giulia, Veneto, and Trentino-Alto Adige (in the north); Tuscany, Marche, and Lazio (in the centre); and Campania and Calabria (in the south). Gender balance was impossible to attain, because only five female party representatives granted an interview. The party representatives and intellectuals were contacted via email and the response rate was low, which may be explained by their busy schedules.

Interview data are complemented by anecdotal evidence gathered from party manifestos, valuable to identify the ideological elements of the populist radical right projected externally to the electorate. Being the façade of parties, manifestos provide the official image parties construct and present to voters (Harrison and Bruter 2011: 58), in the attempt to enlarge their electoral gains. They also portray a unitary image of parties, thus overcoming the diversity of opinions inherent to the interviews (Harrison and Bruter 2011: 54). The manifestos analysed contain interesting elements related to the party's official ideology, focusing on reactionary values, the importance of a strong state, the nation, opposition to the elites, and to immigration. However, manifestos do not include references to fascist and colonial memory, which are not popular themes that would sell to the electorate. Another downside of manifestos is that the external image of the party they represent may be more moderate than it is in reality (Harrison and Bruter 2011: 58), due to strategic calculations to appeal to a larger electorate. Additionally, party manifestos present a unitary ideological position, concealing the ideological heterogeneity of views among party representatives (Harrison and Bruter 2011: 54). Nevertheless, the interviews uncover the party's latent ideology, and the individual ideological preferences making up the parties under scrutiny.

The manifestos scrutinised were obtained through the Manifesto Project Database, an extensive database of party manifestos from 50 different countries spanning in time from 1945 to today, as well as through local coders. The manifestos were created for national elections campaigns and cover the timespan from 2013, the beginning of so-called "migration crisis," to 2021. In this timeframe, only one national election was actually contested. Therefore, the Lega's 2018 manifesto and the FdI's 2018 manifesto are analysed, and insights are added as anecdotal evidence, complementing the bulk of the data garnered from the in-depth interviews with the Italian populist radical right's representatives.

Semi-structured interviews are then examined through CDA, which understands discourse as reflecting social relationships, which are in turn constituted by power dynamics. Hence, discourse ultimately mirrors power dynamics. In particular, CDA focuses on how "social power abuse, dominance, and inequality are enacted, reproduced and resisted by text and talk in the social and political context" (Van Dijk 2008: 352). CDA has a two-fold advantage. First, it is especially useful in unmasking discursive tools used by the populist radical right, elucidated below (Wodak 2015). Second, CDA considers the wider historical context in which discourse is inserted.

Specific features of political discourse that are expedient to unearth the populist radical right's ideology are binary conceptualisations (Chilton 2004: 201–204), clear in the dichotomy between the Italian Self and the immigrant Other; the strategy of coercion, whereby participants induce fear of the other (Chilton 2004: 118); metaphors, hyperboles, mitigation, and euphemisation of the dominant group's crimes (Van Dijk 2008: 362). Wodak, a pioneer of CDA, elucidates further discursive strategies deployed in particular by the populist radical right: through the topos of threat the populist radical right induces fear of the Other, to legitimate its attack on the latter (2015: 53); through the politics of denial, the populist radical right formally denies racism, to appear more moderate, before slipping into racist statements (2015: 58); through the fallacy of sameness and the fallacy of difference, the populist radical right portrays the in-group as homogeneous and as inherently opposed to the out-group (2015: 54); finally, through legitimation through authorisation, the populist radical right resorts to data in order to buttress its own arguments (2015: 6).

References

Berti, C. (2021) "Right-wing populism and the criminalization of sea-rescue NGOs: The 'Sea-Watch 3' case in Italy, and Matteo Salvini's communication on Facebook", *Media, Culture & Society*, vol. 43, no. 3, pp. 532–550.

Cavalieri, A. & Froio, C. (2021) "The behaviour of populist parties in parliament. The policy agendas of populist and other political parties in the Italian question time", *Italian Political Science Review/Rivista Italiana di Scienza Politica*, First View, pp. 1–14.

Chilton, P.A. (2004) *Analysing Political Discourse Theory and Practice*, London; New York: Routledge.

Dierickx, G. (1996) "Ideology: The theoretical construct and its empirical consequences", ECPR Joint Sessions of Workshops, Oslo, March–April.

Harrison, S. & Bruter, M. (2011) *Mapping Extreme Right Ideology: An Empirical Geography of the European Extreme Right*, London: Palgrave Macmillan.

Heller, M., Pietikäinen, S. & Pujolar, J. (2017) *Critical Sociolinguistic Research Methods Studying Language Issues That Matter*, London: Routledge.

Mason, J. (2002) *Qualitative Researching*, London: Sage.

Perrino, S. (2019) "Narrating migration politics in Veneto, Northern Italy", *Narrative Culture*, vol. 6, no. 1, pp. 44–68.

Ruzza, C. & S. Fella (2011) "Populism and the Italian right", *Acta Politica*, vol. 46, no. 2, pp. 158–179.

Van Dijk, T.A. (2008) "Critical discourse analysis", in *The Handbook of Discourse Analysis*, Schiffrin, D., Tannen, D. & Hamilton, H.E. (eds), New York: John Wiley & Sons, pp. 352–371.

Wodak, R. (2015) *The Politics of Fear: What Right-wing Populist Discourses Mean*, London: Sage.

4 "Italians First"
The Ethno-cultural Nation with Civic Undertones

4.1 Introduction

"Prima gli Italiani" ("Italians First") has been dominating the slogans of the Italian populist radical right. Indeed, the Italian populist radical right parties' discourse is studded with references to nationalism. Since its foundation, FdI has styled itself as *"il* partito della Nazione"[1] (Alemanno 2014). The slogan *"Prima l'Italia"* shows FdI's ethno-cultural nationalism, as the party prioritises the *patria* and its national in-group over an implicit out-group (Alemanno 2014: 42). While FdI has always been undeniably nationalist since its inception (Mammone 2018), the Lega has regionalist origins, whose residues are still present.

Since its foundation in 1991 until 2013, the Lega defined its ethno-cultural identity (Rusconi 1993) in regionalist terms, articulated around the socio-economic cleavage separating the north from the south (Gomez-Reino Cachafeiro 2002). The ethno-cultural identity of the Lega was grounded in the so-called *Padania*, the Lega's imagined national community (Huysseune 2010: 4), roughly corresponding to northern Italy. Regionalism coexisted with anti-southern racism, as well as with racism against immigrants from abroad. In the late-1990s, the Lega started to shift its focus from regionalist demands and hostility towards the southern Other to hostility towards immigrants. It is precisely around this time that the Lega began to fashion a nationalist ideology prizing the in-group as opposed to the immigrant out-group (Zaslove 2004: 105). The nationalisation of the Lega culminated with Salvini's ascent to the leadership of the party in 2013 (Albertazzi, Giovannini, and Seddone 2018).

Building on the theoretical foundations of nation and nationalism established in the previous chapter, this chapter sets out to unpack the multiplicity of strands inherent to the Lega's and FdI's nationalism. A copious amount of literature classifies the Italian populist radical right with ethno-cultural nationalism (Curran 2004: 48; Tarchi 2003: 146). In contrast, Gomez-Reino Cachafeiro also traces, within the Lega, some civic elements associated with the north, such as democracy, good government, and hard work, mixed with the predominantly ethno-cultural nationalism grounded in shared culture, language, and ethnicity (2002: 100–102). What results is the Janus-faced nation theoretically outlined in Chapter 2. In fact, the nationalism nourished by the Italian populist radical right

DOI: 10.4324/9781003252597-5

is predominantly ethno-cultural, even though some civic undertones emerge. This notion challenges the widely held view that Italian nationalism is monolithically ethno-cultural.

Nonetheless, faced with the question over who belongs to the Italian nation, the predominantly ethno-cultural nationalism of the Italian populist radical right becomes unsettled. Interestingly, these parties symbolically open up the borders of Italy to regular immigrants. This surprising move is in line with the incorporation of regular migrants into the body of the nation observed by Antonsich (2016). Indeed, this incorporation may be deployed strategically to sharpen the dichotomy between regular immigrants, welcomed into the nation, and evil irregulars, who are doomed to remain cast off from the nation. At the same time, the symbolical integration of regular immigrants into the nation may be interpreted within the Italian populist radical right's "civic zeitgeist" and attempt at mainstreaming, convenient to project themselves as more civic and moderate, thus enlarging their potential electorate (Halikiopoulou, Mock, and Vasilopoulou 2013).

A terminological clarification is needed here: the Lega and FdI more often adopt the term *patria* instead of the term *nazione*, to signify the nation. The term *patria* will be used thereafter, in the analysis of the Italian populist radical right interviews.

4.2 The Ethno-cultural Nation

The equation between *patria* and culture prevails in the discourse of FdI, the Lega, and populist radical right intellectuals. Culture is often linked to the concept of identity, though the latter is controversial and needs further qualification. Identity simultaneously underlines the ethno-cultural homogeneity of the Italian *patria* and its difference compared to the immigrant Other. Although the Italian populist radical right highlights the identity of the *patria*, it is necessary to problematise it. In the interviews not only with the Lega, but also with FdI and intellectuals, the difference between the north and south of the Italian nation often emerges (F20180104F, F20170104M, G20170407P), concerning the mindset (M20170113R), culture (A20180103LC, E20180103G), physical features, dialects, and weather conditions, which, in the words of a Lega representative, "are conducive to productivity in the north and fun in the south" (F20160905L). The emphasis on the difference between north and south upsets the homogeneous identity of the *patria* supported by the populist radical right. One Lega representative even lamented that "Italians have not been made yet," as the only element of cohesion is a shared language, which has obliterated local dialects (G20180105M). The north-south dichotomy further weakens Italian national identity (Verdicchio 1997: 194) and testifies once more to the persistence of the fracture of the peninsula between north and south. What is most remarkable, however, is the emphasis on difference as opposed to national identity that occasionally surfaces not only in the Lega's discourse, but also within FdI, which is officially characterised by the dogma of national unity and identity and formally rejects anti-southern views (Alemanno 2014: 53).

The *patria* is also frequently associated with two related elements: forefathers and history. In the interviews, there are emotional references to the forefathers as the "owners" (see, for instance, C20180109G, G20170407P, L20180105S), "creators and defenders" of Italian territory (E20170404C, G20170109D). This metaphor becomes particularly emotionally invested when the *patria* is said to be too distant and not able to recognise "its children" anymore (S20180108S). As CDA illuminates, the metaphor of "children" to signify Italian citizens is similarly deployed when the *patria* is accused of "not having anything to give to its own children" (C20180109G). Returning to the forefathers, as the interviews reveal, they are the protagonists of national history, which is another pivotal characteristic of the *patria*. Indeed, FdI members stressed the fact that the *patria* is referred to as national history (see, for instance, C20180109G, G20180109C), as "hardships, conquests, victories, and defeats" cemented the nation (F20170408T). However, only one Lega representative gave weight to "the historical roots" that "Italians feel" (G20170112G). Moreover, history is tightly knitted with traditions, which is another element the *patria* relates to in the interviews with FdI, the Lega, and populist radical right intellectuals (see, for instance, F20160905L, F20170111S, R20180111PM). Finally, history is sporadically related to art, which an FdI representative and an intellectual considered as associated with the *patria* (C20180109G, G20170407P).

The connection of the *patria* with the people or the community referenced in the interviews with the Lega and FdI (F20170110F, F20160905L, G20170112G, M20170404F) recalls the Italian populist radical right's excluding populism, which traces the borders of the people along ethno-cultural lines (Aalberg and De Vreese 2017: 10). The Lega and FdI's populism thus becomes intricately mixed with nationalism. These two ideological traits typical of the populist radical right rotate around the empty signifiers of the people and the nation, which are located onto two spatial axes: "populism is constructed on an up-down axis pitting the people against the elites, and nationalism is constructed on an in-out axis opposing the people against the out-group" (Griffini 2019). These empty signifiers become invested with meanings as the concept of people omits the elites and the out-group, and the nation excludes the out-group.

Furthermore, the Italian populist radical right attributes to the *patria* specific moral and physical characteristics which reinforce the ethno-cultural aspect of nationalism. Indeed, the character of Italians apparently consists of being aesthetically beautiful (M20170104G), speaking with hands, being cheerful and hardworking, more like the Greeks than the Scandinavians (L20170104N), unflinching in adversities (M20170104G), and creative (F20160905L). Nevertheless, although character may be assumed to be a manifestation of ethnicity, in the interviews clear references to ethnicity as a defining feature of the *patria* are rare (see, for instance, F20170408T, L20170406C) and are confined to FdI, and populist radical right intellectuals. However, even FdI does not always equate the *patria* with ethnicity. In fact, few FdI politicians and an intellectual took pains to clarify that the *patria* is not necessarily ethnically composed and explicitly eschewed any racial connotation of it (E20170404C, F20170408T, G20170407P, G20170111R, R20180104M).

Additional ethno-cultural elements that demarcate the *patria* are, predictably, the national flag and the national anthem. National symbols, such as the national flag and the national anthem, can be acquired if an immigrant adopts them, but are generally emotionally charged and attached to the ethno-cultural nation. In line with the FdI's adoption of the national flag in their logo, in the interviews, FdI representatives associated the national flag, called the *tricolore*,[2] with the *patria* (F20180104F, F20170111S). Similarly, an FdI representative lamented that children do not know the national anthem (F20170111S).

The association of the *patria* with the home calls for a qualification regarding the classification of the home within the civic or the ethno-cultural camp. Indeed, while the home may be a civic value acquired voluntarily by those willing to be part of the nation, this metaphor, which is generally a rhetorical figure frequently deployed in political discourse (Chilton 2004: 51), is often employed to define a contrast between the Italian *patria* and the Others, i.e., the immigrants, thus assuming ethno-cultural connotations. For instance, one Lega representative's statement that as Christians cannot build a church in the immigrants' countries of origin, then immigrants cannot build a mosque "in our *home*" (E20180103G) equates the home to the Italian ethno-cultural nation characterised by Christianity. Similarly, in the interviews, FdI and Lega representatives circumscribed the home in ethno-cultural terms, by remarking the need to avoid an influx of immigrants into "the home," i.e., Italy (F20180104F, R20180104M), and by requiring that immigrants entering someone's "home," i.e., Italy, respect the rules (F20180104F) and the lifestyle of the host (S20180103F). The metaphor of the home also figures prominently in the security discourse articulated around immigration, whereby the Italian populist radical right highlights the necessity to protect one's own "home," i.e., Italy, "against intruders" (M20170104G, R20180104M), i.e., the immigrants, especially Muslims (P20161219B).

Probing deeper into the interviews with the Italian populist radical right, an interesting grammatical feature emerges from CDA: the usage of the first-person plural possessive *our* to illuminate the contrast between the Italian Self and the immigrant Other. Following Cameron's focus on first-person pronouns suggesting a collective voice (2001: 127), it is worth noting the frequent use of the first-person plural possessive adjective to denote the cohesion of the Italian collectivity vis-à-vis immigrants. Again, while this is not exclusive to the Italian populist radical right, it still illuminates an interesting feature of these parties' discourse. For instance, the interviews are interspersed with phrases such as "*our* laws," "*our* identity," "*our* culture," "*our* forefathers" (F20170104M, F20170111S, G20170405C, G20170411C, G20170112G, G20170111R), which underline the contrast between the Italian *patria* and laws, and the immigrants (A20180103DC, F20170111S, G20180105M, M20170113R), in order to mark the difference between the Self and the Other. The use of the possessives also engenders a sense of commonality with the readers (Ajmi 2013: 157), which may be particularly useful to populist parties, aiming at closing the gap between politicians and the people they claim to represent. Moreover, possessives help construct a coherent group identity, which, as a result, implies a polarisation of representations (Ajmi 2013: 152) pitting the Self against the Other.

4.3 The Civic Nation

The civic undertones of the Italian populist radical right's conception of the *patria*, such as the right to work, progress, and values, are less frequent than the ethno-cultural ones. In the interviews, the right to work surfaces as a civic value (C20180109G), which is rooted in Article 4 of the Italian Constitution (C20180109G), as well as progress (F20170111S), which carries an uncanny resonance to the nationalist and colonial belief that the Italian *patria* supposedly carried the burden of bringing progress to the colonies (Ben-Ghiat 2006: 386). While Italian laws or institutions, typically civic features of the nation, are mentioned only in denigrating terms and not related to the *patria*, the values attached to the *patria* are the civic values of "fraternity, communality, neighbourliness" (F20170111S) and the more ambiguous "Judaeo-Christian values" (L20170406C), which apparently overlap with ethno-cultural connotations of the *patria*.

Nevertheless, territory prevails within the civic understanding of the *patria* in FdI, the Lega, and populist radical right intellectuals. In the interviews, the ways in which territory is referred to are diverse, but they all imply a geographical entity. "The *patria* is a shared territory, which does not necessarily coincide with today's geographical borders, but it is certainly characterised by the land, the soil," an FdI representative argued (F0170408T). Territory is sometimes related to personal history, since it is defined as "where you live" (L20170104N, R20180108D), "where you choose to set your roots" (L20170104N), and "where we grew up" (R20180104M). Other characterisations of territory, despite associating the *patria* with it, add ascribed elements given by birth, which cannot be acquired, as evidenced by the definition of the *patria* as "the place where we/I were/was born" (F20160905L, R20180108D). Therefore, this connotation of the *patria* intricately mixes civic undertones related to the territory with more ethno-cultural tinges linked to birth, which underline the fact that Italian nationalism cannot be categorised as solely civic or solely ethno-cultural. While the Italian populist radical right is interspersing its nationalism with civic elements, in order to enlarge its electoral appeal, it has not eradicated the remnants of ethno-cultural nationalism.

4.4 The Anathema of Multiculturalism

As argued in Chapter 2, multiculturalism is the paradigm of the postmodern age, marked by globalisation and migration: ossified national borders preserving the unity and homogeneity of the ethno-cultural nation are a superseded concept the populist radical right tends to cling to. The Lega advocates a homogeneous community, by reversing the evils of multiculturalism and the deviations of modern and egalitarian society. Also, FdI denounces multiculturalism as a form of tyranny (Mammone 2018: 38). However, the rejection of multiculturalism is not automatically linked to the evocation of a romanticised past, as Caiani, Della Porta, and Wagemann (2012: 132) postulate. In fact, the rejection of multiculturalism does not necessarily equate with the call for an idealised past, which is absent from the interviews and manifestos analysed. Indeed, as the interviews and manifestos reveal, the intellectuals, the Lega and FdI express a strong dislike of multiculturalism, which is considered a risk (G20180109C, G20170109D), and a phenomenon to be avoided (see, for instance, F20170104M, L20170406C, M20170404F, R20180108D, R20180104M). An FdI representative went to extreme lengths to argue that a multicultural civilisation would resemble "anarchy, where everyone feels free to do whatever they like," claiming that "a multicultural civilisation has never existed, apart from the Persians, which were led by an upper caste" (R20180104M).

The reasons behind the hostility towards multiculturalism are multifarious. For instance, apprehension about multiculturalism is rooted in a negative view of "cultural hybridisation" (F20170104M). According to FdI representatives, "it is upsetting to see teenagers who have never been to the Uffizi acting like Harlem rappers" (F20170408T), and to "see kebab shops in Italy and McDonald's outlets in Arab countries" (G20180109C). In a Lega representative's words, "Italy has its own traditions, which cannot be mixed with Muslim ones or, even worse, with the Roma ones" (P20161219B). Other causes of antagonism towards multiculturalism are that it allegedly upsets social peace (M20170113R) and generates overpopulation with all the ensuing demographic strains (S20180103F). The hostility towards multiculturalism is related to the Italian populist radical right's call for the defence of Italian identity, traditions, and customs (M20170404F, P20161219B). A measure commended by the Lega for protecting Italian culture and traditions is the law in force in Lombardy that provides regional dialect classes in some schools, so that "differences and liberty are preserved" (F20170104M). Hence, the Lega praises cultural differences among Italians, but not between Italians and other cultures. Some populist radical right intellectuals, and some FdI and Lega representatives recognised, when interviewed, that multiculturalism is inevitable (see, for instance, C20170106V, G20170405C, G20180109C, G20170112G, G20170407P, G20170111R), with the caveat that it is necessary to defend Italian cultural identity (G20170112G, G20170407P, N20180108C) and "our roots and values, even forcibly" (G20170405C). Only one interviewee, from the Lega, explicitly defined multiculturalism as desirable, "as it implies respect for the Other" (S20180108S). It is important to observe, though, that the Italian populist radical right's explicit rejection of a racially defined *patria* stands in stark contrast with these parties' latent racism that has been theoretically foregrounded in Chapter 2 (see, for instance, Giuliani 2018), and which will be analysed in depth later.

The Italian radical right's aversion to multiculturalism indicates that multiculturalism is not treated as a peaceful and productive project embracing ethno-cultural diversity, but, on the contrary, is perceived as threatening. This perception is also widespread among the local population, which envisages the immigrant as degraded and dangerous, through a process of territorial stigmatisation, exclusion, and segregation (Agustoni, Alietti, and Mantovan 2015: 7). Therefore, the populist radical right panders to the fears of the national in-group and fans the fires of its Othering, but also of its criminalisation of immigrants (tackled in depth in Chapter 6). Italian local residents react to this moral panic either by fleeing those seemingly contaminated spaces, or by protesting in defence of an idealised *locus amoenus* (Agustoni, Alietti, and Mantovan 2015: 8).

The widespread rejection of multiculturalism in Italy appears anachronistic, especially in the light of the massive influx of immigrants that, since the 1990s, have punctuated the predominantly homogenous Italian ethno-cultural nation. The pervasive dismissal of multiculturalism in Italy shaped by the Italian populist radical right taps into the natural disposition of human beings to identify themselves in opposition to the Other, which can be defined in terms of ethnicity, religion, gender, and class, for example. In fact, the Italian populist radical right conceives multiculturalism as the predominant trend associated with immigration (Veugelers 2000: 28–29), and sees immigration as the culprit of the alienation felt by the Italian residents of multicultural spaces.

4.5 Who Belongs to the Italian Nation?

Tightly connected with the definition of *patria* is the question of who can belong to it, which sheds further light on the civic and ethno-cultural connotations of the *patria*. To elicit the views of the Lega, FdI, and the intellectuals over membership of the Italian nation, the question posed in the interviews was "Does the Italian *patria* belong to Italians or to those who love it?"

Part of FdI, and, on a smaller scale, the Lega and populist radical right intellectuals believe that Italy belongs to Italians (see, for instance, F20170110F, F20160905L, G20180109C, L20170410P, N20180108C, S20180103F), thus signalling an ethno-cultural conception of the *patria*, excluding the out-group. However, the predominantly ethno-cultural notion of the *patria* is unsettled by the fact that the Lega, FdI, and populist radical right intellectuals mainly consider that Italy belongs to those who love it (see, for instance, F20180103B, G20170112G, G20180110S, M20170404F, M20170104G, R20180111PM), who are described as those who try to improve it (C20170106V, P20161219B) or defend it (R20180104M). In the words of an FdI representative, the *patria* "must not be a closed concept" (F20180104F); therefore, its borders do not rest on exclusionary ethno-cultural grounds.

The loosening of rigid symbolical ethno-cultural borders of the *patria* to make space for non-Italians by virtue of their love for Italy needs to be qualified. Indeed, one Lega representative stated that even if the *patria* belongs to those who love it, immigrants cultivate a different kind of love (F20160905L). As a result, a hierarchy within the membership of the *patria* is created: immigrants' love for Italy is different from the one cultivated by Italians. Finally, some FdI representatives ambivalently claimed that Italy belongs both to Italians and to those who love it (F20170110F, F20170408T, G20180109C, N20180108C, S20180103F). Therefore, in-depth reading of the interviews, considering their broader context, signals that the conditions for immigrants to belong to the Italian nation are: (1) their love for Italy; (2) their status as regular immigrants, whose regularity is, in the interviews, contingent upon their work and respect for Italy.

Overall, the fact that most of the Italian populist radical right claims that the nation can also encompass immigrants, casts light on the contradiction inherent to its nationalism: while the nation is predominantly demarcated along ethno-cultural lines excluding immigrants, the Italian populist radical right, when explicitly asked who belongs to the nation, strategically resorts to more moderate terms by symbolically opening up the borders of the nation to immigrants. It is only regular immigrants, or those who (vaguely stated) love Italy, that can become incorporated within the nation, as Antonsich notes regarding the normalisation of regular immigrants within the Italian nation (2016: 10).

This symbolic opening up of the borders of the nation can be interpreted as a strategy of the Italian populist radical right to appear moderate, by appropriating civic values, such as inclusiveness, and including them into their otherwise nativist discourse in search for legitimacy and respectability (Halikiopoulou, Mock, and Vasilopoulou 2013). Another interpretation may be found in the populist radical right's willingness to mark the contrast between regular and irregular immigrants. Therefore, according to this interpretation, stating that regular immigrants can be part of the Italian nation becomes an instrumental choice to further exclude the irregulars, thus heightening a sense of fear of the irregular Other.

The symbolic inclusion into the nation of certain kinds of immigrants, pending their fulfilment of precise criteria, is, however, different from granting citizenship. Citizenship laws are outside the scope of this book, but the Lega's and FdI's views on them deserve a brief excursus. Although the Italian populist radical right gives regular immigrants, verbally at least, the possibility of becoming part of the nation, it denies all immigrants, including the regular ones, Italian citizenship even when they reside in Italy. In fact, when it comes to commenting on the law proposal of the *jus soli*,[3] the Lega, FdI, and populist radical right intellectuals take a firm stance against it (see, for instance, F20180104F, G20180109C, S20180808S). In the words of an FdI representative, the *jus soli* is a "swear word," a "folly," and tantamount to "social disintegration" (S20180103F). Predictably, the law aimed at introducing the *jus soli* and abrogating the *jus sanguinis* was defeated in the Senate in December 2017 (Gaita 2018). In the 2018 electoral campaign, the Lega stated that "The acquisition of citizenship should take place in the face of effective naturalization, contingent on socio-economic integration and cultural assimilation" (Lega Manifesto 2018: 23), leaving the meaning and measurement of socio-economic integration and cultural assimilation open for interpretation. Apart from being deployed as a political campaigns tug-of-war, the *jus soli* remains dormant in Parliament.

In the first half of 2022, the Chamber of Deputies discussed the bill to introduce the *jus scholae* to grant citizenship to minors born in Italy by foreign parents, or foreign minors who arrived in Italy before the age of 12, and have completed a cycle of studies in Italy for at least five years. The Lega opposed the bill, contending that, at this time of crisis, pushing to give citizenship to immigrants is disrespectful towards Italians (Il Sole 24 Ore Redazione 2022). FdI supported the Lega's opposition to the *jus scholae* proposal. Meloni branded the proposal as ideological and removed from the concrete problems of Italian citizens, who struggle with an unprecedented economic crisis (Il Sole 24 Ore Redazione 2022). At the time of writing, the proposals for the *jus soli* and the *jus scholae* have been used as a point of contention in political campaigns waged by the Lega and FdI against the centre-left PD.

4.6 Conclusion

This chapter departs from the Italian populist radical right's trademark slogan "Prima gli Italiani" (i.e., "Italians First"). This slogan is not just a skilful marketing strategy, but it well encapsulates the conceptualisation of the nation in the discourse of the Lega and FdI. Overall, the interviews show that nationalism looms predictably large in the discourse of the Lega and FdI, where it is closely interrelated with anti-immigrant sentiment. Indeed, against the background of a perceived decline tied to immigration and the elites' management of it, the Italian populist radical right claims to speak for the people against the out-group, constituted by the elites (especially in relation to their management of immigration), and by immigrants. By exploiting and further exacerbating this sense of decline, the Italian populist radical right projects itself as the saviour of the people against the elites and immigration, and as the saviour of the nation against immigration. Incidentally, in the Lega's and FdI's imagery, the concept of the people becomes largely equated with the concept of the nation, which is predominantly pinned down to the people not belonging to the immigrant out-group. Interestingly, however, the conception of the nation does not exclude the elites that are otherwise excluded from the conception of the people.

Unsurprisingly, the discursive construction of the nation that emerges from the interviews is predominantly delimited by ethno-cultural considerations studded by rare civic nuances. Indeed, some civic undertones complicate this otherwise monotonous picture of ethno-cultural nationalism: the parties sometimes characterise the nation in terms of shared territory, progress, and values. This notion challenges the widely held view that Italian nationalism is monolithically ethno-cultural. Ethno-cultural nationalism features emphasis on shared identity, forefathers, history, culture, language, as well as national symbols, such as the national flag and the national anthem. The Italian populist radical right's attempt to revive the Italian sense of national identity is rooted in these parties' belief that the Italian sense of national identity is feeble.

Crucially, this chapter illuminates a conundrum in the discourse of the Italian populist radical right. Indeed, when explicitly asked who belongs to Italy, the Lega and the FdI representatives implicitly challenge their prevalent ethno-cultural categorisation of the nation related with excluding populism, as they do not bar regular immigrants from belonging to Italy (Griffini 2019). Therefore, predominantly ethno-cultural nationalism is unsettled when the Italian populist radical right symbolically opens the borders of Italy to regular immigrants (Griffini 2019). This ostensible puzzle may be explained by conscious or unconscious slippages of the Lega and FdI into predominantly ethno-cultural nationalism when asked what the nation is, which diverge from the track these parties engineer to project themselves as more moderate and civic when explicitly asked who can belong to the nation (Griffini 2019). The goal is to strategically appeal to a wider range of voters, by offering a polished image of themselves as credible and legitimate, in line with the "civic turn" of the populist radical right (Halikiopoulou, Mock, and Vasilopoulou 2013). Another possible explanation may be that the Italian populist radical right is open to encompass the regular immigrant within the discursive national borders instrumentally, in order to bolster the exclusion of irregular migrants who become the ultimate scapegoat. This strategy is in line with the incorporation of regular migrants into the body of the nation (Antonsich 2016), to consolidate the dichotomy between regular immigrants and evil irregulars, who are, thus, further incriminated.

Notes

1 Literally, "*The* party of the nation." Emphasis added by the author.
2 The name of the Italian flag, composed of three colours (red, white, green).
3 The right to acquire citizenship based on the place of birth. This is the opposite of Italy's established *jus sanguinis*, i.e., the right to acquire citizenship based on the citizenship of one's parents.

References

Aalberg, T. & De Vreese, C. (2017) "Comprehending populist political communication", in *Populist Political Communication in Europe*, Aalberg, T., Esser, F., Reinemann, C., Stromback, J. & De Vreese, C. (eds), London: Routledge, pp. 3–11.

Agustoni, A., Alietti, A. & Mantovan, C. (2015) *Territori e pratiche di convivenza interetnica*, Milan: Franco Angeli.

Ajmi, H. (2013) "Subjectivity in discourse: A CDA approach to the study of adjectives in two political speeches", *Arab World English Journal*, vol. 5, no. 1, pp. 151–166.

Albertazzi, D., Giovannini, A. & Seddone, A. (2018) "'No regionalism please, we are Leghisti!' The transformation of the Italian Lega Nord under the leadership of Matteo Salvini", *Regional & Federal Studies*, vol. 28, no. 5, pp. 645–671.

Alemanno, G. (2014) *Il Partito della nazione*, Rome: I libri del Borghese.

Antonsich, M. (2016) "International migration and the rise of the 'civil' nation", *Journal of Ethnic and Migration Studies*, vol. 42, no. 11, pp. 1790–1807.

Antonsich, M. (2016) "The neoliberal culturalist nation: Voices from Italy", *Transactions of the Institute of British Geographers*, vol. 41, no. 4, pp. 490–502.

Ben-Ghiat, R. (2006) "Modernity is just over there: Colonialism and Italian national identity", *Interventions; International Journal of Postcolonial Studies*, vol. 8, no. 3, pp. 380–393.

Caiani, M., Della Porta, D. & Wagemann, C. (2012) *Mobilizing on the Extreme Right Germany, Italy, and the United States*, Oxford: Oxford University Press.

Cameron, D. (2001) *Working with Spoken Discourse*, London: Sage.
Curran, G. (2004) "Mainstreaming populist discourse: The race-conscious legacy of neo-populist parties in Australia and Italy", *Patterns of Prejudice*, vol. 38, no. 1, pp. 37–55.
Gaita, L. (2018) "Ius soli, promessa mancata: L'Italia resta terra straniera. Dagli States all'Europa, ecco come funziona la cittadinanza", *Il Fatto Quotidiano*. 15 January 2018. Available: https://www.ilfattoquotidiano.it/2018/01/05/ius-soli-promessa-mancata-litalia-resta-terra-straniera-dagli-states-alleuropa-ecco-come-funziona-la-cittadinanza/4073821/ [21 May 2018].
Gomez-Reino Cachafeiro, M. (2002) *Ethnicity and Nationalism in Italian Politics: Inventing the Padania: Lega Nord and the Northern Question*, London: Routledge.
Griffini, M. (2019) "The Italian far right at the crossroads of populism and nationalism", in *Tidal Waves? The Political Economy of Populism and Migration in Europe*, Talani, S. & Rosina, S. (eds), Berlin: Peter Lang.
Halikiopoulou, D., Mock, S. & Vasilopoulou, S. (2013) "The civic zeitgeist: Nationalism and liberal values in the European radical right", *Nations and Nationalism*, vol. 19, no. 1, pp. 107–127.
Huysseune, M. (2010) *Justifications of Centrifugal Regionalism in the European Union: A Comparison Between Flanders and Northern Italy*. Available: https://www.sisp.it/files/papers/2010/michel-huysseune-768.pdf [21 May 2018].
Il Sole 24 Ore Redazione (2022) "La proposta di legge sullo «Ius scholae» spacca la maggioranza". *Il Sole 24 Ore*. 29 June 2022. Available: https://www.ilsole24ore.com/art/la-proposta-legge-ius-scholae-spacca-maggioranza-AEF91CjB?refresh_ce=1 [29 June 2022].
Mammone, A. (2018) "È tempo di patrioti", in *Destra*, Fumagalli, C. & Puttini, S. (eds), Milan: Feltrinelli.
Rusconi, E. (1993) "Will Italy remain a nation?", *European Journal of Sociology*, vol. 34, no. 2, pp. 309–321.
Verdicchio, P. (1997) "Discourse in Southern Italy", in *Revisioning Italy: National Identity and Global Culture*, Allen, B. & Russo, M.J. (eds), Minneapolis: University of Minnesota Press, pp. 191–212.
Veugelers, J.W. (2000) "Right-wing extremism in contemporary France: A 'Silent Counterrevolution'?", *The Sociological Quarterly*, vol. 41, no. 1, pp. 19–40.
Zaslove, A. (2004) "Closing the door? The ideology and impact of radical right populism on immigration policy in Austria and Italy", *Journal of Political Ideologies*, vol. 9, no. 1, pp. 99–118.

5 "I am not racist, but ..."
Problematisation, Differentiation, and Othering of Immigration

5.1 Introduction

A recurring claim made by the populist radical right representatives during the interviews has been the explicit and unsolicited warning that they are not racist. This warning often preceded racist slippages. As the discursive strategy of denial of racism illuminated by Wodak in her analysis of populist radical right discourse suggests, populist radical right parties usually first take their distance from racist attitudes that would be deemed inappropriate by the mainstream, in order to fend off potential denunciations and wrap their nativism in a blanket of acceptability (2015: 58). Then, they succumb to racist affirmations. Faloppa argues that the expression "I'm not racist, but" is widespread: on Facebook there are various groups titled "I'm not racist, but," and his 2010 Google search of the sentence returned 14,000 occurrences (2011). At the time of writing in July 2022, the Google text query run in English returned 75,300 occurrences, while the query run in Italian returned 20,500 occurrences.

Indeed, as outlined in Chapter 2, despite Italy's self-redemptory myth of being extraneous to racism, racism is well engrained in the social and political fabric of the country, as well as seeping into the political arena. However, the clear and voluntary warning that they eschew racism is not surprising among the Lega and the FdI representatives interviewed. Eschewing racism outwardly is to be understood through the prism of the populist radical right's attempt at mainstreaming itself, by blunting its most extreme edges, which would be unpalatable to the wider public. Moderating its discourse is not enough for the populist radical right to mainstream itself, win over a large share of the electorate, and even enter government, as was the case in Switzerland with the Swiss People's Party (SVP), in Austria with the Freedom Party of Austria (FPO), and also in Italy with the Lega's participation in three Berlusconi-led centre-right governments, plus its recent participation in the wholly populist M5S-Lega government. The mainstreaming of the populist radical right can occur when the latter becomes accepted by mainstream parties into coalitions, which often coincides with mainstream parties radicalising their positions, for example when they interpret immigration as a zero-sum game, such as the then centre-right French President Nicholas Sarkozy's de-demonisation of the populist radical right Front National led by Marine Le Pen (Kallis 2015).

DOI: 10.4324/9781003252597-6

Another fitting example of radicalisation of the centre-right is FI's toughened attitude towards immigration in the Berlusconi-led coalition governments, due to, among other factors, the influence of the populist radical right coalition partners Lega and AN. Such radicalisation is manifest in the appropriation of immigration as an issue by the centre-right, resulting in restrictive immigration policies passed under the aegis of Berlusconi as head of the 2001–2006 and the 2008–2011 government coalitions (see Chapter 6).

Therefore, this chapter delves into the populist radical right's discourse on immigration, and highlights the duplicity of overtly civic and moderate statements that cloak racist claims, as well as bringing to light the colonial echoes emerging in the Lega, FdI, and populist radical right intellectuals. The analysis is divided into six categories: problematisation, differentiation, Othering, criminalisation, inferiorisation, and abjectification[1] of immigration. This chapter will focus on the problematisation, differentiation, and Othering of immigration, while the next chapter will deal with the remaining three categories. All these categories thrive on the discursive strategies of simplification and generalisation, which have been documented in various studies in connection with the discourse on immigration (see, for instance, Rivera 2020). The parties at stake, indeed, seem to be blind to the ethnic and religious diversity of immigrants, which are lumped together into a homogenous group. This representation of the immigrant Other echoes Said's point about the colonisers' articulation of the colonised as homogeneous and fixed in time (1978: 1, 108). In the Italian populist radical right's discourse, simplifications and generalisations are at work, in particular, when immigrants are superficially assimilated to Islam, thus ignoring the different religions practised by immigrants and the different hues that Islam can take on. This point is evident in the 2018 Lega's electoral manifesto, when it mentions vaguely "relationship with Islam" in the same section where it discusses issues about immigration. This is symptomatic of the treatment of Islam as monolithic and indissolubly linked to immigration.

5.2 Problematisation of Immigration

Framing immigration as a problem among the Italian populist radical right is not surprising. The nature of such alleged problem is multi-layered: it varies from economic to social and psychological reasons.

The problematisation of immigration becomes entwined anti-elite populism, which is one of the components of populism understood as an ideological feature of the populist radical right (see Chapter 1). The Italian populist radical right's wrath against the government, representing the elites, is essentially due to its alleged miscalculation in dealing with the problem of immigration. The government actions to manage immigration have been deemed as "disastrous" (F20180104F), "embarrassing" (F20180104F), and "shameful" (S20180108S). These qualifications signal a strong anti-elite populism, connected with the problematisation of immigration. Even more so, according to the interviews, the government favours immigration (E20170404C, F20170111S), at the Italians' expense

(F20160905L). The government promulgated "perverse immigration policies" and did not perform the necessary medical checks on newly arrived immigrants (C20180109G, F20160905L, L20170410P). The consequence of the ineptitude of the government is, according to a populist radical right intellectual, the degeneration of immigration into violence (G20170405C) and crime. According to the Italian populist radical right, the nexus between the management of immigration and crime is demonstrated by the major inquests on *mafia capitale*[2] and on the *CARA*[3] in Mineo (M20170113R). The NGOs dealing with the search, rescue, and reception of immigrants are also subject to criticism by the Italian populist radical right, as they are said to represent only some political parties (M20180105M) and to profit from the "immigration business" (R20180104M). For example, in March 2019 Salvini ordered the seizure of the *Mare Jonio*, a rescue vessel operated by the Italian civil society organisation *Mediterranea* carrying 50 migrants. According to Salvini, *Mediterranea* was plotting against the Italian government and aiding irregular immigration (Tondo 2019).

Regarding the political parties attacked by the Italian populist radical right in relation to immigration policies, the usual targets are the centre-left PD, the catch-all populist M5S, and the vague category of the so-called *politically correct* and *buonisti*.[4] In the interviews, the centre left PD was criticised for being lenient towards immigration (F20170111S), while the left at large was blamed for its alleged discrimination against Italians, who lose priority in council housing or social welfare allocations in favour of immigrants (F20170110F). Additionally, the Lega, FdI, and populist radical right intellectuals unanimously condemn the politically correct parties (G20170405C, M20170113R), and those that are often defined as *buonisti*, since they have favoured an open-door policy towards immigration (L20170104N, L20180105S). FdI's criticism also involves the M5S' tolerance for ostensibly unacceptable immigration levels (F20170111S).

In line with two of Canovan's (1999) seminal three characterisations of the people, i.e., *our people* and the *ordinary people*, these quotes reveal once again the Italian populist radical right's claim to side with the ordinary people, especially the disadvantaged, against the incompetent and corrupt elites, but also against those not belonging to the ethno-culturally defined people. The framing of the people as *ordinary* reflects the populist appeal on disaffected voters disenchanted with the corruption reportedly plaguing political parties (Schubel and Ziller 2015). Schubel and Ziller (2015) prove the connection between the perception of politics as corrupt and voting for populist parties: individuals who have experienced corruption in dealing with public officials were more receptive to populist radical right parties' appeals. The framing of the people as *our people* and as *united people* are conceptually similar, although one carries ethnic connotations, absent in the other: *our people* refers to the convergence of the people with the ethnic kith and kin, championing the national in-group against the outgroup (Canovan 1999); the *united people* denotes the unity of the people against divisive factions and fragmentations (Canovan 1999). This notion of the people has not emerged from the interviews and the manifestos analysed in the Italian milieu.

Anti-elite populism entwisted with the problematisation of immigration becomes entwined with anti-EU sentiment, typical of populist anti-elitism: the EU is suspiciously seen as an elite against which the people is juxtaposed (Hainsworth 2008). In the Lega's and FdI's discourse, the EU allegedly "dumps migrants into Italy" (F20160905L), which has been abandoned to manage immigration alone (C20170106V, E20180103G, F20170111S), instead of receiving logistical help from the EU to host immigrants (F20170111S, L20170410P) and adequate financial resources from the EU to invest into immigration management (F20170408T). What is worse, in the words of a Lega representative, the EU rebuked the Lega's attempt to stem clandestine immigration when the Lega was part of government coalitions (M20170404F). Therefore, the EU appears as an accomplice in the immigration crisis, which it apparently exploits to mistreat Italy (M20170104G). It is noteworthy, however, that, in the interviews, only one Lega representative went to extreme lengths, arguing that the EU actually has no role in immigration, because "it does not exist" (G20170112G), thus challenging the very existence of the EU itself. Reportedly, the EU is not able to control and manage borders, which triggers a crisis of political legitimacy so acute that it even undermines the EU's existence.

After this brief contextualisation of the problematisation of immigration in the interaction between racism and anti-elitism against domestic political parties and supranational organisation like the EU, this chapter delves in depth into the connotations and causes of the framing of immigration as a problem. In the early 1990s immigration started to be outlined as a problem in Italian politics (Perlmutter 1996: 229, 233). The triggering event catalysing attention on immigration was the murder of South African activist and political refugee Jerry Masslo in 1989 in Villa Literno (Parati 1997: 169). This murder brought immigration under the spotlight, since it created news coverage, and public and academic debate around it. The murder also cast light on anti-immigrant nationalism and racism married together into nativism, in response to which unions, religious and voluntary associations organised a protest march in Rome attracting 200,000 people (Perlmutter 1996: 234). Jerry Masslo's killing was followed two years later by another event that galvanised public and political attention around immigration: the arrival of 20,000 Albanians on board the *Vlora* in 1991 (Giuliani 2018:198; Parati 1997: 169). Since then, the Italian populist radical right has viewed immigration as a permanent problem. Italian populist radical right representatives from the Lega and FdI, and populist radical right intellectuals problematise immigration by framing it as a generic "issue," but also, more dramatically, as "an explosive problem," "an epoch-making change with obnoxious effects," "a relentless sea," a "damage to Italy," and even "a drama" (see, for instance, E20170404C, F20170110F, F20180104F, G20170405C, G20180105M, L20180105S, M20170113R). The metaphors of the explosion and the unrelenting sea are indicative of the perception of immigration in catastrophic terms.

Immigration is also delineated as a problem in the social realm since immigration without integration apparently creates social issues (G20180105M). This view shifts the blame for the apparent failure of integration policy from the national, regional, and local governments, in charge of immigration policies, to the immigrants themselves, who are blamed for failing to integrate. In doing so, it obscures the responsibility of multi-level governance in devising effective integration policies and the role of institutional racism that excludes immigrants from employment, housing, healthcare, and other welfare provisions.

Moreover, immigration is portrayed as an issue in cultural and religious terms, as it is said to create problematic cultural and religious differences (A20180103DC); in economic terms, as immigration ostensibly implies an enormous waste of money and time (M20180105M); and in demographic terms, since it fosters fears of overpopulation. Indeed, a Lega representative wondered: "In sixty years can we all fit in here?" (F20160905L). According to a 2021 YouGov survey, 77% of Italians still believe that there are too many immigrants, and half of them actually think that immigrant-related crime is increasing, thus lending legitimacy to the populist radical right's discursive problematisation of immigration on demographic grounds, and to the subsequent analysis of the criminalisation of immigration (see Chapter 6). However, from 1999 to 2020 it was reported that the number of immigrants in Italy had increased eightfold, while the crime rate decreased by 80% (Brunelli 2021). Thus, racist language fuels the misplaced perception of the immigrant as equivalent to criminal (Brunelli 2021). On the contrary, it is the lack of access to the labour market and social security that bars adequate integration and pushes foreigners to work illegally, and, in some cases, even to commit crime (Brunelli 2021).

The populist radical right's problematisation of immigration often adopts hyperbole to exaggerate the dimension of the problem (Van Dijk 2008: 362), evidenced, also, in this quote from another Lega representative: "Africa cannot be entirely contained within Italy" (C20170106V). The hyperbolic framing of immigration as a problem by the populist radical right provokes fear of immigration through the topos of threat (Wodak 2015: 53). An additional discursive strategy deployed by the populist radical right is the fallacy of sameness and the fallacy of difference (Wodak 2015: 54), whereby the populist radical right depicts a homogenous in-group inherently different from a seemingly homogenous outgroup composed of problematic immigrants.

In the Italian populist radical right's discourse, the framing of immigration as a problem appears in tandem with the framing of immigration as uncontrollable. The Lega, FdI, and populist radical right intellectuals believe that immigration is out of control (see, for instance, F20180104F, G20170405C, G20170411C). The Italian populist radical right claims that incoming immigrants are not correctly and systematically identified by the police (F20160905L, F20170111S), thus generating an uncontrollable situation. In order to enhance the credibility of their statements, the Italian populist radical right resorts to legitimation through authorisation, whereby political parties legitimate themselves through an appeal to their authority (Wodak 2015: 56), by citing statistics and facts to make their assertions more robust. For instance, to underline the uncontrollability of immigration, an FdI representative stated that "this is communicated to us by data, not by me. I support a non-neutral view, but this is proved by data, these are statistics"

(F20170110F); another one prided himself on the data about unmanageable immigration passed on by acquaintances within the armed forces (F20170111S).

The framing of immigration as an uncontainable problem can be interpreted within what Castelli Gattinara terms the "logic of emergency and exceptionality," through which Italy has dealt with immigration by treating it in "emergential" and exceptional terms, fostering moral panic and requiring special measures (2017: 326). As Calhoun argues, emergency is a way of characterising events as unpredictable, anomalous, and transitory, calling for a restoration of order (2010: 55), in whose name, as anthropologist Albahari claims, further "crimes of peace" are perpetrated by the state against immigrants (2015: 21–22). Before committing "crimes of peace" (Albahari 2015), the logic of emergency leads to the creation of a state of exception, where laws are suspended with the immediate goal of solving a national emergency (Agamben 2003).

This logic of emergency and exceptionality treating immigration as an abnormal, short-lived, and unforeseeable problem slipping out of control and requiring emergency measures, is apparent not only in the Italian populist radical right's discourse referenced in the interviews and the manifestos, but also in the 2017 Minister of the Interior Marco Minniti's campaign against NGOs allegedly collaborating with smugglers while rescuing immigrants (Castelli Gattinara 2018), and in the Minniti-Orlando Decree. The latter was put forward by the PD, with the intention of curtailing illegal immigration through bilateral agreements with north African countries and the expansion of the network of administrative detention (Castelli Gattinara 2017). Adopting Albahari's (2015) interpretive lens, the attempt to stop non-authorised NGOs from rescuing immigrants, bilateral agreements signed with countries with abysmal human rights records, and the boosting of detention centres amount to crimes of peace. Within a system underpinned by the logic of emergency and exceptionality, in the name of the restoration of order following the uncontrollable problem of immigration, the state's pre-emption of the threat of crime, inherent in immigration, results in the crime of denying rescue to immigrants and dooming them to be kept in detention centres in Italy or in Libya.

The COVID-19 pandemic, that started to sweep through Italy in February 2020, represents another kind of emergency Italian politics was faced with. At the beginning of the pandemic, immigration seemed to drift into irrelevance as a theme, given the urgency of managing the healthcare crisis and the rally-round-the-flag effect that brought together divergent political parties in order to fight the common enemy of the nation: COVID-19 (Albertazzi, Bonansinga, and Zulianello 2021: 6). As an interviewee from the Lega admitted: "Immigration has always been a problem, but obviously hundreds of deaths per day shift the focus of the media away from immigration" (E20210504P). However, after this brief period of cohesion and predominant focus on the healthcare crisis, the Lega and FdI went back to their role as opposition, becoming harshly critical of the Conte II government (Albertazzi, Bonansinga, and Zulianello 2021), questioning its management of immigration. Therefore, despite initially taking the backseat vis-à-vis pandemic management, immigration soon regained predominance in the discourse of the Lega and FdI, although to a smaller extent when compared to these parties' discourse before the pandemic. Indeed, the interviews conducted between March 2021 and May 2021 demonstrate that immigration is again a salient issue.

The problematisation of immigration emerges clearly. It is coloured in an alarmist hue that recalls the topos of threat typical of populist radical right discourse, whereby these parties fan the fires of fear of the Other by emphasising the supposed threat it may pose (Wodak 2015).

In the interviews, the Italian populist radical right cloaks its problematisation of immigration under a civic veil: by remarking that immigration in general is theoretically acceptable, but *this* immigration is a problem because of its peculiarities, the Italian populist radical right distances itself from racism and enacts a "civic turn" (Griffini 2021). This way, the Italian populist radical right projects itself as tolerant of immigration in general and only intolerant of the problematic kind of immigration Italy is undergoing now. Therefore, it appears that the Italian populist radical right rejects this problematic immigration on humanitarian grounds, as it is not able to provide shelter to immigrants. Moreover, by adopting a similarly humanitarian logic, immigration is often framed by the Italian populist radical right as a problem harming Italian immigrants themselves. Hence, the parties at stake arise as defenders of Italian immigrants, i.e., immigrants with Italian citizenship, against the new immigrants, who are prioritised in council housing (G20180105M). The civic cloak shrouding the Italian populist radical right's framing of immigration as a problem reaches its peak when an FdI representative stressed how he agrees with the Pope's emphasis on the centrality of human beings, including immigrants, and yet on these humanitarian grounds he deems the current immigration as problematic due to its mismanagement (F20180104F).

The populist radical right's "civic turn" compellingly discussed by Halikiopoulou, Mock, and Vasilopoulou (2013) suggests that populist radical right parties dilute racist rhetoric by appropriating non-racist, civic values and incorporating them into their discourse, in order to gain legitimacy and respectability. As Moffitt (2017: 11) argues,

> The biological racism of older iterations of such parties is no longer electorally successful nor even 'acceptable' on the fringes of mainstream party politics (…), and as a result, these parties have also had to streamline their message, learn to sell it in a more sophisticated way, and adopt both language and positions that bring them closer to electoral success.

Therefore, as just analysed in this category, the Italian populist radical right depicts itself as imbued with the civic values of tolerance of immigration and humanitarian concern for immigrants, in order to appear legitimate and respectable (Griffini 2021). By adopting civic terms, populist radical right parties undergo a process of moderation and mainstreaming. As a result, they become embroiled in the dilemma between office-seeking, achieved through moderating their racism in order to enter into government coalitions, and vote-seeking, accomplished through being loyal to racism (Akkerman et al. 2016: 15). However, while moderation may imply the loss of hard-line voters, it may also enlarge the electorate. Indeed, according to the inclusion-moderation hypothesis widespread in the literature on populism, populist parties in government moderate themselves, to appeal to the median voter, to develop policies, and deliver goods (Berman 2008).

Civic traits are not a novelty in the Italian populist radical right: as Chapter 4 explained, the Italian populist radical right's nationalism blends civic elements with ethno-cultural overtones, where civic features are interpreted as part of a recent civic turn and mainstreaming strategy, in order to appeal to a larger share of the electorate. The "civic turn" of populist radical right racism is not limited to the case of Italy: as Halikiopoulou, Mock, and Vasilopoulou demonstrate (2013), the Swiss People's Party (SVP), the Dutch Pim Fortuyn List (LPF) and Party for Freedom (PVV), and the French Front National (FN)[5] are further examples of the recent incorporation of civic values into racist discourse. For example, regarding the problematisation of immigration portrayed in civic terms, the SVP depicts immigration as a problem that would provoke a clash of civilisations, against which it advocates the protection of the multi-ethnic Swiss national identity characterised as a civic value (Halikiopoulou, Mock, and Vasilopoulou 2013: 116). In a similarly "civic turn," the FN has portrayed its opposition to ostensibly problematic immigration as a civic battle against racism allegedly provoked by immigration (Halikiopoulou, Mock, and Vasilopoulou 2013: 123).

5.3 Differentiation of Immigration

Despite framing immigration *tout court* as an uncontrollable problem, the Italian populist radical right, as revealed by the interviews and manifestos, acknowledges a difference between refugees and economic migrants, when prompted to reflect upon it. Refugees, who according to the 1954 Geneva Convention, are individuals "unable or unwilling to return to their country of origin owing to a well-founded fear of being persecuted for reasons of race, religion, nationality, membership of a particular social group, or political opinion" (UNHCR 1951), are protected by the legal principle of non-refoulement, forbidding the country receiving immigrants to forcibly return them to their country of origin. As suggested by the interviews, the Lega and FdI agree that refugees should be privileged and welcomed over economic migrants (see, for instance, E20180103G, G20170411C, G20180105M, M20170104G, M20170404F, M20170113R, R20180104M), since, according to FdI representatives, "it is evident that those fleeing a war should be considered in a different way from a legal point of view but also from a numerical point of view" (E20170404C), "because this is a matter of human dignity recognised by universal human rights" (G20170111R).

Syrians are the target of particular sympathy. Indeed, a Lega representative argued that "Syrians are our brothers" (L20170104N). These statements, infused with sympathy for refugees, echo Van Dijk's argument about how the populist radical right often covers its racist traits under a cloak of sympathy for immigrants (1996: 98), which is usefully interpreted by keeping in mind the fine line between true, genuine compassion, and strategic compassion: as Fassin warns, episodes of strategic compassion can turn into moments of collective redemption (2005: 375). In fact, Fassin advises that the paradigm of hostility towards and repression of immigration is contradictorily punctuated by instances of sympathy and compassion towards refugees, aimed at helping those expressing these feelings feel more humane (2005: 382), thus leading to their redemption. In a similarly critical vein, Albahari remarks that the *Centri di Identificazione ed Espulsione* (CIE) in Italy are meant to show humanitarian compassion, which can quickly become a government's strategy to redeem itself from the ill treatment of immigrants (2015). Therefore, when the Italian populist radical right projects itself as sympathetic to refugees, it may do so strategically, in order to appear more humane and to redeem itself from the accusation of racism often levelled at this party family.

Hence, refugees are deemed to be qualitatively different from economic migrants, since they escape serious conditions, as well as quantitatively different, since they should be accepted by Italy in greater numbers than economic migrants, who are, by contrast, described in pejorative terms. Indeed, in the interviews and in the manifestos, the Italian populist radical right clearly believes that the reasons leading economic migrants to escape from their countries are less worthy than the reasons motivating refugees to flee. For instance, looking for a better life (A20180103DC, E20170404C) or climate change (F20170110F) do not seem to be valid motivations driving economic migrants to Italy. Economic migrants are framed in derogatory terms, especially when they are blamed for allegedly violating the law in order to come to Italy, while leaving their fellow citizens to starve to death (G20170112G). The disparaging framing of economic migrants is further reinforced by the Italian populist radical right's view that, although Italy is supposedly a welcoming country towards those escaping wars, it cannot be as welcoming towards those fleeing poverty because Italy has to "take care of Italians first, hence those entering our country for economic reasons become a problem" (G20170411C) as "they make money behind our backs" (M20170104G). Curiously, as the last statement shows, the economic migrant is often framed as smart in an insolent way: a "*furbetto*"[6] (F20170408T), generating so much distrust among the Italian populist radical right that a Lega representative doubted that economic migrants are actually escaping poverty, as they are purportedly all well-fed, tall, and muscular (F20160905L).

Despite the tolerance expressed by the interviewees towards refugees, under the Lega-M5S coalition government (Conte I government), Mimmo Lucano, the mayor of Riace (in southern Italy), was arrested on charges of enabling irregular immigration. In fact, Mimmo Lucano welcomed immigrants, including refugees, to his scarcely populated village and integrated them into the local economy (Giuffrida 2018). As a consequence, Salvini ordered the removal of irregular immigrants as well as refugees from Riace (Giuffrida 2018). As part of the radicalising trajectory of the Lega in the Conte I government, in 2018, Salvini introduced a Security Decree that reformed the policies on the status-determination for asylum seekers and immigrants, limiting access to the official reception system for asylum seekers and ensuring that immigrants' status in Italy remains precarious

(Geddes and Pettrachin 2020: 236–237). In 2019 the Follow-Up Security Decree (Decreto Sicurezza Bis) was issued two days after the captain of the NGO ship *Sea-Watch 3*, Carola Rackete, berthed in Lampedusa with 53 immigrants rescued from Mediterranean waters, arguing that it was the "closest safe harbour" (Geddes and Pettrachin 2020: 227). The aim of the Follow-Up Security Decree was to limit access to asylum seekers to Italian territory, by increasing fines on NGOs seeking to bring migrants rescued in the Mediterranean to Italy (Geddes and Pettrachin 2020: 237). NGOs engaged at sea in search and rescue of migrants, including potential refugees, have been a salient topic in the populist radical right: in the 2018 electoral manifesto, the Lega proposed to forbid "1) disembarkment of immigrants from NGOs that are on the margins of Libyan territorial waters [...] which is a prelude to the exploitation of illegal immigration. 2) disembarkment of passengers from NGO boats without identification documents" (Lega Manifesto 2018: 6).

The differentiation of immigration persisted during the COVID-19 pandemic. The distinction eagerly made between seemingly welcome refugees and regular immigrants and seemingly unwelcome economic migrants and irregular immigrants in the interviews remains a staple of the Italian populist radical right discourse on immigration. The current differentiation of immigration evidently comes through when the Lega and FdI launch a scathing attack on irregular immigration, which they define as clandestine: "Clandestine immigration must be banned. (...) It is unacceptable that in a sovereign state anyone can enter and exit as they please," emphatically claimed an FdI representative (P20210422B). The populist radical right is keen on specifying that irregular immigration is a crime, but, as a Lega representative contended,

> Who comes to Italy, even before COVID-19, to seek employment and build a new future is welcome. Those who flee wars or authoritarian regimes are welcome if they comply with Italian laws. Otherwise, they should go back home, or be subject to legal procedures.
>
> (T20210409S)

Clearly, COVID-19 did not defuse attention away from scapegoating irregular immigration and from the apparent embrace of regular immigration. Neither did it stop the populist radical right's support for regular immigration infused with compassion towards immigrants and with the prizing of regular immigrants' contribution to the Italian economy. A Lega representative from the southern region of Calabria, which was initially disparaged by the Lega in its regionalist phase, clarified:

> Controlled immigration is geared towards the protection of migrant dignity. Italy should thank regular immigrants that help us in the agricultural and food industry, and allow us to keep our leadership in this sector. In my region [Calabria], we have around 35% of regular immigrants employed in the agricultural and food industry. (...) Regular immigration is necessary.
>
> (P20210409M)

The simplifications and generalisations[7] at work in the Italian populist radical right's discourse on the differentiation of immigration are patent: these parties are oblivious to the multiple causes beyond war motivating refugees to flee their country and to the fine and blurred line between escaping conflicts, religious, social, political, and ethnic persecution, and fleeing poverty, while looking for better living conditions. Moreover, CDA sheds light on the discursive strategy of denial of racism (Wodak 2015: 58), whereby the Italian populist radical right projects itself as infused by sympathy towards refugees, before slipping into racist comments on economic migrants. In fact, despite the strategy of denial of racism, the Italian populist radical right easily succumbs to the topos of threat (Wodak 2015: 53), by inducing fear of undeserving and insolent economic migrants.

Notwithstanding the differentiation between refugees and economic migrants, the Italian populist radical right, when interviewed, deems that true refugees constitute a minority of the total number of immigrants disembarking onto Italian shores. This attitude, widespread among the Lega, FdI, and populist radical right intellectuals, is indicative of the phenomenon of "migrantisation" of refugees, whereby asylum seekers are framed as economic migrants pending approval of their refugee status (Giuliani 2018: 223). The distrust of self-proclaimed migrants in the discourse of the Italian populist radical right is evident in this quotation from an FdI representative: "If they were true refugees, undoubtedly [we should welcome them]" (G20170109D). Therefore, it is the status of refugees that is doubted, thus creating an atmosphere of suspicion and misgiving. Indeed, the Italian populist radical right, while ignoring the broader causes working as push factors for refugees, believes that immigrants from Asia, and Bangladesh in particular, are not affected by wars, hence they do not deserve the status of refugees (F20170111S). Eritrea and Gambia (L20170104N), along with Senegal (F20170408T), are also categorised as relatively peaceful states, thus showing the Italian populist radical right's ignorance of the havoc wrought by decades of civil war tearing local politics, economy, and society apart.

In emphasising the difference between the alleged minority of deserving refugees and the majority of undeserving economic migrants, the Italian populist radical right avails itself of data, resorting to the strategy of legitimation through authorisation (Wodak 2015: 56), whereby populist radical right parties use data, especially statistics, in order to corroborate the validity of their claims. Interestingly, there is a wide discrepancy among the data provided by the Italian populist radical right in the interviews: some hold that refugees are only 20% of asylum seekers while the rest are called "clandestines" (L20180105S), others contend that refugees represent 25% of asylum seekers while the rest must leave (C20170106V, M20170404F), finally others claim that the cacophony of statistics also includes the figures 3% (E20180103G, M20170404F) and 5% (R20180104M). The strategy of legitimation through authorisation (Wodak 2015: 56) is not just deployed by using data, but also by emphasising one's own professional standing. For instance, an FdI representative, who is a lawyer by trade, described with detail the "unmanageable," "time wasting," and "crazy" legal process asylum seekers are subjected to, involving seven judicial steps, including several possibilities for appeal, and a prioritisation of demands for asylum over other cases (M20180105M).

Moreover, while the distinction between refugees and economic migrants prevails in the Italian populist radical right's discourse, this party family also distinguishes between regular and irregular immigrants. Chapter 4 shed light on the Italian populist radical right's inclusion of regular immigrants into the predominantly ethno-cultural nation. In the interviews, this view is widely shared among the Lega, and FdI, who highlight the difference between undeserving irregulars and regulars who, instead, are worth of respect (F20170110F, F20170111S, G20180105M, L20170104N). Hence, the Italian populist radical right deploys a differential conceptualisation and treatment of immigrants: first, they differentiate between apparently worthless economic migrants and deserving refugees; second, they operate a further distinction between unwelcome irregular immigrants and welcome regular immigrants. Interestingly, these two distinctions do not automatically coincide, as there may be regular economic migrants, who have regularised their stay in Italy through an employment contract or family reunification motives.

Therefore, as revealed by the categories of problematisation and differentiation of immigration, the Mediterranean becomes transfigured from a *Mare Nostrum*, i.e., a cherished space of colonisation under fascism, to what I define as "Mare Vostrum." The latter is a space that is dreaded by these parties, which frame it as a source of an uncontrollable problem mainly orchestrated by deceitful economic migrants that lead Italy to sharp decline.

5.4 Othering of Immigration

The third category, Othering, acts as an umbrella category, including the following three: criminalisation, inferiorisation, and abjectification. Othering is a recurrent theme in studies of colonialism (see, for instance, Fanon 1963; Said 1978; Todorov 1984), and immigration (see, for instance, Faso 2015; Gandesha 2003; Giuliani 2018). The dichotomy between Self and Other is masterfully described by Said in his book *Orientalism*, where he explains how colonialism was grounded in the irreconcilable ontological and epistemological dichotomy between the coloniser Self and the colonised Other, which was produced by the Self as different, irrational, childlike, immature, and depraved (1978: 3, 39–40). Similarly, Fanon, in *The Wretched of the Earth*, illuminates the colonisers' construction of the colonised Other as inherently inferior, animalised, prone to violence and criminality, thus misconceiving the mental pathologies triggered by colonial oppression (1965: 41, 250, 308). Again, Todorov in *The Conquest of America* illustrates how the natives were perceived as Others, generous and peaceful first, then violent and dangerous (1984: 38–40). This colonial dichotomy is lingering in the Othering of the immigrant (Faso 2015; Giuliani 2018) onto which the Self projects its own denied Otherness, turning it into something fearful and dangerous (Gandesha 2003: 4). The Othering of immigrants recalls the 1970s French Nouvelle Droite's principle of the right to cultural difference, ambiguously linked with the need to separate different races (Zaslove 2004: 104). Indeed, the Nouvelle Droite dissimulated biological racism, replacing it with the right to cultural difference and the aversion to the mixing of races, which would have been apparently conducive to segregation, discrimination, cultural decadence, and delinquency (Zaslove, 2004: 104). Indeed, a Lega representative stated that "through the mixing of races cultural roots get lost" (M20170104G). As Lentin explains, a new racism in the 1980s blended nature with culture, biology with history (2004: 95).

On the Italian populist radical right, Othering is illustrated by the following examples. In the interviews, FdI and the Lega concurred that immigration threatens Italian national identity (see, for instance, F20180103B, L20170104N, N20180108C, P20161216B, R20180108M, R20180108D). As Guibernau explains, the perceived threat to national identity motivates the populist radical right's success among the electorate (2010: 10). The differentiation made between refugees and economic migrants is carried over into the category of Othering, as an FdI representative claimed that refugees do not endanger national identity, contrary to other kinds of immigrants (F20170404T). Moreover, the anti-elite populist ideological component of the Italian populist radical right's discourse resurfaces in the category of Othering, since the Italian populist radical right argues that immigration can menace national identity if it is mismanaged, thus hinting at the current mismanagement on the part of politicians (C20180109G, F20180104F).

In the interviews, the Othering of immigrants in the Lega, FdI, and populist radical right intellectuals, manifests itself also through the conviction that immigration, made up of Others, undermines social cohesion (see, for instance, F20170104M, G20180109C, N20180108C, R20180104M), which is linked to endangered social peace (S20180103F). The latter, in the words of a Lega representative, "is based on ethno-cultural homogeneity" (M20170111R). Therefore, according to the Lega and FdI, immigration generates a pervasive sense of alienation and uneasiness (see, for instance, G20170112G, M20170104G, P20161219B, S20180103F) at the expense not only of Italians, who feel discriminated against in favour of the immigrants (G20170111R), but also of the Italian immigrants trumped by the newcomers (G20180105M).

Another frequent emotion harboured by the Lega, FdI, and populist radical right intellectuals is fear towards immigrants (see, for instance, F20180104F, F20170408T, G20170405C, G20170411C), often associated with exasperation (F20170111S, M20170113R) and a sense of injustice (C20170106V, M20170104G) due to the perceived discrimination in favour of immigrants (F20170110F, F20170104M, G20170111R, G20170405C), especially in the applications for council housing or other welfare services (F20170110F). This exasperation is evident in the resentment affecting the population at large and in the turn to the right of the lower classes (R20180104M). As a solution, FdI advocates the criterion of residence, whereby an applicant for council housing must have resided in Italy for five years before being able to apply (F20170110F).

The neoliberal beliefs of the Italian populist radical right, alongside the intersection of race and class, produce the racist and elitist belief that the poorest immigrants bring the most serious decadence (F20170104M). The Italian populist radical right's belief that immigrants endanger social cohesion and bring alienation and decadence is conceptualised not only at a macro level but also at a micro level constituted by interpersonal relationships, as a few Lega representatives seemed to be averse to having immigrants as neighbours (M20170104G, P20161219B).

In the interviews and in manifestos, the Italian populist radical right believes that immigration also poses an economic threat. Indeed, Italy is said to be a country with no need for low-cost labour (C20180109G). As a consequence, immigration puts pressure on the labour market (G20170411C), steals jobs (S20180103F) and benefits (F20160905L, M20170104G), and drains the state of economic resources (C20170106V, P20161219B), thus further exacerbating Italians' poverty (F20170110F, G20170411C, G2017011R, P20161219B) and creating a "war among the poor" (M20170104G). In the 2018 manifesto, the Lega claimed that for the alleged "refugee,"

> the State will not be able to commit more resources than those destined for a 100% disability pension for an Italian citizen. Also, it will not be possible to establish higher contributions for the reception of foreigners than those aimed at policies in support of Italians in poverty.
> (Lega Manifesto 2018: 7)

Moreover, the Lega, FdI, and populist radical right intellectuals blame immigration for driving labour standards down, for instance forcing Italians to be exploited like immigrants by the system of *caporalato*[8] (F20160905L, M20180105M), for decreasing wages (E20180103G, R20180104M, S20180103F), and for substantially worsening labour conditions (F20180103B, F20180104F, F20170408T, G20180109C).

As suggested by the interviews and the manifestos, the Lega and FdI advocate the policy of "Italians First" as a blanket answer to the perception of the social and economic menace brought about by immigration (see, for instance, C20180109G, F20160905L, L20170104N), by prioritising Italians in social housing, other kinds of welfare provisions, and employment. In line with the Italian populist radical right's inclusion of regular immigrants into the nation discussed in Chapter 4, in the interviews, a Lega and an FdI representative encompassed the immigrants who acquired Italian citizenship and are now working (C20170106V), or the immigrants that are regular (F20170111S), within the Italians put first on the party's agenda. This policy of prioritising the national in-group is classified by various studies as exclusionism, which responds to concerns about the alleged harm inflicted by the out-group on the welfare state, social housing (Mammone 2015), and employment, by embracing adverse attitudes against ethnic minorities (Gijsberts, Hagendoorn, and Scheepers 2004: 1) and barring their access to these state services and the job market.

According to the interviews, among the Lega, FdI, and populist radical right intellectuals, immigrants are perceived as completely different in terms of culture, education, and lifestyle, and this difference is irreconcilable and intolerable (see, for instance, A20180103DC, E20170404C, F20170111S, G20170411C, G20170407P). This belief echoes Said's description of the mechanisms of colonialism, predicated on the ontological dichotomy between Self and Other (1978). Indeed, according to Said, colonialism worked by constructing the colonised as the Other, diametrically opposed to the colonising Self, in order to maintain the colonial domination of the former (1978). One Lega representative claimed that one of the most problematic cultural differences between Italians and immigrants is the lack of the concept of private property among immigrants from Africa, where tribes are unfamiliar with this notion (F20160905L). Similarly, an FdI representative added that immigrants "are odd people, not totally fitting with our rule of law" (M20180105M). The rule of law and private property are not the only values seemingly seen as exclusively "European": "Europe is undergoing a kind of immigration that often rejects European democratic values that have been shaped throughout the years. (…) Broadly speaking, I believe that Muslim extremist immigrants have no respect for our social and democratic conquests" (P20210422B). Unexpectedly, given the turn away from biological racism, skin colour is mentioned in an interview with an FdI representative, who argued that "Difference in skin colour and in language can be frightening" (P20210422B). These claims reproduce the colonial rhetoric crystallising the Other into a position of difference from the Italian Self.

The Othering of immigration takes on even greater magnitude when the Lega juxtaposes the deprivation of liberties and economic security experienced by Italians to the implied economic resources spent for immigrants: immigrants appear even more Other than usual, when compared to the Italians experiencing economic hardships. This view resonates with the erroneous opinion, widespread in populist radical right circles, that immigrants cause or precipitate the economic crisis (Anelli, Colantone, and Stanig 2019). In this novel scenario where Italy is facing economic hardships due to the disastrous impact of the COVID-19 pandemic, the accusation that immigrants worsen the economic crisis becomes even more acute. An FdI representative emphasised that

> Due to COVID-19 500,000 people lost their job! It is certainly not reassuring to know that there are immigrant workers available to sell their labour at half price compared to the average, almost always on the black market, through the myriad of migrant cooperatives that are intoxicating our job market.
>
> (B20210517M)

However, the populist radical right is favourable towards the inclusion of regular immigrants as recipients of COVID-19 economic aid, according to this Lega representative: "Regular immigrants have been receiving the same healthcare and vaccinations as any Italian citizen. Therefore, no regular migrant has been discriminated and they all benefit from social welfare, economic aid, furlough, and guarantees against dismissals" (B20210517M).

5.4.1 Reasons for the Othering of Immigration

The representation of immigrants as essentially different Others posing a multidimensional threat has been widely explored by various authors. Indeed, as briefly outlined in Chapter 1, vast scholarly attention has been devoted to the widespread conviction among the populist radical right that immigrants negatively change the socio-demographic makeup of a community, bringing about isolation, alienation (Zaslove 2004: 103), and *anomie* (Arzheimer 2009: 260). In the discourse of the populist radical right, the poor and the working class are in a precarious economic situation and find themselves negatively impacted also by a loss of community unity and cohesion (Zaslove 2004: 103). Arzheimer demonstrates a positive correlation between socio-demographic change and support for the populist radical right's racism (2009: 273).

According to a 2018 survey, in Italy the belief that immigration has created social division is widespread (Dixon et al. 2018: 80). Therefore, the populist radical right deploys the socio-demographic argument to justify its racist scapegoating of immigrants, in order to attract the losers of this socio-demographic change and gain electoral support (Sprague-Jones 2011: 539).

Norris and Inglehart theorise the seminal cultural backlash thesis, using distrust in politics to measure the younger generations' approval of populism (2019). This cultural backlash would explain the recent rise of populist attitudes: first, as a reaction to a shift towards more liberal values; second, because of the tendency of older generations to be more conservative in their voting choice, while younger ones are less interested in participating in the political life (Norris and Inglehart 2019). Moreover, concerning the point about younger generations, although Norris and Inglehart support that younger generations are more liberal, they also argue that younger people who have been raised in a less liberal environment might feel cast aside in a libertarian landscape. This would explain why even younger generations perceive liberal values as a threat and give their support to the populist radical right (Norris and Inglehart 2019). This theory is, however, criticised by Schäfer who claims that distrust in politics is not equivalent to populist support (2021: 9). Furthermore, there is no relevant evidence supporting the idea that older generations display more populist attitudes nor there is any significant difference in the level of political distrust between older and younger generations (Schäfer 2021: 8).

Nonetheless, the socio-demographic explanation is controversial, as there is no unanimous view on the relationship between immigration levels inducing socio-demographic change and racism. Knigge proves that the populist radical right makes sizeable electoral gains where immigration levels are high (1998: 249), which demonstrates a positive correlation between socio-demographic change and the populist radical right's support. However, the socio-demographic justification for racism is flawed: Mudde claims that although the "typical" voter is concerned about immigrants, and one of the main characteristics of the fourth wave is this fear of the immigrant Other, this feeling only constitutes a minority of the radical right electorate, and there is no correlation between the two (1999; 2019).

Furthermore, Perrineau sensibly argues that high levels of immigration may foster closer contact between the national in-group and the out-group, thus increasing tolerance, which does not translate into support for the populist radical right (1985). Therefore, the interviews with the Italian populist radical right exposed in this chapter may indicate that racism based on the socio-demographic argument is exploited by the Italian populist radical right, which, by offering racist discourse a political platform, ultimately contributes to its legitimisation in wider society.

The political psychological explanation for racism provides useful insights into the tendency inherent in human beings to identify themselves positively and in opposition to an out-group, which can be defined in terms of ethnicity, but also gender, social class, religion, and other social markers. Realistic group conflict theory posits that ethnic conflicts are rational and motivated by inter-group competition over scarce resources (Tajfel and Turner 1979). By applying this theory to the populist radical right's racism, it is plausible that the ethnic majority group protected and represented by the populist radical right, i.e., the national in-group, dominant in terms of economic and political power (Gijsberts, Hagendoorn, and Scheepers 2004: 6), enters into conflict with the ethnic minority groups constituted by immigrants. This competition triggers racism and depends on demographic conditions, namely on the size of the out-group competitors, on economic conditions, such as scarcity of employment and welfare, and political conditions, like social security and policies assisting immigrants (Gijsberts, Hagendoorn, and Scheepers 2004: 35). Nevertheless, the fact that in-groups tend to oppose themselves to out-groups, does not mechanically translate into racism. In fact, the contra-identification of the out-group at times of economic scarcity may be a natural predisposition, but racism is not innate.

Abundant scholarly attention has focused on economic reasons for the success of the populist radical right's racism. Zaslove identifies the popularity of the Italian populist radical right's anti-immigrant ideology with the decentralisation and downsizing of factories relying on highly skilled workers, which made it hard to employ immigrants (2004: 101). This analysis, however, lacks explanatory power as the difficulty of hiring immigrants, who are usually unskilled workers, does not automatically translate into hostility towards them. More convincing economic explanations for the rise of the populist radical right focus on contexts of scarcity of resources. In fact, the populist radical right prospers with high rates of unemployment (Arzheimer 2009: 273; Anelli, Colantone, and Stanig 2019). In particular, the introduction of robots in industries forces well-paid workers to perform low-wage jobs and, in general, diminishes their opportunities to be employed (Anelli, Colantone, and Stanig 2019). In general, economic anxieties, including job insecurity and the economic crisis, are correlated with the success of the populist radical right (Dal Bò et al. 2019). According to Cordero et al. (2021), when immigrants are qualified, not only low-educated natives are more likely to vote for populist radical right parties, but also educated ones perceive the Other as a threat, which then fuels their support for the populist radical right. Cordero et al. link this voting behaviour to the current labour market competition: low-educated natives view immigrants in general as a menace, whereas high-skilled ones perceive a pressuring competition with the educated part of the immigrant population (2021: 4).

According to a 2018 survey, 52% of Italians consider the economic impact of immigration to be negative (Dixon et al. 2018: 80). This is a relatively high percentage with more than half of the population sample seeing immigration as damaging the economy. In Germany, for instance, in 2019, 40% of the population sample saw immigration as negative for the economy, and the percentage of people believing that the costs of immigration outweigh the benefits decreased to 38% in Spain (YouGov 2019). Furthermore, according to a 2021 Ipsos survey, 37% of Italians agree that immigrants "take jobs away from the citizens of their own country," while 40% think that Italy would be stronger without immigration. In fact, the populist radical right appeals to those resenting the competition with immigrants in the job market at times of shortage of resources. Realistic group conflict theory gives a psychological grounding to economic explanations for the success of the populist radical right's racism, as it claims that at times of paucity of resources the national in-group, which is dominant in terms of economic and political power, fears the loss of its economic superiority, thus competing with immigrants in order to retain such status (Gijsberts, Hagendoorn, and Scheepers 2004: 6, 35). Therefore, according to this explanation, the lower strata of the population find themselves competing with immigrants for scarce resources, such as jobs and welfare, while desperately trying to retain their economic status. However, Guibernau contends that it is not just the working classes who are the economic victims of immigration; the bourgeoisie, especially in rich regions such as Italy's north-east, also compete with immigrants (2010: 8–10).

Nevertheless, the economic explanations for the success of the populist radical right's racism are controversial: historically not all countries experiencing economic crises, such as Spain and Portugal after the 2008 recession, saw a rise of the populist radical right's racism; on the other hand, Austria and Switzerland, for instance, witnessed the increasing success of populist radical right racism, despite being creditor countries in the 2008 recession (Hopkin 2020). Moreover, a study by Mutz highlights that economic hardships do not play a role in fomenting support for the populist radical right's racism (2018).

In the Italian case, King argued that, in the 1990s, immigrants did not compete for jobs with Italians, as they performed low-wage low-skills niche jobs unpalatable to the national in-group (1993: 287). A more recent study of employment in Italy shows that immigration has a minimal or null impact on the employment of Italians (Fusaro and Lopez-Bazo 2018). While more-educated Italian workers do not suffer from economic competition with immigrants, less-educated Italian workers do (Fusaro and Lopez-Bazo 2018). Overall, however, immigrants do not seem to displace native workers (Fusaro and Lopez-Bazo 2018). According to a 2019 survey, in Italy immigrants occupy low-wage and low-skill jobs, especially in the industrial, agricultural, construction, and care-taking sectors, while Italians tend to perform skilled jobs in the third sector (Leone Moressa 2019), thus competition for employment seems uncorroborated. In 2020, the International Labour

Organisation (ILO) reported that, in Italy, immigrants earn around 30% less than Italians (Amo-Agyei 2020).

Therefore, in order to comprehensively understand the success of the Italian populist radical right's racism, it is necessary to adopt a multifaceted approach: individuals tend to identify themselves positively vis-à-vis the out-group, and this psychological aspect is exacerbated at times of scarcity of resources, such as economic crises. Social change, blamed on the out-group, further contributes to negative attitudes towards immigrants. Nevertheless, political parties such as the populist radical right play a key role in catalysing anti-immigrant racism. As Pelinka notes, populism searches for a culprit (2013: 8), personified both by the elites' mismanaging immigration and by the out-group. The two culprits are configured as inextricably linked to each other. In so doing, populism panders to the fear of the Other, namely the out-group, and instrumentalises it, by heightening the perception of economic and social crisis (Wodak 2015: 5), to legitimise its attack on the elites and its promotion of anti-immigration sentiment.

5.4.2 The Civic Turn in Othering

The Lega's and FdI's views, though, are not monolithically extreme regarding the Othering of immigrants. Indeed, as the interviews suggest, a minority within the Italian populist radical right reject a black and white picture, by arguing that it is not immigration but rather Islam that threatens national identity and social cohesion (F20160905L). They also state that some immigrants adapt themselves to "our" national identity (L20180105S), and do not trigger a loss of a sense of national identity (E20170404C) or do not cause the economic crisis (F20160905L, G20170112G). Moreover, concerning the question of having immigrants as neighbours, the Italian populist radical right predominantly accepts them, as long as they adapt themselves (F20160905L, L20170104N, C20170106V). As a Lega representative clarified, "Some Muslim immigrants can be our neighbours. What is important is that they adapt themselves to at least 60% of our lifestyle since they are guests in our country" (F20160905). This project interprets these moderate statements as part of the "civic turn" of the Italian populist radical right, whereby these parties strive to achieve credibility and legitimacy by toning down their most extreme traits (Halikiopoulou, Mock, and Vasilopoulou 2013). By adopting civic terms, populist radical right parties undergo a process of mainstreaming, diminishing racism and embracing mainstream parties' more moderate views while being caught in a dilemma between vote-seeking and office-seeking (Akkerman et al. 2016: 15).

Despite this civic turn, a close CDA of the interviews and the manifestos illuminates the predominant use of negative vocabulary in the Othering of immigration, such as the words "threat," "alienation," "fear," "exasperation," "injustice," "discrimination," "decadence," "ghettoisation," "stealing jobs and benefits," and "triggering a war among the poor." These negative lexical choices evoke the topos of threat (Wodak 2015: 53): populist radical right parties over-emphasise the danger posed by the scapegoated group (i.e., the immigrants) to instil fear in the population and enhance their electoral gains. This stratagem is similar to Chilton's point about the strategy of coercion used in political discourse, which induces fear of the Other (2004: 118). Furthermore, Wodak's concepts of fallacy of sameness and fallacy of difference (2015: 54) seem particularly useful to analyse the discursive Othering of immigrants, which crudely assumes that Italians constitute a homogenous group, distinctively different from the threatening immigrants' group. Through the fallacy of sameness, the Italian populist radical right is blind to the ethnic diversity within the in-group and the out-group.

5.5 Conclusion

In the March 2018 national elections, the Lega, one of the Italian populist radical right parties analysed in this chapter, scored 17% of the votes and formed a coalition government with the M5S. In November 2018, Salvini, the Lega's Deputy Prime Minister, boisterously welcomed 51 refugees from Niger that had just landed in Italy, announcing that "our doors are open to those fleeing wars, while they are shut to those bringing war to Italy" (Piccolillo 2018). This statement is a telling example of the intertwining of civic and racist tones in the Italian populist radical right's discourse.

The civic turn of the Lega and FdI is not an isolated issue, but is representative of a broader trend, whereby populist radical right parties adopt civic elements to punctuate their otherwise racist discourse (Halikiopopulou, Mock, and Vasilopoulou 2013). Due to the scarcity of scholarly attention devoted to such civic turn in the Italian political milieu, this chapter has contributed to the existing literature on racism and civic discourse, through the CDA of Italian populist radical right interviews and manifestos. As this chapter illustrated, the Italian populist radical right has enacted a civic turn by incorporating civic values into its discourse, in order to forge coalitions with mainstream parties, with a view to achieving seats in government. Moreover, the civic turn may enlarge the share of votes cast for the Italian populist radical right, by extending its appeal to mainstream voters. On the other hand, the Italian populist radical right runs the risk of losing its core voters, attracted to, and bound to this party family through racism. The 2018 national elections seemed to confirm the usefulness of the civic turn, in order to enlarge the share of the electorate, and enter government through coalitions, with the caveat that in the 2018 elections, Lega's government coalition party was not a mainstream party but rather the catch-all populist M5S.

Not just the Lega, but also FdI have interspersed their otherwise racist discourse on immigration with civic values. As a result, immigrants are alleged to be a problem on humanitarian grounds. Similarly, while economic immigrants are disdained and distrusted, refugees are the target of compassion and solidarity. Consequently, with the goal of appearing legitimate and credible, the Italian populist radical right has injected civic elements into its racism.

Departing from the usual Italian populist radical right's self-distancing from racism, this chapter has uncovered both the civic and the racist elements making up the ambivalent discourse on immigration articulated by the Lega and FdI.

First, these parties construct immigration as a problem of unsurmountable magnitude; different reasons are summoned to support the framing of immigration as problematic: (1) From the economic point of view, the Italian populist radical right contends that immigrants are stealing Italians' jobs and economic resources, which becomes a particularly severe issue at times of economic distress. However, the economic arguments made by the populist radical right to justify racism are essentially flawed because, as this chapter argues, immigrants are not reported to take away jobs from Italians. (2) From the socio-demographic point of view, the populist radical right in Italy holds that immigrant inflows negatively alter the socio-demographic composition of a community, where the national in-group supposedly perceives isolation and alienation. According to this line of argument, the poor and the working class especially, who are already affected by the economic damage of immigration, are further socially marginalised, as immigrants allegedly steal jobs and precipitate a loss of a sense of unity and cohesion.

Second, the Lega and FdI differentiate between allegedly deserving refugees and undeserving economic migrants; in doing so, they often map the deserving v. undeserving dichotomy onto the separation between regular and irregular immigrants. Their discourse is infused with an exhibited sense of compassion towards refugees, who escape wars through perilous journeys across the Mediterranean. However, this humanitarian concern must be read critically, as it may be part of the "civic turn" of the populist radical right, in search of legitimacy and accountability (Griffini 2021).

Third, the Lega and FdI irremediably depict the immigrant as an Other, which bears resonance with the construction of the colonised as the colonisers' Other. The Othering of immigrants is grounded on economic and social reasons, which recall the economic and socio-demographic arguments used by the Italian populist radical right to justify the problematisation of immigration. Therefore, the very fact that immigrants are perceived as Others underpins the perception of immigration as a problem. The caveat that regular immigrants and refugees are, instead, welcome to Italy appears as a mere veneer, since the discourse of the Lega and FdI on immigration generally lumps together all immigrants into one group, which is criminalised, inferiorised, and abjectified, as Chapter 6 will show.

Notes

1 The author coined the term *abjectification* by merging the root *abject* (meaning cast off), deployed by the literature on race (see, for instance, Kristeva 1982; Gandesha 2003), with the suffix -*ification* signifying the action of casting off somebody.
2 *Mafia Capitale* is the title of a major police investigation that detected the infiltration of the mafia into Roman governance, including the management of the immigration system.
3 *CARA* stands for *Centro di Accoglienza per Richiedenti Asilo*, i.e., a first-hand reception centre. The *CARA* in Mineo was at the centre of a parliamentary inquest showing the connections between the reception centre and Roman mafia, as well as electoral corruption and bid-rigging.
4 The English translation *do-goodery* does not fully capture the pejorative connotation attached to the Italian *buonismo*.

5 Now National Rally (*Rassemblement National*), since 2018. This book has adhered to the original name of the party Front National, since the project started before the renaming of the party, and the literature deployed on the Front National largely dates back to the period previous to 2018.
6 Meaning "brazenly smart."
7 For a critical analysis of the discourse on immigration, see, for instance, Rivera (2020).
8 System of daily labour operating in southern Italy, characterised by exploitation, meagre pay, long working hours, dehumanising working conditions, and daily recruitment of labourers.

References

Agamben, G. (2003) *Stato di eccezione*, Turin: Bollati Boringhieri.
Akkerman, T., de Lange, S.L. & Rooduijn, M. (2016) *Radical Right-wing Populist Parties in Western Europe: Into the Mainstream?*, London: Routledge.
Albahari, M. (2015) *Crimes of Peace: Mediterranean Migrations at the World's Deadliest Border*, Philadelphia: University of Pennsylvania Press.
Albertazzi, D., Bonansinga, D. & Zulianello, M. (2021) "The rightwing alliance at the time of the Covid-19 pandemic: All change?", *Contemporary Italian Politics*. https://doi.org/10.1080/23248823.2021.1916857.
Amo-Agyei, S. (2020) "The migrant pay gap: Understanding wage differences between migrants and nationals", International Labour Organisation. Available: https://www.ilo.org/wcmsp5/groups/public/---ed_protect/---protrav/---migrant/documents/publication/wcms_763803.pdf [14 December 2020].
Anelli, M., Stanig, P. & Colantone, I. (2019) "We were the robots: Automation in manufacturing and voting behavior in Western Europe", *CReAM Discussion Paper Series, no. 1917*.
Arzheimer, K. (2009) "Contextual factors and the extreme right vote in Western Europe, 1980–2002", *American Journal of Political Science*, vol. 53, no. 2, pp. 259–275.
Berman, S. (2008) "Taming extremist parties: Lessons from Europe", *Journal of Democracy*, vol. 19, no. 1, pp. 5–18.
Brunelli, R. (2021) "Sondaggio YouGov sull'immigrazione: 'Per il 77% degli italiani è troppo alta'", *La Repubblica*. 23 December 2021. Available: https://www.repubblica.it/esteri/2021/12/23/news/immigrazione_sondaggio_you_gov_focus_italia-331331594/ [23 December 2021].
Calhoun, C. (2010) "The idea of emergency: Humanitarian action and global (dis)order", in *Contemporary States of Emergency: The Politics of Military and Humanitarian Interventions*, Fassin, D. & Pandolfi, M. (eds), New York: Zone Books, pp. 29–58.
Canovan, M. (1999) "Trust the people! Populism and the two faces of democracy", *Political Studies*, vol. 47, no. 1, pp. 2–16.
Castelli Gattinara, P. (2017) "Framing exclusion in the public sphere: Far-right mobilisation and the debate on Charlie Hebdo in Italy", *South European Society and Politics*, vol. 22, no. 3, pp. 345–364.
Castelli Gattinara, P. (2018) "Europeans, shut the borders! Anti-refugee mobilisation in Italy and France", in *Solidarity Mobilisations in the 'Refugee Crisis'*, Della Porta, D. (ed.), London: Macmillan, pp. 271–297.
Chilton, P.A. (2004) *Analysing Political Discourse Theory and Practice*, London; New York: Routledge.

Cordero, G., Zagórski, P. & Rama, J. (2021) "Give me your least educated: Immigration, education and support for populist radical right parties in Europe", *Political Studies Review*, pp. 1–8. https://doi.org/10.1177/14789299211029110

Dal Bò, E., Finan, F., Olle. F., Persson, T. & Rickne, J. (2019) "Economic losers and political winners: Sweden's radical right", *Working Paper*.

Dixon, T., Hawkins, S., Heijbroek, L., Juan-Torres, M. & Demoures, F. (2018) "Attitudes towards national identity, immigration and refugees in Italy", *More in Common Papers*.

Faloppa, F. (2011) *Razzisti a parola (per tacer dei fatti)*, Rome-Bari: Laterza.

Fanon, F. (1963) *The Wretched of the Earth*, Paris: Presence Africaine.

Faso, G. (2015) "La costruzione sociale dell'immigrato e del richiedente asilo in italia. Colti, democratici e razzismo colonialista", *Iperstoria*, no. 6.

Fassin, D. (2005) "Compassion and Repression: The Moral Economy of Immigration Policies in France", *Cultural Anthropology*, vol. 20, no.3, pp. 362–387.

Fondazione Leone Moressa (2019) "Gli stranieri ci rubano il lavoro?", *Coffee Break*. Available: http://webcache.googleusercontent.com/search?q=cache:MQZzZZ2P3x8J:www.fondazioneleonemoressa.org/2019/11/11/coffee-break-lavoro/&cd=2&hl=en&ct=clnk&gl=uk&client=safari.

Fusaro, S. & López-Bazo, E. (2018) "The impact of immigration on native employment: Evidence from Italy", *Research Institute of Applied Economics working paper, no. 22*.

Gandesha, S. (2003) "The political semiosis of populism", *The Semiotic Review of Books*, vol. 13, no. 3, pp. 1–12.

Geddes, A. & Pettrachin, A. (2020) "Italian migration policy and politics: Exacerbating paradoxes", *Contemporary Italian Politics*, vol. 12, no. 2, pp. 227–242.

Gijsberts, M., Hagendoorn, A. & Scheepers, P.L.H. (2004) *Nationalism and Exclusion of Migrants: Cross-national Comparisons*, Aldershot: Ashgate.

Giuffrida, A. (2018) "Matteo Salvini orders removal of refugees from Riace", *The Guardian*. 14 October 2018. Available: https://www.theguardian.com/world/2018/oct/14/matteo-salvini-orders-removal-of-refugees-from-riace [21 November 2018].

Giuliani, G. (2018) *Race, Nation and Gender in Modern Italy: Intersectional Representations in Visual Culture*, London: Palgrave Macmillan.

Griffini, M. (2021) "The civic discourse: Representing immigrants in the Italian far right", in *Approaches to Migration, Language, and Identity*, Auer, A. & Thornburn, J. (eds), Berlin: Peter Lang.

Guibernau, M. (2010) "Migration and the rise of the radical right", *Policy Network*, vol. 1.

Hainsworth, P. (2008) *The Extreme Right in Western Europe*, London, New York: Routledge.

Halikiopoulou, D., Mock, S. & Vasilopoulou, S. (2013) "The civic zeitgeist: Nationalism and liberal values in the European radical right", *Nations and Nationalism*, vol. 19, no. 1, pp. 107–127.

Hopkin, J. (2020) *Anti-System Politics: The Crisis of Market Liberalism in Rich Democracies*, Oxford: Oxford University Press.

Ipsos (2021) *Sistema economico e politico in crisi: Visioni populiste, anti-élite e nativiste*. 29 July 2021. Available: https://www.ipsos.com/it-it/sistema-economico-politico-crisi-visioni-populiste-anti-elite-nativiste [29 July 2021].

Kallis, A. (2015) "When fascism became mainstream: The challenge of extremism in times of crisis", *Journal of Comparative Fascist Studies*, vol. 4, pp. 1–24.

King, R. (1993) "Recent immigration to Italy: Character, causes and consequences", *GeoJournal*, vol. 30, no. 3, pp. 283–292.

Knigge, P. (1998) "The ecological correlates of right-wing extremism in Western Europe", *European Journal of Political Research*, vol. 34, no. 2, pp. 249–279.

Kristeva, J. (1982) *Powers of Horror. An Essay on Abjection*, New York: Columbia University Press.
Lentin, A. (2004) *Racism and Anti-racism in Europe*, London: Pluto Press.
Mammone, A. (2015) "Right-wing nationalism and scapegoating migrants", *Al Jazeera*. 15 August 2015. Available: https://www.aljazeera.com/opinions/2015/8/15/right-wing-nationalism-and-scapegoating-migrants [13 August 2022].
Moffitt, B. (2017) "Liberal illiberalism? The reshaping of the contemporary populist radical right in Northern Europe", *Politics and Governance*, vol. 5, no. 4, pp. 112–122.
Mudde, C. (1999) "The single-issue party book: Extreme right parties and the immigration issue", *West European Politics*, vol. 22, no. 3, pp. 182–197.
Mudde, C. (2019) *The Far Right Today*, Cambridge, UK: Polity Press.
Mutz, D. C. (2018) *Status Threat, not Economic Hardship, Explains the 2016 Presidential Vote*, New Haven: Yale University.
Norris, P. & Inglehart, R. (2019) *Cultural Backlash. Trump, Brexit, and Authoritarian Populism*, Cambridge: Cambridge University Press.
Parati, G. (1997) "Strangers in paradise: Foreigners and shadows in Italian literature", in *Revisioning Italy: National Identity and Global Culture*, Allen, B. & Russo, M.J. (eds), Minneapolis: University of Minnesota Press, pp. 169–190.
Pelinka, A. (2013) "Right-wing populism: Concept and typology", in *Right-wing Populism in Europe: Politics and Discourse*, Wodak, R., Mral, B. & KhosraviNik, M. (eds), London: Bloomsbury, pp. 3–22.
Perlmutter, T. (1996) "Immigration politics Italian style: The paradoxical behaviour of mainstream and populist parties", *South European Society and Politics*, vol. 1, no. 2, pp. 229–252.
Perrineau, P. (1985) "Le Front National: Un électorat autoritaire", *Revue Politique et Parlamentaire*, vol. 87, no. 918, pp. 24–31.
Piccolillo, V. (2018) "Salvini accoglie 51 migranti del Niger: 'Porte spalancate a chi scappa dalla guerra, chiuse a chi la porta da noi'", *Corriere della Sera*. 14 November 2018. Available: https://roma.corriere.it/notizie/cronaca/18_novembre_14/roma-salvini-accoglie-51-i-niger-arrivati-corridoi-umanitari-448ad8e8-e801-11e8-b8c4-2c4605eeaada.shtml [29 April 2019].
Rivera, A. (2020) "Un decennio d'infamie razziste, fino all'estremo", in *Cronache di ordinario razzismo*, Lunaria (ed.), Rome: Lunaria, pp. 9–18.
Said, E. (1978) *Orientalism*, London: Penguin.
Schäfer, A. (2021) "Cultural backlash? How (not) to explain the rise of authoritarian populism", *British Journal of Political Science*, vol. 52, no. 4, pp. 1–17.
Sprague-Jones, J. (2011) "Extreme right-wing vote and support for multiculturalism in Europe", *Ethnic and Racial Studies*, vol. 34, no. 4, pp. 535–555.
Tajfel, H. & Turner, J.C. (1979) "An integrative theory of intergroup conflict", in *The Social Psychology of Intergroup Relations*, Austin, W.G. & Worchel, S. (eds), Monterey: Brooks/Cole, pp. 33–47.
Todorov, T. (1984) *The Conquest of America*, New York: Harper and Row.
Tondo, L. (2019) "Italian authorities order seizure of migrant rescue ship", *The Guardian*. 20 March 2019. Available: https://www.theguardian.com/world/2019/mar/20/italian-authorities-order-seizure-migrant-rescue-ship-mare-jonio [21 May 2019].
Van Dijk, T.A. (1996) "Discourse, power and access", in *Texts and Practices. Readings in Critical Discourse Analysis*, Caldas-Coulthard, R.C. & Coulthard, M. (eds), London: Routledge, pp. 84–104.
Van Dijk, T.A. (2008) "Critical discourse analysis", in *The Handbook of Discourse Analysis*, Schiffrin, D., Tannen, D. & Hamilton, H.E. (eds), New York: John Wiley & Sons, pp. 352–371.

Wodak, R. (2015) *The Politics of Fear: What Right-wing Populist Discourses Mean*, London: Sage.
YouGov (2019) *Globalism All Markets*. Available: https://d25d2506sfb94s.cloudfront.net/cumulus_uploads/document/u2x0ae6is9/Globalism2019_immigration_softpower_general.pdf [2 March 2020].
Zaslove, A. (2004) "Closing the door? The ideology and impact of radical right populism on immigration policy in Austria and Italy", *Journal of Political Ideologies*, vol. 9, no. 1, pp. 99–118.
Ziller, C. & Schübel, T. (2015) "'The pure people' versus 'the corrupt elite'? Political corruption, political trust and the success of radical right parties in Europe", *Journal of Elections, Public Opinion and Parties*, vol. 25, no. 3, pp. 368–386.

6 Echoes from Colonialism
Criminalisation, Inferiorisation, and Abjectification of Immigration

6.1 Introduction

Continuing with the meticulous unpacking of the Lega's and FdI's racism started in the previous chapter, this chapter sets out to focus on three subsets of Othering. These three subsets are criminalisation, inferiorisation, and abjectification of immigration, which are copiously referred to in the literature on colonialism (see, for example, Fanon 1963; Said 1978; Todorov 1984) and racism (see for example Giuliani 2018; Guibernau 2010; Maneri 2009; Rivera 2020). As sketched in Chapter 2, the analysis of nativism in the populist radical right cannot be divorced from a deeper historical contextualisation stretching its chronological confines back to colonialism, especially in its fascist phase, when the colonised Other became the pillar of the definition of Italian national and racial identity.

Therefore, this chapter will probe how the Lega and FdI discuss immigration and the extent to which colonial tropes emerge in these discussions. This is not an easy task. The complexity, and, at the same time, the originality of the strand of argument inherent to this chapter lies in the detailed exploration of the depths of the intricacies between colonial echoes, covert or open racism, and the civic discourse in the Lega's and FdI's interviews and manifestos.

This chapter will first examine the equating of immigrants with crime, focusing, especially, on the intersectionality between race, gender and religion, and the association of Muslim immigrants with criminality. It will proceed by delving into the framing of immigrants as inferior. In this category intersectionality comes into play again, by providing a conceptual tool to grasp the entanglement of race, gender, and religion on the one hand, and the association of these three identity markers with the construction of inferiority. The chapter will conclude by teasing out the discursive linkage between immigrants and illness, which is an especially topical issue at the time of writing, during the COVID-19 pandemic. Each section will disentangle the intertwined strands of racist, colonial, and civic discourse.

6.2 Criminalisation of Immigration

Through criminalisation, the immigrant is represented as an intrinsically criminal Other opposed to the seemingly honest Self. Criminalisation echoes the colonial representation of the colonised as inherently suspicious, depraved (Said 1978: 39–40), deceitful (Todorov 1984: 40), and naturally prone to violence (Fanon 1963: 308). Italian fascist colonial discourse also depicted the colonised African as essentially disposed to violence (Conelli 2014: 164).

The colonial criminalisation of the Other is crystallised in the discourse of the Italian populist radical right on immigration since the immigrants are framed as fundamentally inclined to crime (see for example Giuliani 2018; Guibernau 2010; Maneri 2009; Rivera 2011). Immigrants today are subject to a kind of double criminalisation, because their crimes are considered more serious than the crimes committed by the national in-group. In this respect, Giuliani explains the centre-left PD representative Debora Serracchiani's statement deeming the rape of a woman in Trieste even more heinous as it was committed by an immigrant who had breached his hospitality agreement with Italy (2018: 243). In such a way, immigrants are criminalised because of their immigrant status, and their crimes are aggravated by such immigrant status. The criminalisation of immigrants is to be interpreted against the backdrop of the binarism between hypervisualisation and invisibilisation of immigrants: the former takes place when immigrants gain excessive visibility as they are the real or alleged perpetrators of crimes, while the latter steps in when immigrants are the victims of crimes (Giuliani 2018: 11). This discursive strategy is correlated to the frequent omission in media discourse of crimes targeting immigrants (Rivera 2011: 16).

The criminalisation of immigrants is rife in the Italian populist radical right, which links them to the crime of invasion, terrorism, and a wide array of other crimes. When in June 2003 more than 2500 immigrants landed on Lampedusa's shores, Bossi provocatively suggested that they should be shot out of the water (Horowitz 2003). Furthermore, the literature has reported that the Lega generally depicts immigrants as criminals who steal territory and freedom from Italians (Zaslove 2004: 102) and organises vigilante squads to protect local areas against crime. The latter is deeply racialised (Avanza 2010), as the Lega believes that immigrants tend to commit crimes more than Italians.

Fast forward to 2018. In its 2018 electoral manifesto, the Lega presented immigrants as an everyday threat to the security of Italian citizens, despite admitting that there are no official data confirming their thesis: "In Lombardy the rate of foreign drivers involved in accidents (5.6 per 1000 inhabitants) doubles those of Italian drivers (there is no national data)" (Lega Manifesto 2018: 17). This statement was meant to function both as a remark on the criminality of immigrants, and as a rebuke to the Italian state. In fact, the populist radical right's typical call for a strong state that strictly imposes law and order is articulated mainly in the context of immigration, often associated with crime, especially terrorism. In its 2018 manifesto, the Lega states, "The current massive and uncontrolled immigration flows destabilise our country from a social point of view, and offer opportunities for terrorist infiltrations and extremist propaganda," which is a warning that immigration may not only unsettle Italian society (which is an argument unpacked in the preceding chapter), but may also enable terrorists to penetrate into the Italian nation. The Lega's concern for crime and terrorism is echoed in the FdI 2018 manifesto, which demands "Protection for the dignity of the Police and Armed Forces with decent salaries, adequate staffing, means and technologies suitable for combating crime and terrorism," where terrorism is linked to immigration.

According to the Lega and FdI, the dire consequence of the present laxity of laws, whereby arrested immigrants are released after a very short time (F20160905L), is a generalised sense of impunity that encourages crime and terrorism (F20160905L, G20170405C, L20170410P). The Lega contrasts the lenient Italian legal system, where, in the words of a Lega representative, "immigrants exercise only rights but not duties" (F20160905L), with the rigid laws in place in the immigrants' countries of origin (A20180103DC). Through this contrast, authoritarian systems in the immigrants' countries of origin are refigured by the Lega into admirable beacons of legality. Within the broader category of immigrants, the irregular ones chiefly preoccupy the interviewed parties, who are concerned about irregular immigrants expelled from Italy multiple times, but "still hanging around smuggling drugs" (F20160905L). This concern ties back to the differentiation of immigration tackled in the preceding chapter. Interestingly, the need for law and order is expressed with regards to the immigrant population, while the need for Italians to comply with law and order was mentioned only once in the interviews (S20180108S). In so doing, the Other is discursively delegitimated *a priori*, while the Self undergoes an *a priori* legitimation, which is a discursive strategy often observed in political discourse (Chilton 2004).

In the interviews and manifestos, metaphors evoking natural catastrophes are deployed by the Lega and FdI to depict immigration as an invasion (see, for instance, C20170106V, F20170104M, F20170111S, G20170109D). According to the populist radical right, this invasion has been sweeping through Italy since the 1990s (C20170106V) and has escalated since 2013 (M20170113R). The criminalisation of immigrants moves a step further when it represents immigration not only as an invasion, but also as "a mass of silent and quiescent troops" (C20170106V) like "the Barbaric invasions" that spelled the end of the Roman Empire (F20160905L). In a typically anti-elite populist vein, the Italian populist radical right blames this invasion on the EU, where, in the profoundly Eurosceptic words of an FdI representative, "there is someone who prays that every day some desperate individual disembarks on Lampedusa so that they can fill up the hotels that have been up for auction for forty years" (F20170408T). The EU, therefore, is seen as culpable of orchestrating the invasion of immigrants into Italy for economic motives, to assuage the economic insecurity of hotel owners. Another anti-elite populist target of the Lega's and FdI's criminalisation of immigration are the NGOs involved in sea-rescue operations in the Mediterranean, and then docked in Italian ports (Berti 2021). The stance assumed by the populist radical right, but also by the centre-left towards search-and-rescue NGOs has been discussed at length in the preceding chapter, under the category of problematisation of immigration.

While not implying a neo-fascist identity for the current Italian populist radical right, it is worth recalling that under fascism fear of invasion from African races was rife, as Mussolini vented his concerns about the fact that: "The white race will be submerged by races of colour" (Ben-Ghiat 2006: 384). Mussolini's statement expresses the fascist fear that Africans would reproduce at an unprecedented rate and invade Europe, which was already affected by a condition of decline. The metaphor of the invasion is often accompanied by the discursive strategy of hyperbole, whereby the Italian populist radical right exaggerates the dimensions of the phenomenon, by claiming that "Africa" or "everyone" is moving to Europe (F20160905L, R20180103D).

The criminalising metaphor of invasion also takes the form of an inverse colonisation, for which immigrants are blamed in the interviews and in the manifestos. "Inverse colonisation creates advantages for a few and social costs for everyone," the Lega's 1992 and 1994 manifestos already claimed. It seems that such metaphor has not died out yet: several Italian populist radical right representatives implicitly maintained that immigration is an inverse colonisation. "You don't have to be Einstein to understand that in the next twenty years the majority (of the population) in Europe will be Arab, Muslim, and African" (F20170408T), stated one FdI representative, expressing the Italian populist radical right's concern about immigrants' fertility rate. Similarly, the Lega's 2018 manifesto emphasised that the fertility rate among immigrants is around two to four children per woman, while the fertility rate among Italians is around one to two children per woman. The fear of being colonised by immigrants becomes linked with the Lega's and FdI's criminalisation of the reproductive capacity of immigrant women, which discursively criminalises women's bodies in typically colonial style (see, for instance, Giuliani 2018). However, in line with the heterogeneity of voices that the interviews allow to distinguish, one FdI representative deviated from the trend of defining immigration as an inverse colonisation, contending that we cannot apply obsolete concepts to a modern phenomenon (F20180104F).

Departing from the broader criminalising metaphor of invasion and focusing on more specific crimes, in the interviews and the manifestos, among the Lega, FdI, and populist radical right intellectuals, there is wide consensus around the belief that immigrants increase criminality, such as prostitution, rape, theft, drug-smuggling, drug-dealing, and pickpocketing (see, for instance, F20170408T, G20170405C, G20170411C, G20170112G, G20170407P, L20170406C). Even the mafia is ostensibly caused by immigrants, especially Ghanaians, importing their own mafia into Italy (L20170104N). An otherwise relatively moderate Lega representative claimed that increasing numbers of immigrants translate into increasing numbers of "people with the intention to destroy" (S20180108S). Irregular immigration, which was explored in the previous chapter, seems to be particularly linked to crime in the Italian populist radical right's view. The alleged increase in criminality due to irregular immigration is used by the populist radical right to justify anti-immigrant sentiment and the crime of irregular immigration.

In Italy, the association of immigrants with crime in general goes back to the 1990s, when Albanians landing in the country were considered as bearers of criminality (C20170106V, F20170111S). As Dal Lago argues, "the figure of the brutal Balkan bandit predominates, reactivated by the media coverage of the Yugoslav wars in the 1990s" (2006: 191). However, one intellectual associated to the populist radical right disagreed with the connection between immigration and crime, by contending that "There is not a security emergency in Italy. This idea that there is a link between immigration and lack of security has been often spread by the media" (L20170406C).

The view of this intellectual is at odds with the fact that security has become a catchword in the interviews with the Italian populist radical right (see, for instance, G20170109D, M20180105M). Indeed, as mentioned earlier in this chapter, the call for a strong state, which is to be firm in countering criminality and in ensuring security through policing, robust laws, and law enforcement, is one of the defining ideological features of the Italian populist radical right. Hence, against the backdrop of the "civic turn" of the populist radical right (Halikiopoulou, Mock, and Vasilopoulou 2013), the Italian populist radical right arises as the defender of security, a potentially civic value applied both to the in-group and the out-group, which, in fact, is tightly connected with hostility towards immigration, since the Italian populist radical right emphasises the need to protect the people mainly against crime committed by immigrants (Griffini 2021). Consequently, security is not divorceable from racism: the security state fears immigration and multicultural society, which are framed as threats to national security in typically racist fashion (Fekete 2004: 21).

The Italian populist radical right, in the interviews, offers a wide array of reasons that may potentially act as a justification for the reportedly high rate of criminality among immigrants: lacking a proper job, immigrants need to resort to other means for their subsistence and sustenance (A20180103DC, L20170410P, S20180103F). Criminality, in addition, is seen as a necessity for immigrants to find something to do when they are "left in hotels idling all day" (F20170110F, F0180104F). The populist radical right's emphasis on the idleness of immigrants, linked to their criminality, is reported by various authors (see, for instance, Guibernau 2010: 12). In the interviews, the supposed idleness of immigrants is linked to their alleged motivation to come to Italy in search of fun (F20160905L, M20180105M, P20161219B), happy hours (F20160905L), satellite TV (F20160905L), fashionable clothes (S20180103F), and the latest phones (F20180408T, M20180105M, S20180103F), instead of looking for a job (C20170106V). The view of immigrants draining Italian state resources for their own leisure is uncorroborated by statistical and academic sources. It is just built off ideologically impregnated anecdotes that are blind to the complexity of the socio-economic and personal struggles of immigrants.

Additionally, sometimes, criminality is attributed to immigrants because of their own nature, as they were supposedly criminals also in their own countries (C20170106V, L20170104N, M20170404F), or come from countries where compliance with laws is uncommon (M20180105M), to such a degree that immigration, in the words of a Lega representative now looks like "the forced export of the worst people from English society to Australia" (C20170106V). Similarly, an FdI representative claimed that immigrants are "the worst of their countries of origin" (S20180103F). Hence, the criminalisation of immigrants operates on two levels:

on the one hand, immigrants are criminalised because they are linked to real or presumed crimes by virtue of their status as immigrants; on the other hand, the latter aggravates the crimes they really or supposedly commit. The association of immigrants' innate proclivity to crime bears an uncanny resonance to the fascist and colonial belief that the colonised African was, biologically, prone to crime (Galeotti 2000).

In the interviews, criminality is also blamed on the fact that immigrants know that they can do whatever they like, due to the laxity of Italian laws (F20160905L, N20180108C, R20180104M). This point harks back to the call for a strong state vehemently voiced by the populist radical right. According to a Lega representative, "there are people who have received three or four expulsion orders and are still around, maybe smuggling drugs" (F20160905L). Additionally, the Italian populist radical right attributes the responsibility for the immigrants' penchant for crime to the so-called "Alfano bonus," i.e., the pocket money given by the then Italian Minister of Foreign Affairs Angelino Alfano (2016–2018) to immigrants, allegedly exploited by the latter to maximise their profits (F20170408T).

The criminalisation of immigrants is emphasised by the strategy of legitimation through authorisation (Wodak 2015: 56), whereby the Italian populist radical right buttresses its racist statements by resorting to statistics showing the percentage of crimes committed by immigrants. As an FdI representative argued, to show the scale of the link between immigration and criminality in Florence, the police arrested 60 heroin dealers, out of which 56 were asylum seekers (F20180408T). Another FdI representative claimed that 34% of the total population in jails is made up of immigrants (G20170112G), while a Lega representative opined that 50% of the population in jails comes from non-European countries (G20170411C), and a different FdI representative corrected that figure to 60% (S20180103F). These discordant data recall the cacophony of statistics adduced by the Lega and FdI about the number of irregular immigrants in Italy, examined in the previous chapter.

Also in pandemic times, the association of immigrants with crime is still rife in the discourse of the Italian populist radical right. Immigrants tend to be associated with the crime of irregular immigration (as analysed in Chapter 5), and with other kinds of crime. In the interviews, immigrants are connected to prostitution, *caporalato*, and unfair competition in the workplace (P20210422B). Adding to that, they are seen as deserving expulsion and as the embodiment of the crime of irregular migration.

The criminalisation of immigration in Italian policy-making stretches its roots to the 2009 Security Package, introduced by the 2008–2011 Berlusconi-led coalition government. This policy has to be contextualised within the background of immigration policy-making in Italy under coalition governments led by the centre-right FI and including the populist radical right partners AN and Lega. In the 2001–2006 Berlusconi-led coalition government, the 2002 Bossi-Fini Law[1] authorised the expulsion of irregular immigrants. Although it was accompanied by a massive regularisation of irregular immigrants (Rosina 2022:22), this law represented a step towards harsher immigration policy and manifested the radicalisation of the centre-right under the influence of the populist radical right. The trajectory of radicalisation of the mainstream continued in 2009 with the promulgation of the Security Packages,[2] which introduced the crime of irregular immigration (Carvalho 2014). The criminalisation of immigration at a policy level initially envisaged punishment in the form of imprisonment ranging from six months to four years, which was then amended and replaced by a monetary sanction of an amount ranging from 5000 Euros to 10,000 Euros (Rosina 2022). This punitive policy was meant to act as a deterrent to irregular immigration (Rosina 2022).

Furthermore, the Italian populist radical right has been strenuously championing the civic value of individual security through the call for a reform of the Law of Legitimate Defence, which, however, takes on subtle racist remarks. Indeed, when discussing the reform of the Law of Legitimate Defence, the Lega and FdI explicitly or implicitly refer to immigrants as the threat to individual security. The topic of legitimate defence aroused the interviewees' passions, as they indulged in lengthy tirades in favour of legitimate defence, but also against the 2017 version of the reform to the Law of Legitimate Defence (see, for instance, C20170106V, F20170104M, F20160905L, M20170104G, P20161219B, S20180103F). Indeed, although the new law was finally approved by the Chamber of Deputies in May 2017, it did not make it to the end of the legislative journey. Indeed, the new law did not appease the populist radical right's desires to promote the outwardly civic value of individual security. The Lega and FdI bitterly criticised the 2017 law proposal for being too lenient, since it established that reactions to intrusions into private property, even with the use of weapons, would be legal only at night, and in response to violence towards people or things. The person exercising the right to legitimate defence would not be sued if they are reacting to dangers posed to life and health, and to personal and sexual harassment. According to an FdI representative, "Defence is always legitimate; the PD Legitimate Defence Law is bullshit" (S20180103F), and according to a Lega representative, "The Legitimate Defence Law protects criminals against citizens" (F20170104M). The Lega and FdI, in fact, put on a show of strength in Parliament displaying posters mocking the Law as "incomplete," and wearing t-shirts carrying the slogan "Defence is always legitimate" (F.Q. Redazione 2017).

The populist radical right's protests were not lost. In fact, the 2018 electoral campaign by the Lega and FdI vehemently promoted the tightening up of the Law of Legitimate Defence (AGI 2018), and, in the first wholly populist government formed by the Lega and the M5S, Salvini, then Vice-Prime Minister and Minister of the Interior, managed to have a stricter Law of Legitimate Defence passed in January 2019.[3] The law, compared to the 2017 law proposal, did not limit the legitimacy of self-defence to night-time. It increased the amount of the fine to be paid by the trespasser in case of violations of private property threatening individuals and personal belongings; the law also extended the length of jail sentence served by the trespasser.

6.2.1 Criminalisation, Religion, and Gender

The discussion of the criminalisation of immigrants cannot be divorced from wider intersectional considerations on gender and colonialism. Indeed, the

Italian populist radical right's insistence on the prostitution of immigrant women (M20180105M, P20161219B) echoes the colonisers' belief that the colonised were inherently depraved (Said 1978: 39–40). The assumption about the depravity of the colonised was intertwined with the hypersexualisation of colonised women's bodies, represented with large lips and large breasts (Pinkus 1997: 136–137): through the complex and ambivalent nexus of attraction and repulsion typical of the white male gaze on the black female, in Italian colonies black women provided sexual satisfaction to the colonising white Italian males, while posing the risk of immorality, impurity, and racial degeneration (Giuliani 2018: 77). As for men, black and Muslim immigrants and refugees are still hypersexualised, represented as sexually repressed, aggressive, and as natural-born rapists (Giuliani et al. 2020: 167). The same hegemonic white male gaze of colonial reminiscence, therefore, resurfaces in the discourse of the Italian populist radical right on immigrants' prostitution: the discursive articulation of the black body as repellent, immoral, impure, and degenerate reveals a surreptitious sense of complacency and attraction towards it. The idea of a foreign immigrant invasion is supported by these colonial ideas of the dangerousness of the black male "Other" (Giuliani et al. 2020: 177).

The hypersexualisation of immigrant women, sitting uncomfortably with the saving rhetoric of the populist radical right (analysed later in this chapter), often makes recourse to the use of coarse language. While the use of such language is not limited to the populist radical right, it is however a typical sign of populist style, which is direct, simple, and aimed at closing the gap between the politicians and the people they address (Cavazza and Guidetti 2014: 537). Additionally, cursing increases the effectiveness of male politicians, whose public perception improves (Cavazza and Guidetti 2014: 537, 540). For instance, the catch-all populist M5S made cursing its trademark (Bordignon and Ceccarini 2013), by which it attempted to neutralise the distance between itself and the people, and boosted the effectiveness of its male politicians. Similarly, the Lega and FdI display their populist style, by interspersing their discourse with coarse language. For example, an interviewee from the Lega coloured his replies with frequent swear words and vulgar phrases mainly targeting immigrant women, qualified as "whores who end up in nightclubs or, the most miserable, end up in the streets" (P20161219B) to "prostitute[4] themselves" (P20161219B). In this entanglement of populist style, racist ideology, criminalisation of immigration, and gender discrimination, non-immigrant Arab women are also beleaguered and discursively hypersexualised. This point is evident in the following quote by a Lega representative who was talking about (not better specified) "Arab women": "[They are] whores wearing Fendi clothes, full of henna, and gold everywhere" (P20161219B).

A differential criminalisation demarcated along religious lines emerges in the Italian populist radical right. As the interviews indicate, the Lega and FdI representatives created a hierarchy of immigrants based on their proclivity to crime, maintaining that some groups are more prone to crime than others. For instance, they believed that delinquency is more frequent among African immigrants

(F20170111S, C20170106V), while Filipinos (F20170111S, R20180108D) are more docile due to their professing of Catholicism. Indeed, according to an FdI representative, "It is clear that it is easier to live together if people have similar religious identities" (E20170404C). This notion of docility recalls the discourse on the domesticability of the Other: the more easily tameable the Other is, the more easily it can be cannibalised into the borders of the nation, whitened, and included, yet kept different (Sharnma 2003).

In particular, in the interviews, the Lega, FdI, and populist radical right intellectuals think that Muslims are more dangerous or worrying than other ethnic or religious group (see, for instance, A20180103LC, E20170404C, E20180103G, F20180104F, G20180109C), especially as Islam is associated with radicalism (E20170404C). Indeed, the Italian populist radical right almost unanimously agrees that Muslim immigrants, infiltrating the boats crossing the Mediterranean, bring terrorism to Italy (see, for instance, A20180103DC, F20170104M, G20170405C, G20170109D, G20170407P, L20170410P). As a Lega representative emphatically added, in order to highlight the contrast between honest Italians and seemingly criminal Muslim immigrants, "There is nobody from Pavia with Pavese blood and nobody from Milan speaking the Milanese dialect who have blown themselves up as a kamikaze around the world" (G20170411C).

The Italian populist radical right finds explanations for why immigrants bring terrorism. According to the Lega and FdI representatives, and populist radical right intellectuals, terrorism is driven by economic motives (A20180103DC, F20170104M, S20180103F), social alienation caused by the ghettoisation of Muslims (F20170104M), the clash of civilisations between the West and Islam (A20180103DC, C20170106V, G20170109D, G20180109C), and Muslim immigrants' hatred of the West (A20180103DC, F20170111S, S20180103F), further compounded by the allegedly inherent violence of Islam (G20170111R, G20170112G, M20170404F). In the words of the Lega representatives, Islam was founded by Mohammed who was a "murderer" (M20170104G), as "he converted people by slashing throats with his sword" (M20170404F). Finally, in a typically anti-elite populist fashion, whereby the populist radical right criticises the state for its laxity towards crimes related to immigration, an FdI representative blamed Muslim terrorism on the Italian state for having loose rules facilitating the infiltration of terrorists (L20170410P).

For the Italian populist radical right, Muslim immigration is linked not only to terrorism but also to a holy war, as indicated by the interviews (see, for instance, F20160509L, F20170104M, G20180105M). According to the Lega and FdI, on the boats crossing the Mediterranean there are people from ISIS (G20170109D), and Muslim immigrants in general strive to convert the infidels (F201160905L, G20170411C, M20170104G) and maintain supremacy over the Christian world (A20180103LC, L20170104N). Thus, they perpetuate Muslim attempts to conquer the West, going back as far as the medieval Muslim conquest of Sicily and Spain (E20180103G), and their efforts to subjugate Vienna and Lepanto, inscribed in historical archives as the bulwarks of the West (C20170106V). Medieval imagery looms large in the Italian populist radical right's discourse on Muslim immigration, to such a degree that a Lega representative compared the current Muslim immigration to the army that clashed against the Christian crusaders in the Holy Land (C20170106V). Similarly, another Lega representative praised the Christian crusaders for having stopped the Islamisation of the Western world and went to great lengths to assert that "Today we need a crusade to combat the Muslim world" (L20170104N). The belief about a supposed Muslim holy war is compounded by the conviction widespread among the Italian populist radical right that Muslims do not condemn terrorism, but rather condone it (A20180103LC, F20180104F, G20180105M, R20180104M), which resonates with the view that radicalism, in the Lega representatives' words, is the true face of Islam (L20170104N, M20170113R), as it is dictated by the Koran (L20170104N, E20180103G). By deploying the strategy of legitimation through authorisation, the engagement of the Italian populist radical right's representatives with the Koran lends an aura of authority and credibility to their claims. Indeed, by using the Koran as evidence, the Italian populist radical right buttresses its claims using ostensibly trustworthy research, which, though, is always aimed at disparaging the Koran, especially in comparison with the gospels, which are apparently devoid of any violence (F20180104F).

Mosques are a powerful symbol representing Muslim immigrants in the discourse of the Italian populist radical right. According to the interviews, mosques appear as a serious issue (C20170106V, L20170104N). The reasons for their concerns for mosques, among the Lega and FdI, lie in the association of mosques with Islamic radicalism, as they are reportedly "funded by Wahhabis from Gulf countries" (S20180103F), and with terrorism, as they "organise and train terrorists" (see, for instance, A20180103DC, L20170104N, R20180108D, S20180108S). Moreover, mosques seem to be worrying places, as they are allegedly ghettos denying access to Westerners (C20170106V), and are both religious and political places (F20180104F, L20170104N, M20170404F), unlike churches that are just places of worship (F20180104F).

The danger attached to mosques also derives from their being "dark and obscure places" (A20180103DC) located in mysterious sites, such as basements and cellars (E20180103G) proliferating uncontrollably (F20170111S) without council authorisation (F20170111S). Therefore, mosques become disquieting because of their association with an urban security issue, as they are overcrowded and "invade entire blocks of flats and entire streets" (F20170111S). Hence, it is patent that the metaphor of the invasion criminalising immigrants disembarking into Italy is also applied to mosques apparently sprouting everywhere: in an FdI representative's words, "in Tor Pignattara there are seven mosques, in the Esquilino five, we are having an invasion of mosques; this is unacceptable" (F20170111S).

As a solution, the Italian populist radical right proposes either to shut down or to control mosques. In the interviews, FdI and Lega representatives expressed their belief in the freedom of religion (E20170404C, F20170404M, F2017011S). Despite their professed freedom of religion, some Lega and FdI representatives suggested mosques should not be open and those already existing should be closed down (see, for instance, C20180109G, F20170110F, M20170111R, P20161219B), while others believed that mosques should be controlled. The measures to carry out such control are: requesting that imams give sermons in Italian (see, for instance, A20180103DC, C20180104V, F20160905L, F20180104F, S20180103F); establishing an imam register (C20180109G, F20170111S, G20170411C, R20180104M, S20180103F); tracking funding for mosques (C20180109G, F20170408T); controlling IDs at the entrance (G20170109D); and finally, defining the relationship between Islam and the Italian state (G20170411C). In its 2018 manifesto, in the section dedicated to terrorism, the Lega tackled the issue of mosques, presenting some solutions to fight terrorism, such as imposing the use of Italian language in mosques, forbidding the use of Arabic, and asking mosques to "Provide a compulsory theological training for imams, who need to be recorded in a national register of imams" (Lega Manifesto 2018: 18).

Therefore, from the characterisation of mosques mentioned above, and from the solutions purported, it can be inferred that the mosque becomes, in the eyes of the populist radical right, the emblem of Muslims' fusion between religion and politics, which is regarded with fear especially after 9/11 (Zaslove 2004: 106). Already in 1999, the Lega's newspaper *La Padania* criminalised the mosque and linked it to the holy war, by defining it as a "sweetened version of jihad" (Zaslove 2004: 108). As *La Padania* reported in March 2001, the mosque's threat lies in its being a religious space that houses political discussions (Redazione la Padania 2001). Muslims in Italy have been at the centre of acrimonious debate especially after the bewildering effect of 9/11 (Burdett 2005: 2). Indeed, 9/11 presented the West with such an unreal and incandescent threat that it could not be faced with the usual response mechanisms, and triggered a deep fear of Islam (Burdett 2005: 24).

The perception of mosques as threatening places is widespread in Italian society: according to a 2018 survey, only 24% of Italians stated that they did not mind if a mosque was built near their home (Dixon et al. 2018). Writer and journalist Oriana Fallaci contributed to the construction of the perception of mosques as dangerous places offering a breeding ground for terrorists. "They want to build damn mosques everywhere," she said, commenting on the plan for building a mosque in Colle di Val d'Elsa (Tuscany) in 2006, and she promised to blow it up in case it was built (cited in Talbot 2006). Also, the right-wing intellectual Magdi Allam, who underwent a conversion from Islam to Christianity, criticised a "mosque-mania," for brainwashing Muslims and converting them into terrorists (2005).

Fallaci, a prominent journalist and writer, stoked the fires of the fear of Islam in the aftermath of 9/11, achieving immense popularity due to her prestigious reputation as a journalist, her straightforward manifestation of emotions (Burdett 2005: 25–26), and her rough and colloquial style (Orsini 2006: 448, 458). Her first book *La rabbia e l'orgoglio* published as a reaction to 9/11 sold one million copies across Europe and the US (Orsini 2006). Although Fallaci did not identify with any party and harshly criticised a wide range of politicians, including the former Lega's leader Bossi (Orsini 2006), the Lega wanted Fallaci to become a senator and distributed her books (Burdett 2005: 45).

Fallaci enjoyed favourable reception not only by the right, but also by intellectuals, such as Sergio Romano (former diplomat and columnist for *Corriere della Sera*), Ernesto Galli della Loggia (historian and columnist for *Corriere della Sera*), and Giovanni Sartori (political scientist and columnist for *Corriere della Sera*). She also elicited admiration by left-wing politicians, such as Francesco Rutelli (mayor of Rome between 1993 and 2001, Minister of Culture and Deputy Prime Minister in the second Prodi government between 2006 and 2008), and Riccardo Nencini (governor of Tuscany between 2000 and 2010) (Cousin, Vitale 2014). Rutelli, mindful of Fallaci's experience as a young anti-fascist partisan in the Resistance in Italy, praised the journalist's abrasive criticism of totalitarianisms ranging from fascism to Muslim fundamentalism (Conti 2007). Nencini eulogised the writer's deep attachment to Florence, her birth town (Eduati 2016).

Fallaci's ideas voiced anti-Muslim feelings catalysed by 9/11 and, at the same time, played upon them, by propagating phobia towards Islam, which became interpreted monolithically as a "jihad" (Fallaci 2001: 78). Fallaci's interpretation of Islam evokes Huntington's argument about a clash of civilisations, where Western civilisation is overtaken by more economically and demographically dynamic ones (1996). In particular, both Fallaci and Huntington locate the major fault line between different civilisations along the border between the Muslim world and the West (1996). What distinguishes Fallaci from Huntington is that her views are characterised by her belief in the rigidity of a violent and monolithic Islam, which the journalist does not justify in academic terms, but purely through her experience as a witness of certain events or through media reports on those events (Burdett 2005: 29). Fallaci's interpretation criminalises Islam by framing it as intrinsically and relentlessly violent and expansionist, thanks to the complicity of a West blinded by the need to import crude oil (Burdett 2005: 34). Fallaci warned that Muslims were enacting a "religious and cultural conquest" of the West (2004: 201), made possible not only by their political and religious drive to conquer, but also by their high fertility rates that made them "multiply like rats" (2001: 87). Even Magdi Allam, a right-wing intellectual close to the populist radical right, criticised Fallaci's triggering of Islamophobia after 9/11, which apparently hindered a rational analysis of the real threat posed by Islamic radicalism (2005).

Along with the clash of civilisations, another reason explaining the framing of Muslims as inherently hostile Others may be rooted in the Western search for an enemy after the Cold War, as *The New York Times* already noted in 1996 (Sciolino 1996). Indeed, the demise of communism and the collapse of the Eastern bloc deprived the West of an enemy to fight against. This void was quickly filled by Muslims. According to G.W. Bush's adviser Bernard Lewis, Islam shares similarities with communism, as they are both forms of totalitarianism that hold answers to the question of the afterlife (cited in Kundnani 2014: 66). Furthermore, both Islam and communism, as totalitarian ideologies, adopt terror as a founding principle of the state and control individuals' lives (Kundnani 2014: 97–99). Therefore, after the end of the Cold War and especially after 9/11 and the start of the *war on terror*, the political enemy of the West, communism, was replaced by Islam, in particular Islamic terrorism. The Italian populist radical right exploited this reconfiguration to fight Muslim immigration through securitisation: the imposition of hard borders, the policing of immigration, and harsh laws against immigrants. Furthermore, the Italian populist radical right, through Islamophobia, implicitly champions the return to an idealised past characterised by culturally and ethnically homogenous national communities unspoilt by multiculturalism. This reconfiguration of the political enemy of the Italian populist radical right is indicative of these parties' flexibility and adaptability to different historical contexts. In fact, the Lega and FdI are not static parties with fixed ideological components, but rather adapt dynamically to contingencies, to maintain a large voting base.

Moreover, as the above-mentioned quote by Fallaci about Muslims reproducing "like rats" (2001: 87) demonstrates, the inimical representation of Islam is aggravated by the Western fear of Muslims' fertility rate, which recalls the point made in section 6.3.1 on the criminalisation of immigrants' fertility. This precipitates the fear of "Eurabia," which is the Muslim cultural and political subjugation of a declining Europe and is based on the Eurabianists' interpretation of the work by writer Bat Ye'or (2005) on the diplomatic rapprochement between European countries and Arab states in the 1970s, after the oil crisis, and read as a plot for the Muslim conquest of Europe (Carr 2006). In fact, Ye'or puts forward a racist conspiracy argument claiming: "Europe is rapidly being transformed into 'Eurabia', a cultural and political appendage of the Arab/Muslim world that is fundamentally anti-Christian, anti-Semitic, anti-Western and anti-American" (2005). The conspiracy theory of Eurabia is mirrored in Camus's work. Camus feared that European civilisation risked being subverted by massive immigration flows, principally from Muslim countries, and by low fertility rates among native French people (Bergman 2018). As Bergman (2018: 127) acutely observed in the study of conspiracy theories, "This notion of replacement, or of white genocide, has echoed throughout the rhetoric of many anti-migrant far-right movements in the West."

This claim is highly controversial, since, first, it conflates Arabs with Muslims, who are actually two separate entities that do not necessarily coincide. Second, Ye'or's argument mistakenly assumes that the Arab/Muslim world is intrinsically against Christianity, Judaism, the West, and the US. Eurabianists' anxiety over a Muslim takeover of Europe, due to their alleged violence and fertility, was further fuelled in 2017 by Erdogan's invitation to Turkish people to increase the number of children per family (Eatwell and Goodwin 2018), thus confirming the supposed Muslim conspiracy to invade Europe not only through force but also through reproductive power. However, the Eurabianist fear is unfounded, as even Eatwell and Goodwin, who are unsympathetic to criticism of the populist radical right's racism, contend that it is unlikely that the Muslim population in Europe will grow so quickly (Eatwell and Goodwin 2018).

Hostility towards mosques is widespread beyond Italian borders. For instance, in 2009, in Switzerland a referendum to prohibit the construction of minarets on mosques passed by 57.9% (Halikiopoulou, Mock, and Vasilopoulou 2013: 118). The populist radical right SVP's campaign against minarets represented them as missiles attacking the country and as the emblem of the Muslims' imposition of their ideas of law and order, allegedly incompatible with the Swiss values

88 *Echoes from Colonialism*

of freedom and equality (Halikiopoulou, Mock, and Vasilopoulou 2013: 119). Similarly, the British National Party (BNP) contrasted the building of mosques with the British civic values of modernity, secularism, and democracy, and concluded that mosques should not be built (Halikiopoulou, Mock, and Vasilopoulou 2013: 121).

6.2.2 The Civic Turn in the Criminalisation of Immigration

The interviews show that the nexus between Muslim immigration and danger, terrorism, and holy war is nuanced. The civic turn of the populist radical right is evident in the following quotation by an FdI representative: "If a young woman ends up as a prostitute on a road, then (…) we allowed her exploitation. This kind of immigration favours human trafficking and benefits those who need cheap labour to exploit" (R20210426S). By equating immigration to human trafficking and exploitation, the Italian populist radical right arises as a defender of the rights of immigrants, thus appearing inclusive and moderate. In this instance, the FdI representative interviewed even took the responsibility of allowing prostitution of immigrant women upon themselves.

Moderation surfaces, in particular, in discussions over the link between immigration, religion, and crime. Part of the Italian populist radical right believes that Muslims are not more dangerous than other immigrants (L20170401P, N20180108C). Moreover, a few prudently qualified their statements on the connection between immigration and terrorism by claiming that it is simplistic, while the link between non-integrated immigrants and terrorism makes more sense (G20180109C, M20180105M). Indeed, few Lega and FdI representatives opposed the equating of immigration and terrorism, by contending that not all Muslims are terrorists (G201801089C, L20180105S), but all terrorists are Muslim (C20180109G, G20170111R). Regarding the holy war, a sizeable portion of party representatives similarly expressed moderate views, by dissenting with the generalised representation of Muslim immigration as a holy war (see, for instance, C20180109G, F20170110F, G20170112G, M20170104F, S20180103F). Instead, they put forward the view that the holy war is only waged by some Muslims (E20170404C, G20180109C, G20170407P) against everyone else who is not Muslim (E20170404C, G20170109D). In the words of an FdI representative, "A big portion of radical Islam believe they are in a state of war against all those who are not Muslims" (E20170404C).

Despite some strains of moderation belonging to the populist radical right's trajectory towards civicness, within the category of criminalisation, negative vocabulary linked to war is frequently used to denote immigrants, especially Muslim ones. This is symptomatic of racist hues. In fact, terms such as "invasion," "troops," "ghetto," "crusader," "terrorism," "holy war," "hatred," "radicalism" often emerge from the interviews. These terms reveal the recurrent topos of threat (Wodak 2015: 53) that the populist radical right deploys to fan the fires of fear, by associating immigrants with a menace to security on a macro level through invasion, terrorism, and a holy war, and on a micro level through crimes such as thefts, burglaries, pickpocketing, rapes, prostitution, drug-smuggling, and drug-selling.

The topos of threat is particularly evident regarding Muslim immigrants, as the Italian populist radical right deploys quotations by Muslim leaders to induce anxiety. For instance, a Lega representative claimed that in an interview with ISIS he watched, ISIS declared that they "will bring camels to drink from the Trevi fountain" (P20161219B), and both the Lega and FdI representatives reported Erdogan's alleged assertion: "We will conquer you with our women's wombs" (F20180408T, L20170401N). Similarly, already in 2008, the Lega manifesto warned that immigrants' fertility may lead to the eclipse of Europe. These anxiety-generating statements resonate in the Italian populist radical right as an ominous prediction: Muslims will invade Europe in great numbers and conquer it not just through a holy war, but also through the fertility of Muslim women. Finally, the legitimation v. delegitimation discursive strategy mapped onto the Self v. Other contrast goes hand-in-hand with the discursive strategy of the omission of the dominant group's crimes (Van Dijk 2008: 362): crimes committed by Italians are rendered invisible in the discourse of the Italian populist radical right. Further discursive strategies are in operation in the criminalisation of immigration: the fallacy of sameness and the fallacy of difference (Wodak 2015: 54), becoming blatant when the Italian populist radical right frames immigrants, especially Muslim ones, as a homogeneous group, intrinsically criminal, thus being oblivious to the vast array of ethnic and religious diversity inherent to Muslim immigrants.

6.3 Inferiorisation of Immigration

As documented in the literature on colonialism (see, for instance, Cassata 2008; Fanon 1963; Matard-Bonucci 2008; Said 1978) and on immigration (see, for instance, Giuliani 2018), inferiorisation figures prominently in the rhetoric of Othering, where immigrants are depicted as essentially inferior Others opposed to an ostensibly superior Italian Self. The colonial belief that Africans lacked logic, critical ability, and progress (Cassata 2008: 231, 234), and were doomed to remain in a child-like state (Matard-Bonucci 2008: 128) reverberates in the Italian populist radical right's inferiorisation of immigrants. Furthermore, the inferiorisation of the immigrant Other recalls Fanon's point about the dehumanisation of the colonised orchestrated by the colonisers (1963: 41) and Said's argument about the Western construction of the East as naturally irrational and child-like, in need of Western illumination and progress (1978: 40).

Inferiorisation depicting immigrants as backward is rife on the Italian populist radical right. Even in the early 1990s, La Malfa, representative of the Partito Repubblicano Italiano (PRI), believed that immigration would damage democracy and provoke a "barbarisation" of civil life (cited in Iraci Fedeli 1990: 7), thus suggesting the association of immigrants with inferior Barbaric people. Similarly, as suggested by the interviews, the Lega claims that immigrants are lazier than Italians (F20160905L) and not willing to work (M20170104G,

P20161219B), which carries an uncanny resonance of fascist and colonial tropes about Africans being lazier than Italians (Conelli 2014: 164). Moreover, Said's argument that the West produced the East as intrinsically lethargic and opposed to an energetic, initiative-driven West (1978: 39–40) clearly comes through. Inferiorisation also emerges from the Italian populist radical right's characterisation of immigrants as slaves (M20170104G, M20170111R, N20180108C), which is a metaphor, conveying the supposed inferiority of immigrants and their partial loss of humanity.

The inferiorisation of immigrants, whereby immigrants are portrayed as inferior, is also present in the discourse of the Lega and FdI in the spring of 2021. While the notion of immigrants as inferior human beings is implicit in the discourse of the Italian populist radical right, the FdI's and the Lega's cloaking of this inferiorisation under a civic veil, which feeds into these parties' effort to come across as democratic, is more patent. This is exemplified in the following quotation from an FdI representative: "They live in an inhuman way. Italy cannot treat people as beasts, which must always be condemned" (P20210422B). The interviewee is in this case referring to immigrants who live in deplorable conditions lacking essential services, and is attacking the Italian government for treating immigrants in such a reprehensible way, thus depicting himself as the protector of migrant individual rights. The use of metaphors, such as beasts, is widespread in the populist radical right discourse (Van Dijk, 2008).

Another common metaphor still used in the 2021 interviews is slaves, as immigrants are said to be part of a "slave trade" (R20210426S), which is tied to the above-mentioned notion of immigrants as victims of human trafficking. The metaphor of slaves implies that immigrants are involved in illegal labour and available to sell their labour cheaply, with a negative impact on the employment of Italians. Berti's analysis of Salvini's posts in the wake of his ban on the *Sea-Watch 3* from docking in the harbour confirms that immigrants are depicted as victims of a slave trade (2021). Muslim immigrants are the major target of inferiorisation since the populist radical right shapes its image as promoter of human rights and democracy against allegedly undemocratic Muslim ideas. For instance, an FdI interviewee referred to radical Muslim immigrants as a threat to Italy's social progress: "When we face radical Muslim immigrants, it is often hard to make them comply with what is normal civil Western democratic life" (P20210422B). Interestingly, the contrast made is between Western democratic life, taken as a benchmark of "normality," and the apparently undemocratic habits of radical Muslim immigrants.

6.3.1 Inferiorisation, Religion, and Gender

Within the category of the inferiorisation of immigrants, Islamophobia looms large. First, as the interviews indicate, the Lega and FdI believe that Muslims lack respect for women (see, for instance, G20170109D, M20170404F, M20170111R, R20180104M), and recall the seventeenth- or eighteenth-century condition of women in Europe (E20170404C). "Civil rights for women are extremely limited [in the Muslim religion]," a Lega representative argued (M20170404F). The examples used to support this belief are that Muslim women cannot wear the clothes they like (S20180103F) and cannot drive or walk alone without their husband in Saudi Arabia (G20180109C). The allusion to the belief that Muslim women supposedly cannot choose what to wear is an implicit criticism of Muslim women's veil.

The veil has become a symbol of Muslim oppression of women. For instance, the Lega instrumentally depicts itself as the champion of women's rights, by abrasively criticising Muslim women wearing the veil (Spruce 2007: 123), seen as the embodiment of the inferiority of Muslim principles, as it supposedly strips women of their dignity. In the interviews, a populist radical right intellectual, in order to underline the inferiority of Muslim customs and their fixation with headscarves, made the example of a girl who had her head shaved when she refused to wear the veil (G201170405C). However, an FdI representative claimed that women wearing a veil do not pose any problem, provided that the veil is not a burka (F20180407T), thus demonstrating awareness of the fact that there are different kinds of veils, although Islamophobic discourse often offers an undifferentiated conception of the veil as an instrument of exclusion of women (Navarro 2010: 101). This interpretation of the veil is grounded in the view of Islam as monolithically oppressive towards women, given its alleged imposition of the veil asphyxiating women (Hirschkind and Mahmood 2012). According to the populist radical right, the veil is the embodiment of Muslim men's subjugation of women to Islamic traditions, and, as a consequence, as a sign of misogyny and patriarchy. This is seen as clashing with Western values protecting gender equality. This clash is deployed strategically as an ethical justification for the populist radical right's demand for "the need to protect our women" (Dietze and Roth 2020; Havertz 2021). The use of feminist arguments supporting women's rights and gender equality, in support of racism and Islamophobia, is labelled "femonationalism" (Mudde 2019; Walia 2021). For instance, in France, a number of French feminists, advocating gender equality, believed that the veil symbolised the submission of women (Navarro 2010: 106) and supported the 1994 law that banned the veil from public schools (Hirschkind and Mahmood 2012: 351–352). This ruling was followed by a 2010 law that prohibited full-face covering in public places (Wolfreys 2018: 33).

The inferiorisation of Muslim immigrants, linked to gender and religion, also extends to popular culture. Indeed, a Lega representative used Bello Figo, an immigrant rap singer mocking Italians' racism against immigrants, to denigrate Muslims' lack of respect for women: "He earns money saying such things, where are the feminists?" (L20170104N). In fact, Bello Figo deploys in a sarcastic way several swear words that are offensive to women, with the ultimate goal of deriding the Italians' racist misconception of how immigrants view women. As Giuliani notes in her analysis of the contemporary reception of Bello Figo, Salvini, the Lega's leader, suggested the rap singer should go to work on cotton plantations (2018: 232), thus deploying a colonial discourse to blame the singer's alleged impertinence towards women. The emphasis on Muslim women's denied

92 *Echoes from Colonialism*

rights can be read as a subtly double inferiorisation. In fact, the populist radical right remarks on the inferiority of Muslim women who supposedly lack rights, but also on the inferiority of Muslim customs at large that deny such rights to women. In doing so, the populist radical right projects itself as a benevolent defender of Muslim women's rights, in line with the civic turn of the populist radical right probed in depth in the next section.

This double inferiorisation of Muslim women acted out under the guise of a benign protection of them can be interpreted, adopting Spivak's quote, as a case of "white men defending brown women from brown men" (1998: 92), thus exploiting issues revolving around femininity in order to construct the Other as inferior. This discursive strategy is embodied in "pseudo-emancipatory gender politics" promoting women's rights against Islam (Wodak 2015: 22) and results in what Ramirez defines as "neo-colonial sexism"[5] (2006), whereby Muslim women are constructed as Others in order to maintain and buttress Western superiority (Delphy 2008; Hirschkind and Mahmood 2012). Therefore, Islamophobia is curiously entangled with the protection of women's rights (Mayer, Ajanović, and Sauer 2020: 108), as Muslims are perceived as a threat to the women's emancipation achieved by the immigrants' host countries (Spierings 2020: 45). Particularly, the populist radical right condemns the alleged patriarchal and misogynist attitude of Muslim men, which leads to a stigmatisation of the Muslim Other, irreconcilable with the gender equality reportedly characterising Western societies (Sauer 2020: 27).

Ironically, it is in the context of Islamophobia that the populist radical right turns its attention to women's agency and addresses the question of gender equality (Mudde 2019: 304). This stands in stark contrast with the Lega's and FdI's traditional view of the woman encased in traditional gender roles. More specifically, Scrinzi reports that women in the Lega discourse are conceived as the mothers of the nation, divided between their work outside of the domestic sphere, and their social reproductive work (Scrinzi 2017: 874).

Second, the Lega, FdI, and populist radical right intellectuals, when interviewed, denigrate Muslim immigrants because they supposedly lack the principle of reciprocity between different religions characterising tolerant societies. An example of the lack of reciprocity is immigrants insisting on building mosques in Italy, while they do not let Christians build churches in the immigrants' countries of origin or they do not let Christians exhibit religious symbols in Italy, such as the crucifix in schools (see, for instance, F20170110F, G201704045C, L20170410P, P20161219B, P20170404L, S20180108S). While discussing the topic of mosques, an FdI representative added that, "The [Italian] state gives funds to all religions, but it is not fair that I am barred from opening a church in some [Muslim] country" (L2017001P).

Third, the Italian populist radical right underlines the poor human rights record of Muslim immigrants. Indeed, the human rights identified as faring poorly among Muslims are the respect for the notion of life itself (C20180109G), respect for secularism (G20170109D), respect for other human beings, forgiveness (G20170111R), liberty (M20170404F, L20170104N), solidarity (L20170104N), and respect for homosexuals (S20180103F). Interestingly, the attack on Muslim immigrants by virtue of their alleged lack of respect for homosexuals shines light onto the contradictory discourse articulated by the Italian populist radical right with regards to LGBTQ+ rights. The Lega and FdI display a reactionary position towards LGBTQ+ rights when it comes to Italians. While they depict themselves as defenders of LGBTQ+ rights supposedly trumped over by Muslim immigrants, they relentlessly fight against the homosexual family. An emblematic case is the Lega's and FdI's opposition to the 2020 Zan Law Proposal,[6] named after the PD member of Parliament Alessandro Zan. Zan proposed an amendment to the Mancino Law that condemns discriminations based on race, ethnicity, and religion, to include the protection of the LGBTQ+ community, women, and people with disabilities. The Lega and FdI (among other parties) rejected the proposal, while the Vatican suggested modifying the proposal, leading to the Zan law proposal not being approved (Il Post Redazione, 2021). This contradictory stance on LGBTQ+ rights resonates with the civic turn of the populist radical right, which is explored in depth in the following section.

6.3.2 The Civic Turn in the Inferiorisation of Immigration

The Italian populist radical right's protection of women's rights, reciprocity, and, broadly speaking, human rights against Islam is a *leitmotif* in the civic turn of the European populist radical right's discourse. The Swiss SVP, the Dutch LPF, the French FN, and the British BNP also depict themselves as defenders of tolerance against intolerant Muslim immigrants (Halikiopoulou, Mock, and Vasilopoulou 2013: 119–123). In the SVP, Muslims appear particularly dangerous, due to their supposed inability to integrate into civic Swiss society, since they allegedly infringe the Swiss civic values of religious freedom and freedom of thought (Halikiopoulou, Mock, and Vasilopoulou 2013: 116–118). Similarly, the Dutch LPF frames Muslim immigrants as a problem triggering a clash between Dutch freedoms, identity, and values, and Muslim intolerance (Halikiopoulou, Mock, and Vasilopoulou 2013: 119). Less successfully, the BNP portrays Muslim immigrants as a danger to civil liberties and secular modern democracy (Halikiopoulou, Mock, and Vasilopoulou 2013: 121). Similarly, the FN champions French national identity and secularism inherited from the French Revolution: civic values that are ostensibly menaced by problematic Muslim immigrants (Halikiopoulou, Mock, and Vasilopoulou 2013: 122).

Indeed, by letting the civic value of respect for women's rights trickle down into an otherwise racist discourse, the populist radical right aims to gain respectability and legitimacy (Halikiopoulou, Mock, and Vasilopoulou 2013: 108). This "civic turn" can be interpreted again as an attempt at mainstreaming (Akkerman et al. 2016: 15). Interestingly, in the interviews, the same Italian populist radical right parties, when tackling gender questions within the in-group, abandon civic values. In fact, the latter are replaced by reactionary attitudes championing the so-called "traditional family," i.e., the heterosexual one grounded on traditional gender roles, which is a typical feature of the populist radical right (Wodak 2015:

152). The "traditional family" emphasises masculinity and commodifies women as the Other, relegated to the role of carers and reproducers (Campbell 2014: 4).

The inferiorisation of Muslims, infused by both racism and civic values, goes beyond political parties and reverberates in Fallaci's books, scathingly criticising Muslims' seemingly obscurantist attitudes towards women and emphasising the under-development of Islam, allegedly alien to democracy and secularism (Burdett 2005: 29–30). Therefore, in Fallaci's books, widely appreciated by a broad spectrum of political parties, spearheaded by the populist radical right, Islam is depicted as an inferior antithesis to the lifestyle, freedom, and mentality of the West (Burdett 2005: 39). While Fallaci projected the West as the defender of freedoms, the Italian populist radical right portrays itself as the guarantor of reciprocity and human rights, typically civic values. The image the Italian populist radical right projects, hence, is indicative of its "civic turn" intended to increase credibility and legitimacy (Halikiopoulou, Mock, and Vasilopoulou 2013).

CDA provides a fruitful prism through which to analyse the inferiorisation of immigrants. First of all, once again negative terms, such as "lazy," "slave," and "lack of respect," are used by the populist radical right to denote the Other. These terms also highlight the topos of threat (Wodak 2015: 53) to induce fear of the supposedly lazy, misogynistic, intolerant, and disrespectful Other. Moreover, another discursive strategy at work in the discourse of the Italian populist radical right is the fallacy of sameness and of difference (Wodak 2015: 54), whereby the Italian populist radical right frames immigrants, especially Muslim ones, as a homogeneous group, intrinsically different from and inferior to the in-group, thus being oblivious to the vast array of ethnic and religious diversity present among Muslims. Finally, the strategy of denial (Wodak 2015: 56), through which populist radical right parties strategically frame themselves as distant from racism, while slipping into racist statements, is evident in the Italian populist radical right's claim that all people are equal, but immigrants are lazier. By denying their own racist prejudices, these parties project their criticism of the minority group as objective, or factual, thus legitimising themselves.

6.4 Abjectification of Immigration

The category of Othering also includes abjectification, whereby the Italian populist radical right represents immigrants as naturally abject Others (etymologically, "cast off" from the Self due to dirt and contagion) as opposed to the ostensibly human, clean, and healthy Italian Self. Several scholars of colonialism (see, for instance, Galeotti 2000; Giuliani 2018) and race (see, for instance, Gandesha 2003; Giuliani 2018; Kristeva 1982) have documented the connection between abjection and the Other. Thoroughly explored by Kristeva (1982), the abject is a stranger, alien from the body of the Self, but at the same time impossible to completely cast off. The abject is now personified by the immigrant Other, associated, as Gandesha (2003) convincingly shows, to bodily fluids and dirt in the writings of Fallaci (2001: 128–129).

The abject Other, however, is not just located within the external Other, i.e., the immigrant, but is signified to a lesser degree by the internal Other, i.e., the southerner in the case of Italy. The latter, despite being whitened in the national and racial imaginary under fascism, in the 1970s and 1980s, and finally with the reconfiguration of Italy from being an emigration country to an immigration country, still cannot emancipate itself from its own abjection forced upon it by the peculiar Italian articulation of national and racial identity (Giuliani 2018). As discussed in Chapter 4, anti-southernism has not disappeared yet from the ideology of the Italian populist radical right. The category of abjectification, be it targeted at an internal or an external Other, recalls the abjectification of the colonised Other driven by the colonisers' fear of being contaminated. For instance, Mussolini banned inter-racial marriages due to the fear of pollution of the Italian race and contagion of leprosy and cholera (Galeotti 2000: 96–98), condemned madamism in the 1936 *Legge Organica per l'Impero*,[7] and denied citizenship to mixed race offspring in a 1940 law (Giuliani 2018: 78).

The Lega often links immigrants to their supposed disturbing uncleanliness (Rivera 2009: 14). Abjectification is uncovered by the interviews not only with the Lega, but also with FdI. The Lega and FdI claim that immigrants bring illnesses, such as scabies and tuberculosis (see, for instance, C20180109G, C20170106V, E20170404C, F20160905L). In the words of an FdI representative, "It is undeniable that in Italy there is an established vaccination and hygiene system. Even the World Health Organisation, which is a neutral institution and not a xenophobic party, reckons that Africa is less healthy than Italy" (E20170404C). The solution seems to be to enforce strict health controls on a manageable number of immigrants (C20180109G, F20170408T), including compulsory vaccinations upon arrival (E20170404C). The culprit, again, in a typically anti-elite populist way, is the state that neglects health controls on the newly arrived immigrants (F20160905L, L20170410P). Moreover, immigrants are depicted as alien to hygienic measures (F20170104M, P20161219B), in contrast with Italians who, in the words of an FdI representative, are "a civil and clean people living in clean environments" (N20180108C). A few Lega representatives believed that the alleged lack of hygiene is so serious that immigrants should not work in school canteen kitchens (M20170104G, P20161219B). The phenomenon of immigration was itself abjectified by one FdI representative who characterised it as "an epidemic problem" (F20180104F).

Nonetheless, not all the Italian populist radical right connects immigration to illnesses. Indeed, a few Lega and FdI representatives argued that there is no straightforward connection between immigration and illness (C20180109G, G20170109D, L20170104N, M20170404F). Regarding the 2017 outbreak of meningitis in Italy, the Italian populist radical right predominantly rejects a correlation between this illness and immigration (C20170106V, F20170104M, G20170112G, P20170404L).

The Italian populist radical right deploys a negative vocabulary to indicate the range of illnesses uncommon in Italy, and lack of hygiene, brought by immigrants. In doing so, the populist radical right panders to the fear of dirt and illnesses carried by immigrants, and unleashes panic over immigration, through the topos of threat (Wodak 2015: 53). Moreover, the fallacy of sameness and the fallacy of difference (Wodak 2015: 54) operate in the discourse of the Italian populist radical right, which lumps immigrants as a coherent whole, sharing the germs of contamination with disease and dirt. Finally, legitimation through authorisation (Wodak 2015: 58) serves the purpose of validating the link between immigration and illnesses, by resorting to data received from medical doctors (F20170111S, G20170111R, L20170104N, M20170113R).

The abjectification of immigration is particularly worth studying during pandemic times. The Italian populist radical right showed a contradictory approach to the question of the relationship between immigration and the COVID-19 pandemic. Immediately upon the breakout of the COVID-19 pandemic in Italy in February 2020, the Lega and FdI momentarily showed national unity and set aside the issue of immigration, which deeply polarises politics and society. However, after a short rally-round the flag period, they soon started to blame immigrants and Chinese residents in Italy for spreading the virus to the Italian peninsula (Albertazzi, Bonansinga, and Zulianello 2021). More generally, during pandemic times, immigrants are still seen as carriers of contagion:

> Migrant arrivals are still going on, but we cannot exit our towns. We cannot go and visit our partner living in a nearby town, because the police could catch me red-handed. However, an immigrant can still move to Italy, maybe even carrying illnesses. This is something that enormously irritates and infuriates me!

exclaimed an FdI representative, also highlighting the contrast between seemingly free to roam immigrants, and Italians locked in their homes (R20210426S).

6.5 Conclusion

In October 2018, Pierre Moscovici, the European Commissioner for Economic and Financial Affairs, warned that the Italian government led by the Lega and the M5S was Eurosceptic and racist (Gagliardi 2018). Salvini replied to this accusation by bitterly accusing Moscovici of "talking nonsense" as there is "no risk of racism in Italy, just a government finally chosen by the citizens" (Gagliardi 2018). One month earlier, the UN High Commissioner for Human Rights Michelle Bachelet declared that she would send UN staff to Italy in order to investigate the increase in racist episodes. Salvini retorted that he was considering cutting Italy's economic contributions to the UN, which, according to the Lega's leader, is corrupt. He ended his rebuttal by claiming that "if they [the UNHCR staff] want just to stay in a nice hotel in Rome, then we will welcome them," thus deriding Bachelet's intentions (Di Caro 2018). To establish whether or not the rise in racism in Italy in the second half of 2018 – conceptually defined in this book as part of nativism – was driven by the Lega-M5S government elected in March

2018 is beyond the scope of this project and will be the focus of future scholarly enquiry.

However, for the purposes of this book, it is essential to highlight that Moscovici's and Bachelet's words of caution testify to the fact that racism is alive and well in Italy and has been thriving in 2018 both at government and grassroots level. Therefore, Italy's self-redeeming narrative of immunity to racism (Burgio 2000) is clearly challenged by the pervasive existence of racism on the populist radical right. This assertion is corroborated by data: during the Lega-M5S government, and in particular in the period between June 2018 and August 2018, there were 33 episodes of racist violence across Italy, including physical aggression, aggression with weapons, and murders (De Luca 2018). Not only immigrants, but also black Italians have been targeted, such as the athlete Daisy Osakue, who was egged by youths in Turin (Il Post 2018). At the time of writing, according to the most recent study conducted by UNAR, 709 cases of aggressions for racial reasons were reported in 2021 (Alliva 2022). Emblematic is the heinous crime that happened, in July 2022, to 39-year-old Nigerian Alika Ogorchukwu, who was murdered on the street in Civitanova Marche, by a white Italian, while the witnesses were grotesquely filming the scene (Repubblica 2022).

This chapter, as the preceding one, interpreted racism drawing on Hall's (1997) definition of this concept as dynamic and contextual, and on Balibar's (1991) belief in the inextricability of racism and nationalism, which conceptually form nativism. Hence, racism in Italy is to be understood in conjunction with the predominant ethno-cultural nationalism, from which it flows, and against the historical background of the Italian fascist conception of racial and national identity. Even if racism against the colonised Other already existed under liberal Italy, it was under fascist colonialism that it became a constitutive element for the articulation of Italian national and racial identity: the blackness of the colonised Other was necessary for the construction of Italian whiteness and for the emancipation of the latter from the inferiority complex affecting it, whereby Italians were backward due to the interbreeding of the Latin/Roman race with black races (Giuliani 2018: 26). The Italian Mediterranean racial and national identity that became pivotal to fascism distinguished itself from the African Mediterranean national and racial identity of the colonised. At the same time, Italian Mediterraneanness turned the alleged interbreeding of Roman and African races into an advantage that valorised the Italian identity as a unique and superior melting pot (Giuliani 2018: 26). In the second half of the1930s, the prizing of Mediterraneanness and interbreeding was replaced by the accent on Aryanness (Giuliani 2018: 28).

Therefore, as revealed by the interviews and manifestos analysed in Chapters 5 and 6, the related categories of criminalisation, inferiorisation, and abjectification of immigration flow seamlessly from the umbrella category of Othering (explored in Chapter 5). The result is that the Mediterranean in the Italian populist radical right's discourse is a far cry from the fascist *Mare Nostrum*. It is no more a *Mare Nostrum*, i.e., a space to exhibit Italian prestige. Quite to the contrary, the Italian populist radical right feels that immigration is now plunging

Italy into a steep political, economic, and social decline, and fears the high fertility of immigrants, which further exacerbates their representation as criminal and threatening Others. Furthermore, the Italian populist radical right perceives immigration as bringing a whole host of different kinds of crime, including a holy war; inferior cultural practices outraging human rights, and women's rights in particular; and illnesses and lack of hygiene. Therefore, since the rise of a conspicuous immigrant population in Italy in the early 1990s, the Lega, FdI, and populist radical right intellectuals have viewed the Mediterranean as what I call a "Mare Vostrum," i.e., a source of immigrant Others, inherently criminal, inferior, and abject.

In conclusion, the fascist colonial construction of national and racial identity vis-à-vis the colonised Other becomes a useful lens through which to analyse today's Italian populist radical right's nativism. Indeed, the immigrant has now taken the place of the colonised as the Other against which the Italian populist radical right defines a predominantly ethno-cultural Italian national identity, strictly connected with racism.

Although the analysis of Italian racism between 1945 and 1990 falls outside the scope of this project, it is necessary to remember that the racism characterising fascist colonialism did not disappear with the end of fascism and colonialism before abruptly resurfacing in the 1990s with the rise of the Italian populist radical right. In fact, the neo-fascist MSI that emerged from the ashes of fascism firmly retained a fascist legacy, while operating within democracy (Furlong 1992: 345). Officially, biological racism was eschewed by 60% of the MSI (Ignazi 1996: 707), but this neo-fascist party believed in the need to separate different cultures to preserve Italian national identity (Griffin 1996: 132). This belief mirrored the Nouvelle Droite's concern about the mixing of cultures and its cultural view of racism strategically moving away from the biological one. In fact, by emphasising culture rather than race, the Nouvelle Droite and the MSI were projecting a more respectable image of themselves. Although immigration was not prominent in Italy before the 1990s, the MSI was undoubtedly racist, since it argued that immigrants were bringing social problems to Italy (Furlong 1992: 351) and threatened national identity (Ignazi 1996: 707). As a consequence, the MSI advocated the expulsion of immigrants (Ignazi 1996: 707) and indulged in their violent aggression in bars and hostels (Furlong 1992: 351). After the demise of the MSI in 1994, the prominence of racism shaped during fascist colonialism and preserved by the MSI was maintained with the rise of the Italian populist radical right parties AN, the Lega, and, later, FdI.

Even if the racism making up nativism, in conjunction with nationalism, is tangible in Italy, such racism is masked in the Italian populist radical right's discourse under a civic mantle. Indeed, in order to appear more legitimate, credible, and palatable to a wider range of potential electors, the Italian populist radical right blends purely racist remarks with civic overtones, whereby it portrays itself as a protector of migrants' human rights, refugees, security, tolerance, women's rights, and human rights more broadly (Griffini 2021). This civic turn of the Italian populist radical right, also observed in other European countries, contributes to making the populist radical right appear more mainstream, thus maximising its chance to be elected into office. The process of mainstreaming of the populist radical right has been witnessed in other European countries (Akkerman et al. 2016: 15) and appears even more relevant in Italy after the election, in March 2018, of the Lega as a party in the government coalition with the M5S, headed by Salvini and Luigi Di Maio as Deputy Prime Ministers. Whether the Lega, according to the debated inclusion-moderation theory (Akkerman et al. 2016), whereby parties in government moderate their racism, has further mainstreamed itself while in government or not, is open to future research.

Currently, it is clear that the Lega has not abandoned racism and has even further radicalised itself, thus proving Akkerman and Rooduijn's (2015) argument that the inclusion of populist radical right parties into government coalitions does not necessarily lead to their moderation. Indeed, it seems that the Lega has deployed a civic coat to cover racism in order to appear mainstream and enter into government. Its civic turn was, therefore, purely strategic, in order to increase the size of its potential electorate. Once the Lega achieved its desired position at the helm of Italian politics, it shifted to outright radicalisation. Such radicalisation becomes evident when analysing Salvini's claim in September 2018 that the alleged invasion of immigrants has triggered the comeback of tuberculosis (Corriere 2018). Furthermore, radicalisation is clear when considering that in the summer of 2018 Salvini banned the ships *Aquarius* and *Diciotti* carrying hundreds of immigrants from docking in Italian ports (Hardt and Mezzadra 2018). A further instance of radicalisation is Salvini's order to remove immigrants from Riace after the arrest, on the grounds of favouring illegal immigration, of the town's mayor in October 2018. Riace was well-known for its successful model of integration of immigrants which also aimed at replenishing the demography of a small southern town badly hit by emigration (Giuffrida 2018). These three examples testify to the discourse and policies erring on the racist side that were deployed by Salvini since gaining power in March 2018. The Lega, when it was in a government coalition with a non-mainstream party, the M5S, missed the incentives to deradicalise that might have been provided by mainstream parties. Instead, it walked on a tightrope between achieving further radicalisation, thus alienating the moderate electorate, and retaining significant electoral consensus.

Crucially, racism has also been fostered by mainstream right and left parties, as well as the media and the educational system, which all contribute to its normalisation in political and popular discourse in Italy. Through normalisation, racism appears common-sense and logical (Mondon 2013). In fact, as Chapter 1 showed, mainstream right and mainstream left parties, such as FI and the PD, have inserted anti-immigrant statements into their discourse. Popular culture has further normalised racism. Indeed, immigrants in Italy are framed as dangerous invaders and hypervisibilised when they are the real or presumed perpetrators of crime, while they are invisibilised when they are the victims of crime (Giuliani 2018). Whereas the invisibilisation of immigrants is an implicitly racist practice aimed at stripping them of their agency, the hypervisibilisation of immigrants that is rampant in political talk shows, such as *Dalla Vostra Parte*, is more explicit in the show's panicked reporting of the alleged refugees' invasion, of rapes committed by immigrants, and of evictions targeting Italians in favour of immigrants (Giuliani 2018: 222).

Racism is also patent in the popular reception of immigrant singers in Italy, such as Bello Figo and Cecile. The latter, who denounces Western inferiorisation and eroticisation of the female black body, has been pejoratively referred to as "Cameroonian," despite having been born in the Italian town of Ostia (Giuliani 2018: 225). Similarly, Bello Figo, who mocks the Italians' stereotyping of immigrants, has been under fire in TV shows. Even Salvini commented that Bello Figo should be sent to work on banana and cotton plantations (Giuliani 2018: 232). The discussion of racism at popular level requires reflection on its relationship with the populist radical right parties' racism. While there is no scope in this project to deal extensively with this matter, it is useful to note that racism does exist at popular level, also thanks to its normalisation through the radicalisation of the mainstream. In turn, the populist radical right taps into popular racism, by portraying itself as the expression of the voice of the people, making the issue of immigration more salient and exploiting such salience for electoral gains. Although not all media and the whole educational system are racist, the media's indulgence of populism and the simplistic portrayal of race in the Italian educational system shape public opinion and young minds, thus fanning the fires of racism, which becomes combined with nationalism in the explosive cocktail of nativism.

Notes

1 For the full text of the 2002 Bossi-Fini Law, consult the following webpage: https://web.camera.it/parlam/leggi/02189l.htm.
2 For the full text of the 2009 Security Package, consult the following webpage: www.meltingpot.org/app/uploads/2009/02/00393348.pdf.
3 For the full text of the 2019 Law of Legitimate Defence: www.gazzettaufficiale.it/eli/id/2019/05/03/19G00042/sg.
4 The original Italian word *battono* definitely sounds more vulgar than *prostitute*.
5 This book believes that the term *postcolonial* is more appropriate here, as it illuminates the legacy and continuation of colonialism, without attributing neo-colonial aspirations to the populist radical right.
6 For the full text of the 2020 Zan law proposal, consult the following webpage: www.camera.it/leg18/126?tab=&leg=18&idDocumento=0569.
7 Literally, "Imperial law."

References

Akkerman, T., de Lange, S.L. & Rooduijn, M. (2016) *Radical Right-wing Populist Parties in Western Europe: Into the Mainstream?*, London: Routledge.

Akkerman, T. & Rooduijn, M. (2015) "Pariahs or partners? Inclusion and exclusion of radical right parties and the effects on their policy positions", *Political Studies Review*, vol. 63, no. 5, pp. 1140–1157.

Albertazzi, D., Bonansinga, D. & Zulianello, M. (2021) "The rightwing alliance at the time of the Covid-19 pandemic: All change?", *Contemporary Italian Politics*, https://doi.org /10.1080/ 23248823.2021.1916857

Allam, M. (2005) *Vincere la paura*, Milan: Mondadori.

Alliva, S. (2022) "L'epidemia dell'odio: nell'ultimo anno 1.379 aggressioni razziste, omotransfobiche, antisemite e abiliste", *L'Espresso*. 16 February 2022. Available: https://espresso.repubblica.it/attualita/2022/02/16/news/aggressioni_razziste_ omotransfobiche_antisemite_abiliste-337961138/ [17 August 2022].

Avanza, M. (2010) "The Northern League and its 'innocuous' xenophobia", in *Italy Today: The Sick Man of Europe*, Mammone, A. & Veltri, G.A. (eds), London: Routledge, pp. 131–142.

Balibar, E. (1991) "Racism and nationalism", in *Race, Nation, Class: Ambiguous Identities*, Balibar, E. & Wallerstein, I.M. (eds), London: Verso, pp. 37–68.

Ben-Ghiat, R. (2006) "Modernity is just over there: Colonialism and Italian national identity", *Interventions; International Journal of Postcolonial Studies*, vol. 8, no. 3, pp. 380–393.

Bergmann, E. (2018) *Conspiracy and Populism: The Politics of Misinformation*, New York: Springer International Publishing AG.

Berti, C. (2021) "Right-wing populism and the criminalization of sea-rescue NGOs: The 'Sea-Watch 3' case in Italy, and Matteo Salvini's communication on Facebook", *Media, Culture & Society*, vol. 43, no. 3, pp. 532–550.

Bordignon, F. & Ceccarini, L. (2013) "Five Stars and a cricket. Beppe Grillo shakes Italian politics", *South European Society and Politics*, vol. 18, no. 4, pp. 427–449.

Burdett, C. (2005) "Colonial associations and the memory of Italian East Africa", in *Italian Colonialism: Legacy and Memory*, Andall, J. & Duncan, D. (eds), Oxford, Bern: Peter Lang, pp. 125–142.

Burgio, A. (2000) *Nel nome della razza. Il razzismo nella storia d'Italia, 1870–1945*, Bologna: Il Mulino.

Campbell, B. (2014) "After neoliberalism: The need for a gender revolution", *Soundings*, vol. 56, no.1, pp. 10–26.

Carr, M. (2006) "You are now entering Eurabia", *Race and Class*, vol. 48, no. 1, pp. 1–22.

Carvalho, J. (2014) *Impact of Extreme Right Parties on Immigration Policy: Comparing Britain, France and Italy*, London: Routledge.

Cassata, F. (2008) *La Difesa della razza: Politica, ideologia e immagine del razzismo fascista*, G. Turin: Einaudi.

Cavazza, N. & Guidetti, M. (2014) "Swearing in political discourse: Why vulgarity works", *Journal of Language and Social Psychology*, vol. 33, no. 5, pp. 537–547.

Chilton, P.A. (2004) *Analysing Political Discourse Theory and Practice*, London; New York: Routledge.

Conelli, C. (2014) "Razza, colonialità, nazione", in *Quel che resta dell'impero: La cultura coloniale degli italiani*, Deplano, V. & Pes, A. (eds), Milan: Mimesis, pp. 149–168.

Conti, P. (2007) "Oriana, voce della passione antitotalitaria", *Corriere della Sera*. 13 September 2007. Available: https://www.corriere.it/Speciali/Spettacoli/2007/Fallaci /articoli/uno.htht [15 November 2019].

Corriere Redazione (2018) "Salvini: 'Troppi migranti, è tornata a diffondersi la tubercolosi'", *Corriere della Sera*. 12 September 2018. Available: https://www.corriere .it/politica/18_settembre_12/salvini-troppi-migranti-tornata-diffondersi-tubercolosi -8ccc0606-b69a-11e8-83fc-d7dcaceaa02b.shtml [21 May 2019].

102 Echoes from Colonialism

Cousin, B. & Vitale, T. (2014) "Le magistère intellectuel islamophobe d'Oriana Fallaci. Origines et modalités du succès italien de la 'Trilogie sur l'Islam et sur l'Occident' (2001–2006)", *Sociologie*, vol. 5, no. 1, pp. 61–79.

Dal Lago, A. (2006) *Non-persone: L'esclusione dei migranti in una società globale*, Milan: Feltrinelli.

De Luca, D.M. (2018) "L'Italia è diventata una paese razzista?", *Il Post*. 2 August 2018. Available: https://www.ilpost.it/2018/08/02/italia-paese-razzista/ [21 November 2018].

Delphy, C. (2008) *Classer, dominer: Qui sont les autres?*, Paris: La Fabrique.

Di Caro, P. (2018) "Inviati ONU, duello con l'Italia", *Corriere della Sera*. 10 September 2018. Available: https://www.corriere.it/esteri/18_settembre_11/inviati-onu-duello-l-italia-2ec51778-b53c-11e8-9795-182d8d9833a0.shtml [21 November 2018].

Dietze, G. & Roth, J. (eds) (2020) *Right-Wing Populism and Gender. European Perspectives and Beyond*. Bielefeld: Transcript Verlag.

Dixon, T., Hawkins, S., Heijbroek, L., Juan-Torres, M. & Demoures, F. (2018) "Attitudes towards national identity, immigration and refugees in Italy", *More in Common Papers*.

Eatwell, R. & Goodwin, M. (2018) *National Populism: The Revolt Against Liberal Democracy*, London: Penguin.

Eduati, L. (2016) "'Il fuoco dentro' di Riccardo Nencini, scritti inediti di Oriana Fallaci: 'Firenze matrigna con i suoi figli migliori'", *Huffington Post*. 21 March 2016. Available: https://www.huffingtonpost.it/2016/03/21/riccardo-nencini-oriana-fallaci_n_9515600.html [November 2019].

F.Q. Redazione (2017) "Legittima difesa, ok della Camera: Licenza di sparare di notte. Ecco cosa prevede la legge. Show di Salvini ('espulso')", *Il Fatto Quotidiano*. 4 May 2017. Available: https://www.ilfattoquotidiano.it/2017/05/04/legittima-difesa-ok-della-camera-licenza-di-sparare-di-notte-ecco-cosa-prevede-la-legge-show-di-salvini-espulso/3562215/ [21 May 2018].

Fallaci, O. (2001) *The Rage and the Pride*, New York: Rizzoli.

Fallaci, O. (2004) *La forza della ragione*, New York: Rizzoli.

Fanon, F. (1963) *The Wretched of the Earth*, Paris: Presence Africaine.

Fekete, L. (2004) "Anti-Muslim racism and the European security state", *Race and Class*, vol. 46, no. 3, pp. 3–29.

Furlong, P. (1992) "The extreme right in Italy: Old orders and dangerous novelties", *Parliamentary Affairs*, vol. 45, no. 3, pp. 345–356.

Gagliardi, G. (2018) "Chi è Luca Traini, l'ex candidato della Lega che ha sparato a Macerata", *Repubblica*. 3 February 2018. Available: https://www.repubblica.it/cronaca/2018/02/03/news/macerata_luca_traini-187950304/ [05 December 2019].

Galeotti, C. (2000) *Mussolini ha sempre ragione: I decaloghi del fascismo*, Milan: Garzanti.

Gandesha, S. (2003) "The political semiosis of populism", *The Semiotic Review of Books*, vol. 13, no. 3, pp. 1–12.

Gazzetta Ufficiale (2019) *LEGGE 26 aprile 2019, n. 36. Modifiche al codice penale e altre disposizioni in materia di legittima difesa*. Available: https://www.gazzettaufficiale.it/eli/id/2019/05/03/19G00042/sg [30 September 2022].

Giuffrida, A. (2018) "Matteo Salvini orders removal of refugees from Riace", *The Guardian*. 14 October 2018. Available: https://www.theguardian.com/world/2018/oct/14/matteo-salvini-orders-removal-of-refugees-from-riace [21 November 2018].

Giuliani, G. (2018) *Race, Nation and Gender in Modern Italy: Intersectional Representations in Visual Culture*, London: Palgrave Macmillan.

Giuliani, G., José Santos, S. & Garraio, J. (2020) "Online social media and the construction of sexual moral panic around migrants in Europe", *Socioscapes. International Journal of Societies, Politics, and Culture*, vol. 1, no. 1, pp. 161–180.

Griffin, R. (1996) "The 'post-Fascism' of the Alleanza Nazionale: A case study in ideological morphology", *Journal of Political Ideologies*, vol. 1, no. 2, pp. 123–145.

Griffini, M. (2021) "The civic discourse: Representing immigrants in the Italian far right", in *Approaches to Migration, Language, and Identity*, Auer, A. & Thornburn, J. (eds), Oxford, Bern: Peter Lang.

Guibernau, M. (2010) "Migration and the rise of the radical right", *Policy Network*, vol. 1.

Halikiopoulou, D., Mock, S. & Vasilopoulou, S. (2013) "The civic zeitgeist: Nationalism and liberal values in the European radical right", *Nations and Nationalism*, vol. 19, no. 1, pp. 107–127.

Hall, S. (1997) "Race, the floating signifier featuring Stuart Hall transcript", The Media Education Foundation. Available: https://www.mediaed.org/transcripts/Stuart-Hall-Race-the-Floating-Signifier-Transcript.pdf.

Hardt, M. & Mezzadra, S. (2018) "We've launched a migrant rescue ship to resist the racist right in Italy", *The Guardian*. 9 October 2018. Available: https://www.theguardian.com/commentisfree/2018/oct/09/migrant-rescue-ship-racist-politics-italy-us [21 November 2018].

Havertz, R. (2021) *Radical Right Populism in Germany. AfD, Pegida, and the Identitarian Movement*, New York: Routledge Studies. Palgrave Macmillan.

Hirschkind, C. & Mahmood, S. (2012) "Feminism, the Taliban, and politics of counter-insurgency", *Anthropological Quarterly*, vol. 75, no. 2, pp. 339–354.

Horowitz, J. (2003) "Europe: Italy: Immigrant boat sinks", *The New York Times*. 18 June 2003. Available: http://www.nytimes.com/2003/06/18/world/world-briefing-europe-italy-immigrant-boat-sinks.html [21 May 2018].

Huntington, S.P. (1996) *The Clash of Civilizations and the Remaking of World Order*, New York: Simon & Schuster.

Huntington, S.P. et al. (1996) *The Clash of Civilizations?: The Debate*, New York: Council on Foreign Relations.

Ignazi, P. (1996) "From neo-fascists to post-fascists? The transformation of the MSI into the AN", *West European Politics*, vol. 19, no. 4, pp. 693–714.

Il Post Redazione (2021) "Com'è finito il DDL Zan", *Il Post*. 28 October 2021. Available: https://www.ilpost.it/2021/10/28/ddl-zan-fine-bocciato-senato/ [28 October 2021].

Iraci Fedeli, L. (1990) *Razzismo e immigrazione, il caso Italia*, Rome: Acropoli.

Kristeva, J. (1982) *Powers of Horror. An Essay on Abjection*, New York: Columbia University Press.

Kundnani, A. (2014) *The Muslims Are Coming!: Islamophobia, Extremism, and the Domestic War on Terror*, New York: Verso.

La Padania Redazione (2001) "La moschea non è solo un luogo di culto", *La Padania*. 16 March 2001.

Lega manifesto (1992).

Lega manifesto (1994).

Maneri, M. (2009) "I media nel razzismo consensuale", in *Rapporto sul razzismo in Italia*, Naletto, G. & Andrisani, P. (eds), Manifestolibri, Rome: Lunaria, pp. 47–51.

Matard-Bonucci, M. (2008) "D'une persécution l'autre: Racisme colonial et antisémitisme dans l'Italie fasciste", *Revue d'histoire moderne et contemporaine (1954-)*, vol. 55, no. 3, pp. 116–137.

Mayer, S.; Ajanović, E. & Sauer, B. (2020) "Man, Woman, Family. Gender and the Limited Modernization of Right-Wing Extremism in Austria", in *Right-Wing Populism and Gender. European Perspectives and Beyond*, Dietze, G. & Roth, J. (eds), Bielefeld: Transcript Verlag, pp. 101–117.

Mondon, A. (2013) "Nicolas Sarkozy's legitimization of the Front National: Background and perspectives", *Patterns of Prejudice*, vol. 47, no. 1, pp. 22–40.

Mudde, C. (2019) *The Far Right Today*, Cambridge, UK: Polity Press.

Navarro, L. (2010). "Islamophobia and sexism: Muslim women in the Western mass media". *Human Architecture: Journal of the Sociology of Self-Knowledge*, vol. 8, no. 2.

Orsini, F. (2006) "Cannons and rubber boats: Oriana Fallaci and the 'Clash of Civilizations'", *Interventions; International Journal of Postcolonial Studies*, vol. 8, no. 3, pp. 444–460.

Pinkus, K. (1997) "Shades of black in advertising and popular culture", in *Revisioning Italy: National Identity and Global Culture*, Allen, B. & Russo, M.J. (eds), Minneapolis: University of Minnesota Press, pp. 134–155.

Ramirez, A. (2006) "Sexismo Neocolonial", *El Pais*. 7 October 2006. Available: https://elpais.com/diario/2006/10/08/opinion/1160258412_850215.html [26 February 2023].

Repubblica Redazione (2022) "Civitanova Marche, la polizia: 'Alika finito a mani nude'. E i nigeriani bloccano il corso per protesta", *Repubblica*. 30 July 2022. Available: https://www.repubblica.it/cronaca/2022/07/30/news/omicidio_civitanova_marche_finito_mani_nude_protesta_nigeriani-359769374/ [17 August 2022].

Rivera, A. (2009) "Il circolo vizioso del razzismo", in *Rapporto sul razzismo in Italia*, Naletto, G. & Andrisani, P. (eds), Manifestolibri, Rome: Lunaria, pp. 11–19.

Rivera, A. (2011) "Due anni di scena razzista in Italia. Protagonisti e comprimari, vittime e ribelli", in *Cronache di ordinario razzismo*, Lunaria (eds), Rome: Edizioni dell'asino, pp. 6–30.

Rivera, A. (2017) "Dalle politiche migranticide dell'Unione Europea alle comunità del rancore", in *Cronache di ordinario razzismo*, Lunaria (eds), Rome: Lunaria, pp. 10–22.

Rivera, A. (2020) "Un decennio d'infamie razziste, fino all'estremo", in *Cronache di ordinario razzismo*, Lunaria (eds), Rome: Lunaria, pp. 9–18.

Rosina, M. (2022) *The Criminalisation of Irregular Migration in Europe. Globalisation, Deterrence, and Vicious Cycles*, London: Palgrave.

Said, E. (1978) *Orientalism*, London: Penguin.

Sauer, B. (2020) "Authoritarian right-wing populism as masculinist identity politics. The role of affects", in *Right-Wing Populism and Gender. European Perspectives and Beyond*, Dietze, G. & Roth, J. (eds), Bielefeld: Transcript Verlag, pp. 23–41.

Sciolino, E. (1996) "Seeing green; The red menace is gone. But here's Islam", *The New York Times*. 21 January 1996. Available: https://www.nytimes.com/1996/01/21/weekinreview/seeing-green-the-red-menace-is-gone-but-here-s-islam.html [21 May 2018].

Scrinzi, F. (2017) "Caring for the elderly in the family or in the nation? Gender, women and migrant care labour in the Lega Nord", *West European Politics*, vol. 40, no. 4, pp. 869–886.

Sharma, A. (2003) "White paranoia: Orientalism in the age of empire", *Fashion Theory: The Journal of Dress*, vol. 7, no. 3–4, pp. 301–317.

Spierings, N. (2020) "Why gender and sexuality are both trivial and pivotal in populist radical right politics", in *Right-Wing Populism and Gender. European Perspectives and Beyond*, Dietze, G. & Roth, J. (eds), Bielefeld: Transcript Verlag, pp. 41–58.

Spivak, G.C. (1988) "Can the subaltern speak?", in *Colonial Discourse and Post-colonial Theory*, Williams, P. & Chrisman, L. (eds), New York: Columbia University Press, pp. 21–78.

Spruce, D. (2007) "Empire and counter-empire in the Italian far right: Conflicting nationalisms and the split between the Lega Nord and Alleanza Nazionale on immigration", *Theory Culture & Society*, vol. 24, no. 5, pp. 99–126.

Talbot, M. (2006) "The agitator", *The New Yorker*. 5 June 2006. Available: https://www.newyorker.com/magazine/2006/06/05/the-agitator [15 November 2019].

Todorov, T. (1984) *The Conquest of America*, New York: Harper and Row.

Van Dijk, T.A. (2008) "Critical Discourse Analysis", in *The Handbook of discourse analysis*, D. Schiffrin, D. Tannen & H.E. Hamilton (eds), John Wiley & Sons, pp. 352–371.

Walia, H. (2021) *Border and Rule. Global Migration Capitalism, and the Rise of Racist Nationalism*, Chicago: Haymarket Books.

Wodak, R. (2015) *The Politics of Fear: What Right-wing Populist Discourses Mean*, London: Sage.

Wolfreys, J. (2018) *Republic of Islamophobia: The Rise of Respectable Racism in France*, Oxford: Oxford University Press.

Ye'or, B. (2005) "Eurabia - Europe's Future?", Middle East Forum. Available: https://www.meforum.org/696/eurabia-europes-future.

Zaslove, A. (2004) "Closing the door? The ideology and impact of radical right populism on immigration policy in Austria and Italy", *Journal of Political Ideologies*, vol. 9, no. 1, pp. 99–118.

7 Memory and Forgetting

The Colonial Past in the Italian Populist Radical Right

7.1 Introduction

Chapters 5 and 6 uncovered the colonial echoes that are evoked in the interviews and manifestos of the Lega and FdI. Whether these echoes are intentionally or unintentionally used by the populist radical right is outside the scope of this book. Indeed, intentionality is hard to gauge from the interviews and manifestos, and the question of whether colonial echoes are consciously or unconsciously constructed provides an interesting avenue for future political psychological enquiry. Regardless of intentionality, colonial rhetoric is deep-seated in the Italian populist radical right's discourse on immigration, even though the racism marking colonial rhetoric is often covered under a veil of civic rhetoric. This lingering colonial rhetoric is underpinned by a selective memory of Italian colonialism, largely consigning colonial brutalities to oblivion. It seems that the Italian populist radical right does not consciously repeat colonial rhetoric, as the interviewees did not deliberately compare immigrants to the colonised, and they talked about colonialism only when prompted to do so.

Memory is interpreted in this book as selective by definition. Briefly recalling the introduction of the concept of memory in Chapter 1, in its basic definition, it is the mental capacity of an individual or a group to recollect information from the past (Oppenheimer and Hakvoort 2003: 94). These recollections are inherently subjective and biased (Lowenthal 1985: 194, 206), as individuals and groups select which aspects of the past to remember. Hence, it is impossible for memory to offer a complete, objective, and correct account of the past. Memory in this book is intended in its collective connotation: it represents the relationship of a community with its past (Mammone 2006: 212), and depends on individual recollections (Foot 2009: 192), which are shaped by the social context in which they take place (Halbwachs 1992).

Despite memory being selective, the Italian populist radical right's memory of colonialism is noteworthy because it chooses to remember what are considered positive elements, while erasing negative ones. The latter are doomed to forgetting, which is a lack of memory and, more subtly, the obstruction of a loss (Chambers 2001) to guard a hurt identity (Laplanche and Pontalis 1988: 390–394). When forgetting is a deliberate process to remove uncomfortable reminiscences, it works as a self-defence mechanism aimed at protecting a damaged identity (Mellino 2012:

115). Importantly, such selective forgetting, whether conscious or unconscious, has repercussions on the Italian populist radical right's relationship with immigrants, who are the natural heirs to the colonised Other, regardless of whether their country of birth had been colonised by Italy or by another country.

Several studies advance suppositions about a link between attitudes towards immigrants and attitudes towards colonial memory in wider Italian society (see, for instance, Andall and Duncan 2005; Chambers 2008; De Cesari 2012; Galeazzo 1994; Labanca 2002; Ponzanesi 2005), and abroad (see, for instance, Gilroy 2005; Mols and Jetten 2014). In recent years, a number of authors have been increasingly interested in the hitherto understudied analysis of the connections between contemporary populism and colonial memory in the postcolony (see, for instance, the Special Issue "Populism in the Postcolony" published by Kairos in 2020), and in the West (see, for instance, De Cesari and Kaya 2020). For example, in the Netherlands, Couperus and Tortola (2019) note that the populist radical right has highlighted the allegedly most positive aspects of the colonial past and fabricated fake historical colonial narratives. In Italy, Proglio (2019: 15) has produced a pioneering investigation of the Mediterranean as a "ghost" of Italy's colonial past that resurfaces in the contemporary construction of Italian national identity, juxtaposed to the immigrant Other in the discourse of the Lega's leader Salvini. Siddi (2020) has made an innovative move in shedding light on how the Italian foreign policy discourse, during the refugee and migrant crisis of 2014–2018, negated the contentious elements of Italy's colonial past. This selective "silencing" of the colonial past was embedded in Italy's myth of *Italiani brava gente*,[1] which depicted Italians as incapable of any wrongdoing. Siddi (2020) draws on parliamentary speeches, including the Lega and FdI, but limits the focus to foreign policy discourse. Nevertheless, a thorough and comprehensive postcolonial examination of Italian political discourse in the populist radical right going beyond the Lega's leader and the field of foreign policy is still lacking. The intention of this chapter is exactly to fill this gap in the literature, by drawing on interviews with the Italian populist radical right.

The colonial memory shaped by the Italian populist radical right, however, needs to be understood against the backdrop of Italy's post-war experience, marred by the lack of a critical assessment of colonialism, due to the demonising equation of colonialism with fascism (Pinkus 2003), and the myth of *Italiani brava gente* (Del Boca 1992). Furthermore, the perceived inferiority compared to other European countries (Allen and Russo 1997: 3) led Italy to cover up its misdeeds in its quest for prestige. These factors combined to make the emergence of a more critical memory of colonialism and fascism, shedding light on both their positive and negative aspects, impossible to attain among political parties, but also in education and in the wider public.

7.2 The Rejection of the Link between Colonialism and Immigration

The Italian populist radical right espouses a selective memory of colonialism when it fails to acknowledge the link between colonialism, which wrought havoc in the immigrants' countries of origin, and immigration. Several academics have documented this connection. For instance, Werbner and Modood claim there is a mechanical link between colonialism and immigration, as they maintain that immigration often originates from former colonies (1997: 1). Such association is discussed in the case of Italy by De Donno and Srivastava, who argue that immigration has encouraged Italy to think again about its colonial history (2006: 378): in the recent past immigrants from former Italian colonies constituted a sizeable portion of the total number of immigrants arriving in Italy. Indeed, according to the Ministry of the Interior's official data, in 2018 Eritreans were the second most numerous nationality among all the immigrants disembarked into Italy, amounting to 14% of all immigrants (Ministero dell'Interno 2018), while at the time of writing Eritreans account for 3% of migrant arrivals since the beginning of 2022 (Ministero dell'Interno 2022).

Surprisingly, given the robustness of the link between immigration and colonialism, the Lega, FdI, and populist radical right intellectuals believe that immigration occurs regardless of colonial exploitation (see, for instance, A20180103DC, A20170404M, A20180103LC, F20170110F, G20170405C, G2017109D). This widely-held belief reveals a selective memory of Italian colonialism, purged of its violence. "[Immigration] has nothing to do with past colonisation" (A20180803DC) firmly asserted a Lega representative. Instead, the interviewees, when prompted to reflect on a possible link between colonialism and immigration, brush off this topic, and turn the focus onto the causes of immigration they identify. The causes of immigration recognised by the Lega and FdI are Western neo-colonialism (M20170104G, F2170104M) and the dramatic end of colonialism (G20170407P, M20180105M, R20180104M).

The first reason mentioned here, namely Western neo-colonialism, switches the blame from Italian past colonial occupation to contemporary colonialism exercised by Western powers. By "Western powers," the Lega means the US, the UK, and France, allegedly enforcing a new form of colonialism through extraction of resources. Therefore, Italy is once again redeemed. The second reason mentioned here, namely the end of colonialism, is a not-so-covert hint at the beneficial effect of Western past colonialism (which will be examined exhaustively later in this chapter). Here it suffices to add, as evidence used to justify the regret for the end of colonialism, the emphasis posed by an FdI interviewee on the alleged incapacity of formerly colonised people to govern themselves in a "self-sufficient and authoritative" way (R20180104M). This affirmation is drenched in colonial rhetoric, looking at the colonial past through a skewed lens. Therefore, through the discursive strategy of blame reversal often deployed in the populist radical right's discourse (Van Dijk 2008: 352), blame is shifted from past colonialism to contemporary neo-colonial actors, such as the US, and even to decolonisation itself.

A further claim uttered by the populist radical right that again diverts blame away from Italy, is shifting culpability onto France and the UK. It is a case in point that an FdI representative recognised that the link between colonialism and immigration is valid in countries such as France and the UK because they never broke economic and diplomatic relationships with their colonies. While the continuity in economic and diplomatic ties between former colonial powers in the West and their colonies is an incontrovertible fact, this does not amount to a justification for excluding Italy from the countries that wrought havoc on former colonies. Italy's colonialism was much shorter than British and French colonialism, since Italy did not lose its colonies during the decolonisation wave in the 1960s and 1970s, but it was deprived of them during the Second World War; Italy's ties with Eritrea, Ethiopia, Somalia, and Libya were certainly weaker than the intense diplomatic and economic flows between other major European powers and their former colonies. These are unquestionable facts. However, these facts do not imply that Italy's short-lived colonial past and tenuous ties to its former colonies exempt it from having created the conditions for political and economic instability ensuing the end of colonial domination. Italy was not foreign to colonial violence.

As usual, there are exceptions, and the interviews make up a bunch of heterogeneous voices. A few representatives among the Italian populist radical right assert that colonialism created the economic, social, and political instability that now works as push factor for immigrants (F20180104F, M20170113R, D20210329S), as a Lega representative argued: "we (Europeans) deconstructed their economy and society (…) often in a violent way" (M20170111R). In general, few Italian populist radical right representatives recognise the negative impact of colonialism on the economy, society, and politics in the immigrants' countries of origin, regardless of whether they were colonised by Italy or other Western countries.

It is interesting that some Lega and FdI representatives and intellectuals acknowledge that immigration is connected to past colonialism, but they frame this connection as an inevitable consequence of the Western drive to colonise (G20170111R, L20170406C, M20170111R, N20180108C). Therefore, they acknowledge the link between past colonialism and immigration, but they shy away from highlighting the responsibility of colonial powers for economic, social, and political insecurity in the immigrants' countries of origin. "Today those who had been subject to colonialism in the past are trying to break into our home and settle down here" (M20170111R). This statement uttered by a Lega representative is cleansed of responsibility: colonial subjection is not attributed to any agent. Moreover, the language is denigratory towards immigrants, as evidenced by the term "break into," redolent of the criminalisation of immigration tackled in Chapter 6.

7.3 Selective Colonial Memory: What is Remembered

7.3.1 An Idealised Memory of the Colonial Past

A selective memory of colonialism expunged of violence also underpins the melancholia for a golden colonial past and a subtle postcolonial melancholia on the Italian populist radical right. Mols and Jetten's study of Dutch, French, and Belgian populist radical right parties shows that the populist radical right nostalgically idealises the national collective past, pitting it against a fearful present spoilt by immigration, thus legitimising racism against immigrants, seen as the culprits for the end of a golden age (2014: 74). Alarmist narratives about immigration thus induce a feeling of anxiety about the present and a longing for a golden past, and legitimate the harsh treatment of immigrants (Mols and Jetten 2014). Although Mols and Jetten do not specifically allude to the colonial past when mentioning a past golden age (2014), this book applies their argument to Italian populist radical right parties to investigate the interaction between the Italian populist radical right's colonial memory and the Italian populist radical right's racism.

As the interviews suggest, the Italian populist radical right's discourse, which is decisively racist, contains sporadic references to a romanticised colonial past. The then leader of AN (the FdI predecessor) Gianfranco Fini, in 2006, claimed that "Not all colonial history was negative. If we considered how Ethiopia, Somalia, and Libya ended up today and how they fared under colonialism, there would be a re-assessment of our role in those countries" (Casadio 2006). The sun soon set on AN in 2008 and FdI emerged from its ashes in 2012. As transpires from the representatives' statements reported and analysed in the section above about the denial of a link between Italian colonialism and immigration, the populist radical right still has a fairly positive memory of Italian colonial past. Various elements are put forward as corroborations for the argument that Italian colonialism was, after all, *good*. This idealisation of the colonial past producing a specific amalgam of memories of colonialism's positive aspects is not an isolated case that only applies to Italy. In fact, Couperus and Tortola (2019), for instance, identify the glorification of an untainted colonial past in the discourse of the populist radical right in the Netherlands.

Infrastructure, such as roads, bridges, and services, is often mentioned as an example of an idealised glorious colonial past by the Lega, FdI, and populist radical right intellectuals (F20160905L, F20170408T, G20170407P, M20170113R, M20180105M). "There have been times in which Italy moved to the other side of the Mediterranean to bring innovation and infrastructures," poignantly expressed a Lega representative (P20210409M). The construction of hospitals, homes (G20170407P), markets, and schools (M20170104G) is viewed under a positive light as having helped the development of the economy and society in former colonies.

The positive value attributed to Italian colonialism does not stop at material deeds, but spills over into the moral dimension: Italian colonisers are said to have left a good impression on the colonised. As one Lega representative argued, "colonialism brought a more civilised culture, dignity to human beings, protection of the weak and solidarity against abuses" (L20170404N). In a similar colonial rhetoric underlining the supposed inferiority of the colonised Other, another Lega representative regretted that "we haven't been able to transmit our own ideals to the races that are clearly not used to these ideals" (P20161219B). Overall, Italian colonialism seems to have made a positive impact on the colonies, since, in the words of a Lega representative, "I think that bringing our culture to other countries is always something positive. (…) When we were ruling our colonies, everything was going fine" (T20210409S). Adding to that, an FdI representative firmly asserts that "We should not forget the civilisation and progress that Italy managed to leave in its 30-year rule over Libya" (B20210507M). Consequently, the image of Italian colonialism revealed by the interviews is one of an idealised colonialism, devoted to munificently improving the colonised countries without any exploitation. The aura of positivity shrouding colonialism is rooted not only in the conviction about the racial superiority of Italian colonisers, but also in the belief that the colonised countries were *terrae nullius*,[2] lacking any significant civilisation (R20180104M).

Therefore, transferring Mols and Jetten's (2014) study onto the Italian scenario, it is possible to advance the hypothesis that the Italian populist radical right deploys an idealised narrative of a positive colonial past, to emphasise in an alarmist tone the discontinuity between a magnificent colonial past characterised by racial superiority and the bestowing of material and moral improvements on the colonies, and a miserable present tainted by immigration and decline. Such melancholia, in turns, legitimises racism against immigrants.

7.3.2 Postcolonial Melancholia (or the Absence Thereof)

In the literature, prominent postcolonial author Paul Gilroy advances the argument that the idealisation of the colonial past, which implies the forgetting of colonial misdeeds, forms the basis for postcolonial melancholia (2005: 13). The erasure of the memory of colonial brutalities becomes related to a sense of melancholia towards the colonial past. Indeed, the UK, according to Gilroy's argument, lacks the ability to mourn the loss of imperial prestige, which is combined with worries over the arrival of postcolonial immigrants, political and economic crises, and the perception of a loss of a characteristic cohesive national culture (2005). As an unconscious reaction against the loss of imperial predominance, and as a consequence of the lack of elaboration of the imperial past, and the perceived unsettlement of British national identity, for the British the Empire becomes constructed as a source of embarrassment and disquiet. In response to such embarrassment and disquiet, the British colonial past is conveniently forgotten (Gilroy 2005: 81). In such a way, shame and guilt over colonial times are reversed onto the reminders of such colonial past: the immigrants.

Certainly, Italian colonialism represents an exception to the British colonial and postcolonial paradigms that work as a context for Gilroy's theory of postcolonial melancholia (2005). Indeed, Italy did not endure a decolonisation process involving anti-colonial struggles, because it lost its colonies at the end of the Second World War. Moreover, Italian has not been kept as the official language in former colonies, except for Somalia, which retained Italian as an official language until the end of Italy's trusteeship in 1960 (Lewis 1961 cited in Andall and Duncan 2005: 17). However, a less successful colonial experience, less enduring colonial ties, and an earlier decolonisation process involving no anti-colonial struggle does not preclude the possibility for the argument of postcolonial melancholia to be applied to Italy as well, and, especially, to the Italian populist radical right, following the comparatively late wave of immigration into Italy that started in the 1990s, from former colonies as well as from other countries.

Offering a contribution to the existing literature that glosses over the existence of postcolonial melancholia in the Italian populist radical right, this book claims that postcolonial melancholia is not explicit among Italian populist radical right parties. In the interviews, when asked whether Italy should have clung to its colonies at the end of the Second World War, only one Lega representative did express the wish that Italy had retained its colonies (P20161219B). Generally, colonial melancholia is not a feature of the Lega and FdI. Colonialism is seen by the populist radical right as delayed, short-lived and unsuccessful (see, for instance, G20170411C, G20180105M, M20180105M, R20180108D). In the words of a Lega representative, "colonialism was a joke, we went too fast, and we ended up making mistakes" (C20170106V). The view of colonialism as a joke is widely shared among the Lega and FdI representatives, to emphasise Italian colonial failures (C20170106V, F20170104M, P20170404L, S20180103F). Indeed, the Italian populist radical right criticises Italian colonisers for lacking foreign policy skills (F20160905L) and the capacity to profit financially from its colonies (L20180104N, L20180105S, S20180108S).

What emerges from the interviews is not a markedly clear postcolonial melancholia, regretting the demise of colonialism and longing for its return (which would be, nevertheless, an obsolete wish in contemporary times). This signals a discrepancy with the persisting postcolonial melancholia lingering in Italian postwar politics and culture. Triulzi (2005: 157), Pinkus (1997: 152), and Lombardi-Diop (2012: 176) suggest that post-war Italy cultivated melancholia for its colonies, after the abrupt loss experienced at the hands of the Allies. Moreover, the post-war Partito Nazionale Monarchico (PNM) and the Democrazia Cristiana (DC) stubbornly dreamed of regaining the lost colonies. The PNM believed that Italy had the right to reclaim its lost colonies, which was legitimised by Italy's "civilising mission," the quest for international prestige, and the search for a destination for emigration (Ungari 2014: 397). Deploying a similar colonial rhetoric, the DC head of state Alcide De Gasperi desired a return of former Italian colonies, due to the hard work Italy had performed in the Italian *Oltremare* (Pes 2014: 426). The left initially disapproved of the government's colonialist claims, but after 1948 even the Partito Comunista Italiano (PCI) and the Partito Socialista Italiano (PSI) blamed the DC government for ignoring Italian colonial desires (De Michele 2011: 106).

A revealing detail symbolising a lack of postcolonial melancholia in the Italian populist radical right is these parties' reaction to the term *Mare Nostrum*, which was a desired space of colonisation in Roman and fascist colonial times. *Mare Nostrum* has now become a disdained middle passage between the immigrants' countries of origin and Italy: a *Mare Aliorum* as Fogu defines it, to emphasise the dangerous alterity associated with the Mediterranean nowadays (2010: 1). Indeed, as the interviews indicate, the Mediterranean no longer represents a coveted space of colonial conquest associated with the grandeur of the fascist empire: now the term *Mare Nostrum* merely elicits disgust and anger in the Lega and FdI, which link it with the now-dismissed Italian search and rescue programme introduced in 2013 in the aftermath of a tragic shipwreck of migrants in Lampedusa and phased out in 2014. Therefore, *Mare Nostrum* is bitterly described as "an horrendous EU policy" (C20170106V), "a waste of money" (F20170104M), "a dramatic failure"

(G20170109D), "the deathbed of migrants" (L20170104N, M20170104G), and a lucrative immigration "business" (L20170104N, P20161219B). These descriptions of *Mare Nostrum* reveal the complete detachment of this term from the colonial past. Instead, they signal the embedding of this term in present immigration politics, in a typically populist anti-elite fashion, criticising the EU and the Italian government that coordinated the *Mare Nostrum* search and rescue operations.

7.4 Selective Colonial Memory: What is Forgotten

Despite the absence of an explicit postcolonial melancholia within the Italian populist radical right, the subtle idealisation of the Italian colonial past calls for an analysis of the Italian populist radical right's stance on Italian colonial crimes. In fact, the idealisation of colonialism goes in tandem with the selective forgetting of colonial crimes, which is underpinned by a colonial memory that singles out only certain events to be remembered.

Indeed, postcolonial studies have posited that the lack of elaboration of in-group war violence leads to hostility towards the enemy, i.e., the victim of violence, seen as responsible for the sense of guilt nurtured by the in-group (Leone and Sarrica 2014). On the contrary, the process of mourning involves the thorough elaboration of the violence committed and leads to reconciliation, implying the end of the scapegoating of the enemy (Leone and Mastrovito 2014: 17). Reconciliation entails a critical analysis of the past and the end of the stubborn attempt at defending the in-group's identity against the sense of guilt for committing crimes (Leone and Mastrovito 2014: 12–13). Although Leone and Mastrovito's (2014) argument does not explicitly mention colonial crimes and political parties, here I apply it to the Italian populist radical right's lack of elaboration of colonial crimes. Indeed, Leone and Mastrovito's (2014) argument on the connection between the lack of mourning of in-group violence and hostility towards the victims of such violence can be transposed onto the Italian populist radical right. In fact, this party family seems to have avoided the elaboration of colonial crimes through a more nuanced appraisal of the colonial past. As a consequence, colonial crimes are mainly consigned to selective forgetting, which may lead to these parties' hostile stance against the heirs of the victims of colonial crimes: the immigrants.

In the interviews, the Italian radical right largely displays a selective colonial memory that either negates or downplays colonial violence. In fact, fascist colonialism used asphyxiating gas in Ethiopia, napalm to burn villages in Eritrea, and the bombing of rebels' villages in Somalia (Del Boca 2003: 28). In Libya, General Rodolfo Graziani commanded the mass deportation of the population of the Cyrenaic Gebel to concentration camps. Out of 100,000 people deported, 15,000 died in transit out of thirst, starvation, mistreatment, and fatigue, and 40,000 died in the camp (Randazzo 2006: 122). Concerning the utter negation of colonial brutalities, a Lega representative even claimed that "concentration camps in Libya did not exist" (P20161219B). However, it is the belittling of colonial crimes that is more common. Indeed, the Lega and FdI admit that Italians committed colonial wrongdoings (see, for instance, F2017011S, L20170104N, M20170104G), but mitigate their gravity by adopting a relativist perspective, which contends that in the nineteenth and early twentieth centuries colonial violence was commonplace (F20170104M). The emphasis on immigration is a further pretext to downplay the seriousness of colonial wrongdoings. In fact, immigration is allegedly a more serious issue than colonial crimes (A20180103LC).

Another common explanation of the Lega, FdI, and populist radical right intellectuals to justify colonial misdeeds is the comparison with allegedly much more violent crimes committed by other European countries (see, for instance, A20180103LC, F20170408T, G20170111R, L20170406C, L2018015S), for example the Boers in South Africa (C20170106V), the French, the British (see, for instance, C20180109G, E20170404C, G20170109D, G20170411C), and the Belgians (G20170411C). This comparison recalls the negation of the link between Italian colonialism and immigration, which is discordantly joined with the acknowledgement of the connection between the colonial past of other Western major powers, and the immigration flows into the former colonial motherlands.

Therefore, Italian colonial crimes, perpetrated especially under fascism, become normalised, as they are essentially interpreted by the Italian populist radical right as purely symbolic of the violent practices widespread during the age of colonialism. It is useful to note, however, that colonial violence has become normalised not only in Italy, but also in countries that do not have a fascist past. In France, for instance, Sarkozy, on his 2007 trip to Africa, recognised that French colonialism in Algeria brought suffering and injustices, but he asserted no meaningful repentance. On the other hand, he claimed that it was time for France to stop apologising for colonialism and engaging in self-flagellation over the French brutalities committed in the Algerian war against anti-colonial troops (Noussis 2020). Instead, he encouraged the youth to focus on the future and emphasised the good deeds of French colonialism (Reuters 2007). In more recent times, Macron triggered an acrimonious debate after his 2018 admission of the use of torture in the Algerian War. This episode attracted academic attention on the French silence shrouding the Algerian War (Noussis 2020). In such a way, state leaders, by shifting attention from colonial misdeeds to colonial deeds, strategically enacted the selective forgetting of the negative aspects of the colonial past, precluding the possibility for apologies, and accepting the colonial violence that plagued former colonies as normal.

The ignorance or the minimisation of colonial crimes in the Italian populist radical right's memory is also evident when, in the interviews, the Italian populist radical right considers it inappropriate to apologise to former colonies for colonial atrocities. Indeed, in the interviews, some Italian populist radical right representatives utterly refused to recognise the morality and the utility of apologies to former colonies, which are considered "ridiculous" (R20180108D), "stupid" (E20170404C), "crazy" (F20170104M), "superfluous" (G20170411C, N20180108C), "useless" (P20161219B, C20180109G), even "suicidal" (M20170111R) and "pathetic" (S20180108S). In the words of a Lega representative, "we already gave them [the Libyans] back the obelisk, this is enough" (F20160905L). Predictably, the Italian populist radical right bitterly criticises Massimo D'Alema (then Prime Minister) for having apologised in the 1990s (Del Boca 2005: 200) for colonial violence in Libya (see, for instance, A20180103LC, A20170404M, E201810103G, F20180103B). In fact, in the 1990s, politicians timidly admitted colonial crimes. The President of the Republic Oscar Luigi Scalfaro recognised Italian crimes, the Minister of Defence Domenico Corcione admitted the use of gas in Ethiopia (Labanca 2005: 38), and Prime Minister D'Alema deprecated the Italian colonial past in Libya and offered his apologies to the former Italian colony (Del Boca 2005: 200).

As suggested by the interviews, even in the case of incontrovertible evidence of colonial crimes, some representatives from the Lega and FdI emphasised that Italy should apologise only *if* it committed crimes (see, for instance, F20170110F, F20180104F, G20170112G, L20180105S). Hence, they remained vague on whether they believe apologies are actually due or not. Nevertheless, also when apologies are half-heartedly invoked, they have the strategic scope of stopping immigration. In fact, an FdI representative claimed that

> I don't think we have to apologise, but if it becomes fundamental to do so in order to stop migrants' boats from coming to Italy, I will apologise, even if I don't know why, because Italy does not have anything to apologise for.
> (G20170109D)

Therefore, the belittling of colonial crimes is grounded in a selective colonial memory in the Italian populist radical right's discourse, which erases the brutal aspects of the colonial past. By selectively forgetting colonial violence, the Italian populist radical right is declining responsibility for the colonial crimes committed in its former colonies.

The Italian populist radical right's opinion on selective forgetting is interesting. One FdI representative contended that "[colonial history] is characterised by positive and negative elements, on which we must reflect in order to avoid repeating mistakes" (F20170110F). However, in the interviews, the Italian populist radical right generally does not think it urgent to remember the colonial past. Some interviewees recognised the existence of colonial forgetting, but did not seem eager to overcome it (G20170112G, F20160905L), while others did not acknowledge the existence of amnesia and/or aphasia (E20170404C, F20170111S, G20170109D). An FdI representative explicitly advocated the forgetting of the colonial past, showing that, in this case, forgetting was deliberate: "The past is over (…). In order to carry on, we need to set aside what happened. Until we learn how to forget, (…) we won't grow" (L20170410P).

Indifference to colonial history is commonplace, as revealed by the interviews with the Lega, FdI, and populist radical right intellectuals (see, for instance, F20170104M, G20170109D, L20170406C, M20170404F, M20170113R). A Lega representative manifested his lack of interest in colonial history by stating, "I do not think that [colonial history] is a topical theme" (M20170404F). Indifference and forgetting are rooted in a colonial memory that is purified from its colonial violence. In fact, a tendency widespread in the Italian populist radical right is to shift attention from the memory of colonial crimes perpetrated by Italians to the memory of Italians as victims of the left, such as the Italians fleeing Tito's regime from Istria and Dalmatia, who were allegedly mistreated by the Italian left and the trade unions (G20170109D, S20180108S). As a Lega interviewee reported, "Bologna did not even give warm milk to the children [of the Italian exiles]" (S20180108S). The emphasis on Italy's mistreatment of the Italians displaced from Istria and Dalmatia also appears in the writings of Ernesto Galli della Loggia, the prominent journalist and scholar who tried to revive Italian nationalism through a form of neo-patriotism, by highlighting the failures of the Resistance in shaping a cohesive Italian national identity in the post-war period (2003).

7.4.1 Colonial Forgetting beyond the Populist Radical Right

Colonial memory plagued by selective forgetting also permeates the academic realm in Italy. From the end of fascism to the 1980s, colonialism was hidden in history textbooks and political debates (Labanca 2005: 33–35, 37) and the Italian colonial enterprise was seen as incidental to Italian history (Andall and Duncan 2005: 9). Even studies on fascism analyse colonialism imprecisely, as Labanca points out (2003: 37). Only in the 1980s did historiographic interest in Italian colonial history emerge and textbooks started featuring Italian colonialism (Labanca 2005: 37). This void in colonial memory, avoiding uncomfortable reminiscences, hindered the retrieval of historical truth, as Italy silenced the memory of its own colonial mistakes (Del Boca 2003: 19), or confronted them with significant delays. The results of this colonial forgetting are reflected in attitudes towards immigrants in contemporary Italy. Andall and Duncan (2005) and Labanca (2005) warn that attitudes to colonial memory in Italian society at large affect attitudes towards immigrants, while Ponzanesi claims that immigration has crystallised colonial rhetoric (2005). Narrowing down the focus from attitudes towards colonial memory and immigration to a manipulated colonial memory and racism, the lack of memory of the Italian colonial past made public opinion unprepared for the arrival of immigrants in the 1990s (Galeazzo 1994: 15); led to racism against immigrants (Chambers 2008: 7); was conducive to violations of human rights against immigrants (De Cesari 2012: 316).

A prime example of selective colonial memory choosing which aspects of the past to render invisible and forget is the interviewees' attitude towards Indro Montanelli, a notable journalist and writer who, while fighting in the fascist colonial War in Ethiopia, had purchased an Eritrean young girl. This episode elicited marked polarisation in politics: while the racist and sexist behaviour of Montanelli generally aroused disgust and condemnation, the populist radical right was reluctant to express complete repulsion. Montanelli's questionable records came under the media spotlight when, in the wake of the killing of African-American George Floyd by US police in 2020, the Black Lives Matter movement re-ignited its campaigns and joined forces with the anti-colonial movement. The Black Lives

Memory and Forgetting 117

Matter protests created a spill-over effect into the realm of colonial statues, and, in sign of protest, Montanelli's statue in Milan was splashed with red paint. When prompted to offer their reflections on this recent event, the populist radical right was careful not to admit the cruelty of Montanelli's purchase of an Eritrean young girl called Destà. Instead, with their typical strategy of blame reversal, an FdI representative opined that

> I do not justify Montanelli's behaviour, but I understand it from a historical perspective. We need to contextualise the fact within history and within the culture this kid belonged to. Probably she was coming from a Muslim culture, where getting married at 12 years of age was normal. What Montanelli did was not discordant with the historical and social circumstances he lived in.
> (P200210422B)

Therefore, a cruel colonial memory is brushed under the carpet of the historical contextualisation of colonial fascist violence within the milieu of fascist colonialism, ultimately resulting in the absolution of Montanelli and in the forgetting of the related episode.

Colonial memory affected by the selective forgetting of colonial crimes also underlies the diplomatic indifference Italy demonstrated when it failed to intervene in its former colonies in the decades after its forced retreat from colonialism, while these countries were torn apart by wars. In fact, when Ethiopia breached Eritrea's autonomy within the federation, by incorporating it into the Ethiopian Empire in 1964, Italy did not intervene to protect its former colony. Only in 1988 did Italy recognise the need to confront the Eritrean question. In 1992 it sent economic aid, a year after Eritrea's independence was sanctioned by the United Nations (Del Boca 2003: 28–29). Similarly, in Somalia, where Italy retained a UN trusteeship from 1950 to 1960, Italy unsuccessfully intervened only in 1992, 23 years after the dictator Said Barré had subverted the fragile Somali democracy and 15 years after Barré's annexation of the province of Ogaden triggered a disastrous war with Ethiopia, which it ultimately won (Del Boca 2003: 30–31).

7.4.2 Diplomatic Indifference

Diplomatic ties between the Italian motherland and its former colonies have been characterised by a degree of neglect on the part of Italy. As the interviews suggest, the Italian populist radical right is split concerning diplomatic indifference: some representatives recognised it, while others ignored it. Overall, the Italian populist radical right does not regret Italy's lack of intervention in Ethiopia, Eritrea, and Somalia, when these countries were swept through by civil wars. In the interviews, the Lega, FdI, and populist radical right intellectuals justify Italy's diplomatic indifference towards its former colonies by asserting that Italy did not have any responsibility towards them. In the telling words of a Lega representative, "it is as if [the former colonies] had never been our colonies" (M20170104G). Other excuses put forward for diplomatic indifference are that Italy, through intervention, would have appeared to be pursuing some strategic interest in its former colonies (F20170110F, L20180105S), and that intervention would have slowed down Italy's growth (L20170410P) or at least would not have yielded any economic profit (F20160905L, S20180103F). Therefore, contrary to the humanitarian ethos displayed by the populist radical right regarding the protection of refugees escaping "real wars" (analysed in depth in Chapter 5), humanitarianism takes the backseat when the Italian populist radical right is faced with the political turmoil its former colonies underwent.

In fact, intervention motivated by a sense of moral responsibility for formerly Italian territories is dismissed as "fanta-politics" (F20170104M), i.e., a surreal policy that is removed from reality. Hence, moral responsibility does not appear to belong to the realm of real politics, which apparently encompasses only economic interests. Only a few Lega representatives contended that Italy should have intervened, because it had a duty to do so by virtue of its former dominion over those territories (G20180109C, M20170111R). Italy's indifference towards its former colonies is also evident in the lack of condemnation of dictatorships developed in the Italian *Olremare*.[3] Indeed, one Lega representative's convoluted words clearly reveal the Lega's lack of a sense of moral responsibility towards Italy's former colonies: "we need to stop accusing a dictator only because he is a dictator" (M20170104G). Such lack of condemnation of dictators is indicative of the disregard of dictatorial regimes, and of clemency towards dictators, who are apparently not to be condemned. This leniency towards dictators also became clear when a Lega councillor in Regione Lombardia defined the bloody dictator of Eritrea, Isaias Afewerki, who took power in 1991, as "a friend," "a wise and skilful man," who ruled his country "with paternal and firm hand" (Stella 2018). The Lega forbade the Italian military ship *Diciotti*, carrying mainly Eritrean migrants, from mooring in the port in Catania for five days in August 2018 (Camilli 2018), a further example of the Italian populist radical right's denial of the destructive consequences of Afewerki's brutal dictatorship. Therefore, Italy's indifference towards its former colonies testifies to the fact that colonialism was not psychologically processed (Ben-Ghiat 2006: 390), as the memory of it remained obstructed by selective forgetting, resulting in Italy declining any responsibility to aid those countries.

Nevertheless, the case of Libya and its dictator Muammar Gaddafi represents an exception to Italian diplomatic indifference towards its former colonies and, again, demonstrates that the Italian populist radical right does not feel the need to apologise for colonial crimes. This is underpinned by a colonial memory affected by the selective forgetting of colonial crimes in Libya, and by the presence of a sharp strategic purpose steering the relationship with Gaddafi. Indeed, in 1956, Italy grudgingly paid reparations to Libya for colonial exploitation and brutalities. Yet, subsequently, Italy refused Gaddafi's insistent demands for further reparations, arguing that the 1956 Italo-Libya Accord had erased all debts (Del Boca 2003: 26, 27). In 1998, the Italo-Libyan Commission expressed Italy's regret for colonial violence in Libya (Coraluzzo 2008: 121). Shortly after, in 2000, Italy initiated a long thread of agreements with Libya, all centred on cooperation on countering terrorism and irregular migration transiting through Libya and arriving in Italy (Giuffré 2013). Bilateral agreements signed between Italy and its former colony include a 2000 memorandum of intent addressing terrorism, drug trafficking, crime, and irregular migrants; a 2003 agreement on intelligence exchange on migration; and a 2007 agreement to jointly patrol Libyan coasts (Paoletti 2011: 274).

Within this string of bilateral agreements, the Memorandum of Understanding deserves mentioning. In 2017 the then Italian Prime Minister Paolo Gentiloni and Fayez al-Sarraj, leader of the internationally recognised Presidency Council of the Government of National Accord (GNA), sealed the long-standing history of migration-related cooperation with the signature of a Memorandum of Understanding[4] in Rome (Albahari 2017). Among other issues, the Memorandum expresses a commitment to the implementation of the Treaty of Friendship, Partnership, and Cooperation signed in 2008 by the then Prime Minister Berlusconi and his Libyan counterpart Gaddafi (Albahari 2017). Particular emphasis was given to a bilateral fight "against terrorism, organized crime, drug trafficking, and immigration" (article 19); to Italian financial assistance to build and strengthen the capacity of the Libyan coast guard with the objective of externalising border-patrolling activities to Libya; and to the use of detention centres in Libya for irregular immigrants, and re*patria*tion of third country nationals irregularly immigrated into Italy (Albahari 2017). Indeed, since 2017, capacity building by Italy of Libya's security forces has been consolidated, since Libya is perceived by Italy as a "potential transmission belt for criminal activities to the EU" (Ceccorulli and Coticchia 2020: 178).

The 2017 Memorandum of Understanding between Italy and Libya is noteworthy, since it calls for the implementation of arguably the most relevant bilateral agreement between Italy and its former colony in the last two decades: the above-mentioned 2008 Treaty on Friendship, Partnership, and Cooperation.[5] In the 2008 Treaty on Friendship, Partnership, and Cooperation, Italy and Libya pledged to coordinate joint patrolling of Libyan waters. In exchange for improved diplomatic relations, Libya promised to help Italy in the fight against terrorism and to stop immigration to Italy as a strategy to exit international isolation (Coralluzzo 2008: 123). Moreover, the fateful 2008 Berlusconi and Gaddafi Treaty promised Italian investments in Libyan oil, healthcare, education, and highways, in exchange for Libya's cooperation on immigration control (De Cesari 2012: 319–320). Despite being redolent of colonial rhetoric in its promise of financial and logistical assistance in exchange for investment opportunities and immigration control, the 2008 Treaty was largely oblivious to colonial relations between Italy and Libya. It briefly referred to the colonial past, stressing the fact that it was over and was just a "painful chapter of the past" (De Cesari 2012: 317–318). Hence, colonial memory was erased, thus precluding the possibility of raising awareness of colonial abuses and confining them in the past (De Cesari 2012: 318). Indeed, the Treaty did not engender any remembrance days, truth commissions or media debates (De Cesari 2012: 320). As De Cesari argues, the Berlusconi-owned newspaper *Il Giornale* even celebrated the Treaty and glorified the benign and

120 *Memory and Forgetting*

civilising aspects of the Italian colonial mission (2012: 321). Another ambiguity surrounding this Treaty was Italy's pledge to return migrants to Libya, who were then detained in camps, where they were abused and tortured (Del Castillo 2011: 5).

As revealed by the interviews, the Lega, FdI, and populist radical right intellectuals positively review the 2008 Berlusconi-Gaddafi Friendship Treaty, emphasising how it managed to contain immigration into Italy (see, for instance, F201701010F, G20170411C, G20170111R, L20180105S, M20170113R), as well as to channel oil into Italy (A20180103DC). Therefore, economic and political strategy took priority (see, for instance, F20170104M, F20170408T, G20170109D, G20170112G, L20170406C) over a sense of guilt and the need to apologise to Libya for Italy's colonial cruelties (see, for instance, C20180109G, F20170408T, L20170406C, M20170104G). As a Lega representative argued, "the Treaty was purely strategic; this argument [that] it may have been driven by a sense of guilt can be put forward only by some 'innocent soul' of the left that feels perennially guilty towards Africa" (G20180105M). Moreover, in the interviews, the Lega, FdI, and populist radical right intellectuals consider Berlusconi as far-sighted (see, for instance, A20180103LC, F20170110F, G20170407P, L20170104N, S20180103F), even a "genius" (L20170104N) and a "great man" (S20180103B).

The Italian populist radical right is similarly munificent in its judgement of Gaddafi as a pragmatic statesman (see, for instance, A20170404M, F20170408T, F20180104F), who, with his "sharp intelligence" (F20170111S), managed to stave off the danger of the Arab Spring (E20180103G, P20161219B, S20180108S). Only a few Italian populist radical right representatives explicitly recognised the challenge the Treaty posed to moral and ethical principles (G20180109C, G20170112G, R20180108D), as Gaddafi was a dictator. Indeed, in an FdI representative's words, "Gaddafi was a bloody and violent dictator, (…) but the only one capable of stopping this wave of invasion" (R20180103D). Hence, the pure fact that Gaddafi was a dictator is offset by his ability to halt immigration into Italy, which is opportunistically valued more than his moral qualities.

7.5 Conclusion

The analysis of the construction of the Other against which the Italian Self constituted itself casts light on the essential role played by colonial discourse in the Italian production of national and racial identity, as Chapters 5 and 6 have elaborated using a postcolonial theoretical framework. This lingering colonial rhetoric is underpinned by a selective memory of Italian colonialism, largely consigning colonial brutalities to oblivion. Such selective memory is two-pronged: it consists of the idealisation of the colonial past and the concurrent marginalisation of difficult elements of Italy's colonialism (Griffini 2022).

To succinctly sum up the main theoretical pillars of this chapter, it is useful to remind the reader of the definitions that have been adopted for this chapter's buzzwords. First, postcolonialism is understood here as an analytical framework aiming at uncovering and recovering the legacy of colonialism in today's political parties' discourse. Postcolonialism attempts to provide a critical analysis of an otherwise largely neglected topic, i.e., Italian colonial memory. Such neglect is due to the fact that the memory of Italian colonialism drifted out of public debates, education, and politics after Italy's abrupt loss of its colonies during the Second World War at the hands of the Allies. Despite brief and insignificant attempts at reviving Italian colonialism in the immediate aftermath of the Second World War, colonialism remained out of politics and society for long decades, only to be recovered by a thriving strand of postcolonial literature in the last few decades (Lombardi-Diop and Romeo 2012). Second, the concept of memory is central to this chapter, as it is a useful gauge of the kind of national and racial identity articulated by political parties, as well as a helpful indicator of the relationship between the colonial past and attitudes towards today's immigrants. The advantage of deploying the concept of memory is evident: memory is the backbone of the national and racial identity fabricated by political parties, and substantiated by a specific interpretation of the collective past (Cento Bull 2016). Given the mainly ethno-cultural hue of the Lega's and FdI's notion of the nation, interwoven with racism, it is unsurprising that these populist radical right parties create a national and racial identity that is solidly anchored in a sanitised memory of the Italian national past.

It is impossible to glean whether the Italian populist radical right consciously constructs a selective colonial memory, since this task would spill over into the discipline of Political Psychology. Notwithstanding the unsolved question about the intentionality or lack thereof of the crafting of selective colonial memory, it is plausible to conclude that the colonial past, in the Italian populist radical right's discourse, on the one hand materialises through the discursive construction of immigrants. On the other hand, the Italian colonial past undergoes a discursive dematerialisation in the Lega's and FdI's memory. The twin metaphors of materialisation and dematerialisation of the colonial past, instrumental to the advancement of racist anti-immigrant rhetoric drenched in colonial stereotypes, have been proposed in Griffini's (2022) article. This article has been substantially expanded theoretically and empirically in this chapter, which does not have the ambition to establish causal connections between a selective colonial memory and postcolonial racism. What this chapter has strived to obtain is the emphasis on the multiple ways in which the so-far underappreciated colonial memory selectively features in the Lega's and FdI's discourse on immigration.

The line of argument advanced here significantly develops the hitherto limited literature on the link between colonial memory and anti-immigrant sentiment. The core argument put forward in this chapter recalls, expands, and adds evidence for Siddi's (2020: 1035) brilliant thesis that "the new postcolonial encounter between Italian citizens and the disenfranchised ex-colonial subjects" has been influenced by a "selective [colonial] memory (…) [that] has fuelled feelings of cultural and racial superiority." The Lega and FdI selectively shape the memory of Italian colonial past, mainly expunging it from its most difficult aspects and casting light onto those considered as most positive. Even when the Lega and FdI acknowledge the existence of colonial brutalities, they deflect attention away from them and instead redirect blame onto other European colonial powers and onto the Italian left, which are accused of seemingly more serious crimes.

The fact that the Italian populist radical right parties do not fully acknowledge the controversial aspects of Italy's colonial past, which are bracketed off discourse, may contribute to the deployment of a colonial discourse by these same parties, evident in their construction of the image of the immigrant as Other, criminal, inferior, and dirty.

Notes

1 *Italiani brava gente* means literally *Italians good people*.
2 Literally, "no one's lands."
3 Meaning "former overseas territories."
4 For the full text of the 2017 Memorandum of Understanding, consult the following webpage: www.governo.it/sites/governo.it/files/Libia.pdf.
5 For the full text of the 2008 Treaty on Friendship, Partnership, and Cooperation, consult the following webpage: www.meltingpot.org/2008/10/diffuso-il-testo-dellaccordo-italia-libia/.

References

Albahari, M. (2017) "Beyond Europe, Borders Adrift", *Humanity*, vol. 8, no. 3, 523–525.

Allen, B. & Russo, M.J. (eds) (1997) *Revisioning Italy: National Identity and Global Culture*, Minneapolis: University of Minnesota Press.

Andall, J. & Duncan, D. (eds) (2005) *Italian Colonialism: Legacy and Memory*, Oxford, Bern: Peter Lang.

Ben-Ghiat, R. (2006) "Modernity is just over there: Colonialism and Italian national identity", *Interventions; International Journal of Postcolonial Studies*, vol. 8, no. 3, pp. 380–393.

Camilli, A. (2018) "Chi sono le persone bloccate a bordo della nave Diciotti", *Internazionale*. 24 August 2018. Available: https://www.internazionale.it/bloc-notes/annalisa-camilli/2018/08/24/diciotti-guardia-costiera-migranti [21 May 2019].

Casadio, G. (2006) "Fini rivaluta le colonie italiane. Guardate come stanno", *Repubblica*. 26 September 2006. Available: https://ricerca.repubblica.it/repubblica/archivio/repubblica/2006/09/26/fini-rivaluta-le-colonie-italiane-guardate-come.html [20 October 2015].

Ceccorulli, M. & Coticchia, F. (2020) "'I'll take two.' Migration, terrorism, and the Italian military engagement in Niger and Libya", *Journal of Modern Italian Studies*, vol. 25, no. 2, pp. 174–196.

Cento Bull, A. (2016) "The role of memory in populist discourse: The case of the Italian Second Republic", *Patterns of Prejudice*, vol. 50, no. 3, pp. 213–231.

Chambers, I. (2001) *Culture after Humanism: History, Culture, Subjectivity*, London: Routledge.

Chambers, I. (2008) *Mediterranean Crossings: The Politics of an Interrupted Modernity*, Durham, NC: Duke University Press.

Coralluzzo, V. (2008) "Italy and the Mediterranean: Relations with the Maghreb countries", *Modern Italy*, vol. 13, no. 2, pp. 115–133.

Couperus, S. & Tortola, P. D. (2019) "Right-wing populism's (ab)use of the past in Italy and the Netherlands. Debats", *Journal on Culture, Power and Society*, vol. 4, pp. 105–118.

De Cesari, C. (2012) "The paradoxes of colonial reparation: Foreclosing memory and the 2008 Italy–Libya Friendship Treaty", *Memory Studies*, vol. 5, no. 3, pp. 316–326.

De Cesari, C. & Kaya, A. (2020) *European Memory in Populism: Representations of Self and Other*, London: Routledge.

De Donno, F. & Srivastava, N. (2006) "Colonial and postcolonial Italy", *Interventions; International Journal of Postcolonial Studies*, vol. 8, no. 3, pp. 371–379.

De Michele, G. (2011) "'A beautiful moment of bravery and hard work': Italian colonialism in post-1945 history high school textbooks", *Modern Italy*, vol. 16, no. 2, pp. 105–120.

Del Boca, A. (1992) *L'Africa nella coscienza degli Italiani: Miti, memorie, errori, sconfitte*, Rome: Laterza.

Del Boca, A. (2003) "The myths, suppressions, denials, and defaults of Italian colonialism", in *A Place in the Sun: Africa in Italian Colonial Culture from Post-unification to the Present*, Palumbo, P. (ed.), Berkeley: University of California Press, pp. 17–36.

Del Boca, A. (2005) *Italiani, brava gente?: Un mito duro a morire*, Vicenza: N. Pozza.

Del Castillo, L. (2011) "Italian-Libyan relations", *Criminal Justice Matters*, vol. 85, no. 1, pp. 4–5.

Fogu, C. (2010) "From *Mare Nostrum* to *Mare Aliorum*: Mediterranean theory and Mediterraneism in contemporary Italian thought", *California Italian Studies*, vol. 1, no. 1, pp. 1–23.

Foot, J. (2009) *Italy's Divided Memory*, New York: Palgrave Macmillan.

Galeazzo, P. (1994) "La nuova immigrazione a Milano. Il caso dell'Eritrea", in *Tra due rive. La nuova immigrazione a Milano*, Barile, G., Dal Lago, A., Marchetti, A. & Galeazzo, P. (eds), Milan: Franco Angeli, pp. 367–412.

Galli della Loggia, E. (2003) *La Morte della patria*, Bari-Rome: Laterza.

Gilroy, P. (2005) *Postcolonial Melancholia*, New York: Columbia University Press.

Giuffré, M. (2013) "State responsibility beyond borders: What legal basis for Italy's pushbacks to Libya?", *International Journal of Refugee Law*, vol. 24, no. 4, pp. 692–734.

Griffini, M. (2022) "'How can you feel guilty for colonialism? it is a folly': Colonial memory in the Italian populist radical right", *European Politics and Society*. https://doi.org/10.1080/23745118.2022.2058753.

Halbwachs, M. (1992) *On Collective Memory*, ed. and trans. Lewis A. Coser, Chicago: University of Chicago Press.

Labanca, N. (2002) "Le passé colonial et le présent de l'immigration dans l'Italie contemporaine", *Migrations Société*, vol. 14, no. 81–2, pp. 97–106.

Labanca, N. (2003) "Studies and research on fascist colonialism, 1922–1935", in *A Place in the Sun: Africa in Italian Colonial Culture from Post-unification to the Present*, Palumbo, P. (ed.), Berkeley: University of California Press, pp. 37–61.

Labanca, N. (2005) "History and memory of Italian colonialism today", in *Italian Colonialism: Legacy and Memory*, Andall, J. & Duncan, D. (eds), Oxford, Bern: Peter Lang, pp. 29–46.

Laplanche, J. & Pontalis, J. (1988) *The Language of Psycho-analysis*, London: Karnac.

Leone, G. & Mastrovito, T. (2014) "Learning about our shameful past: A sociopsychological analysis of present-day historical narratives of Italian colonial wars", *International Journal of Conflict and Violence*, vol. 4, no. 1, pp. 11–27.

Leone, G. & Sarrica, M. (2014) "Making room for negative emotions about the national past: An explorative study of effects of parrhesia on Italian colonial crimes", *International Journal of Intercultural Relations*, vol. 43, pp. 126–138.

Lombardi-Diop, C. (2012) "Postracial/Postcolonial Italy", in *Postcolonial Italy: Challenging National Homogeneity*, Lombardi-Diop, C. & Romeo, C. (eds), New York: Palgrave Macmillan, pp. 175–190.

Lowenthal, D. (1985) *The Past is a Foreign Country*, New York: Cambridge University Press.

Mammone, A. (2006) "A daily revision of the past: Fascism, anti-fascism, and memory in contemporary Italy", *Modern Italy*, vol. 11, no. 2, pp. 211–226.

Memorandum of Understanding (2017) *Memorandum d'intesa sulla cooperazione nel campo dello sviluppo, del contrasto all'immigrazione illegale, al traffico di esseri umani, al contrabbando e sul rafforzamento della sicurezza delle frontiere tra lo Stato della Libia e la Repubblica Italiana*. Available: https://www.governo.it/sites/governo.it/files/Libia.pdf. [21 September 2022].

Mellino, M. (2012) *Cittadinanze postcoloniali: Appartenenze, razza e razzismo in Europa e in Italia*, Firenze: Carocci.

Ministero dell'Interno (2018) *Cruscotto statistico giornaliero*. Available: http://www.interno.gov.it/sites/default/files/cruscotto_statistico_giornaliero_12-11-2018.pdf [12 November 2018].

Ministero dell'Interno (2022) *Cruscotto statistico giornaliero*. Available: http://www.libertaciviliimmigrazione.dlci.interno.gov.it/sites/default/files/allegati/cruscotto_statistico_giornaliero_15-09-2022_1.pdf [30 September 2022].

Mols, F. & Jetten, J. (2014) "No guts, no glory: How framing the collective past paves the way for anti-immigrant sentiments", *International Journal of Intercultural Relations*, vol. 43, pp. 74–86.

Noussis, G. (2020) "Rethinking colonialism in France's post-Chirac era: From Sarkozy's 'anti-repentance' to Macron's 'crisis of acceptance'", *Modern Languages Open*, vol. 1, no. 30, pp. 1–13.

Oppenheimer, L. & Hakvoort, I. (2003) "Will the Germans ever be forgiven? Memories of the Second World War four generations later", in *The Role of Memory in Ethnic Conflict*, Cairns, E. & Roe, M.D. (eds), London: Palgrave, pp. 94–103.

Paoletti, E. (2011) "Power relations and international migration: The case of Italy and Libya", *Political Studies*, vol. 59, no. 2, pp. 269–289.

Pes, A. (2014) "Coloni senza colonie", in *Quel che resta dell'impero: La cultura coloniale degli italiani*, Deplano, V. & Pes, A. (eds), Milan: Mimesis, Milan, pp. 417–438.

Pinkus, K. (2003) "Empty spaces: Decolonization in Italy", in *A Place in the Sun: Africa in Italian Colonial Culture from Post-unification to the Present*, Palumbo, P. (ed.), Berkeley: University of California Press, pp. 299–320.

Ponzanesi, S. (2005) "Beyond the Black Venus: Colonial sexual politics and contemporary visual practices", in *Italian Colonialism: Legacy and Memory*, Andall, J. & Duncan, D. (eds), Oxford, Bern: Peter Lang, pp. 165–190.

Proglio, G. (2019) "The Mediterranean as a mirror and ghost of the colonial past: The role of cultural memory in the production of populist narratives in Italy", in *European Memory in Populism: Representations of Self and Other*, De Cesari, C. & Kaya, A. (eds), London: Routledge, pp. 112–128.

Randazzo, A. (2006) *Roma predona: Il colonialismo italiano in Africa, 1870–1943*, Milan: Kaos.

Reuters Redazione (2007) "Sarkozy tells Algeria: No apology for the past", *Reuters*. 10 July 2007. Available: https://uk.reuters.com/article/uk-algeria-france-apology-idUKL1063873720070710 [21 May 2018].

Sciubra, A. (2008) "Diffuso il testo dell'accordo Italia –Libia", *Melting Pot Europa*. 27 October 2008. Available: https://www.meltingpot.org/2008/10/diffuso-il-testo-dellaccordo-italia-libia/ [21 September 2022].

Siddi, M. (2020) "Silencing history: Forgetting Italy's past during the refugee crisis in Europe", *International Politics*, vol. 6, pp. 1030–1046.

Stella, G.A. 24 August (2018) "Eritrei in fuga dalla tortura Il ministro aveva promesso: Guanti bianchi per i profughi", *Corriere della Sera*. 24 August 2018. Available: https://www.corriere.it/digital-edition/CORRIEREFC_NAZIONALE_WEB/2018/08/24/6/eritrei-in-fuga-dalla-tortura-il-ministro-aveva-promesso-guanti-bianchi-per-i-profughi_U3020107164405CZF.shtml [21 November 2018].

Triulzi, A. (2005) "Adwa: From monument to document", in *Italian Colonialism: Legacy and Memory*, Andall, J. & Duncan, D. (eds), Oxford, Bern: Peter Lang, pp. 23–40.

Ungari, A. (2014) "I monarchici italiani e la questione coloniale", in *Quel che resta dell'impero: la cultura coloniale degli italiani*, Deplano, V. & Pes, A. (eds), Milan: Mimesis, pp. 393–416.

Van Dijk, T.A. (2008) "Critical discourse analysis", in *The Handbook of Discourse Analysis*, Schiffrin, D., Tannen, D. & Hamilton, H.E. (eds), New York: John Wiley & Sons, pp. 352–371.

Werbner, P. & Modood, T. (1997) *The Politics of Multiculturalism in the New Europe: Racism, Identity and Community*, London: Zed Books.

8 Memory and Forgetting

The Fascist Past in the Italian Populist Radical Right

8.1 Introduction

Colonialism prospered under fascism, and it is indeed under fascism that colonial racism became a constitutive element of Italian national and racial identity. The relationship between the Italian populist radical right and the memory of fascism is interesting to investigate. It is clear that the Italian populist radical right retains an ambivalent relationship to fascism, which was sketched in Chapters 1 and 2, and which will be explored more in depth in this chapter. In fact, the parties at stake recognise the negative aspects of fascism, yet they do not utterly condemn it, tending to exalt its most positive elements. While it would be hasty to conclude that this ambiguous stance on fascism, in turn, generates anti-immigrant racism, it is safe to claim that such ambiguity hinders a critical appraisal of Italy's fascist past by the Italian populist radical right, thus further contributing to the creation of a selective fascist and colonial memory (as fascism represented the most successful period in Italian colonialism).

Moreover, several scholars have studied the vestiges of fascism in the Italian populist radical right, although the interview methods have not been deployed yet for this purpose (see, for instance, Mammone 2018; Manucci 2020; Traverso 2017). Caramani and Manucci (2019), and Manucci (2020) produced a groundbreaking comparative analysis of eight Western European countries to test the connection between the kind of re-elaboration of fascist past and populist radical right success. In the case of Italy, they argue that the country has forged a victimised memory of fascism, where victimisation means that "The country fabricates victimhood of 'external' fascist regimes and denies responsibility" (Caramani and Manucci 2019: 1164). However, this chapter does not hold the ambition of bringing a substantial innovation to the literature on the relationship between the kind of fascist memory nurtured, the acceptability of fascism in contemporary domestic politics, and the success of the contemporary radical right, as Manucci extensively and acutely documents in his book (2020), and as Caramani and Manucci focus on in their article (2019). Instead, this chapter aims at deepening and broadening the analysis of the relationship between colonial memory and contemporary nativism in the Italian populist radical right. Therefore, this chapter should not distract from the main focus of the book, but should be intended as an essential

DOI: 10.4324/9781003252597-9

supplementary analysis to the detailed examination of colonial memory carried out in Chapter 7.

8.2 Fascist Residues in the Italian Right?

Fascist residues in Italian politics came into the limelight during the 2018 electoral campaign, when Attilio Fontana (a Lega representative and the President of the region of Lombardy) claimed to *Radio Padania* that we have to protect the white race from ethnic substitution (Cremonesi 2018). A year earlier, Berlusconi declared that Mussolini was not really a dictator (Stefanoni 2017). Whether these affirmations reflect the true beliefs of their speakers or mirror a mere electoral strategy represents a fertile soil for future research. If they did represent the genuine opinions of Fontana and Berlusconi, then they would signal a marked fascist legacy influencing not only the populist radical right, but also the centre-right. On the other hand, if these statements were just an electoral strategy to attract hardliners, they would demonstrate that both the Lega and FI are willing to compromise the support of their more moderate electorate in order to lure more radical elements. We would, then, witness a radicalisation of the centre-right and a further radicalisation of the populist radical right. What is safe to assume is that these claims, along with Salvini's and Meloni's reaction to the killing of an immigrant by a neo-fascist in Macerata, unveil the populist radical right's ambivalence towards fascism: while these parties cannot be considered fascist in their totality, they may include some leftover fascist elements, showing that they have not yet severed their umbilical cord with fascism, as Traverso argues (2017).

The fascist residues in FdI are not surprising, as the latter is the heir to the MSI, the first and only post-fascist party in the post-Second World War era. The recent case of the *Lobby nera*[1] is an emblematic example of these fascist residues. The *Lobby nera* is an investigative report published at the end of 2021 by the online newspaper *Fanpage* about the FdI member and Member of the European Parliament, Carlo Fidanza, accused of negotiating illegal financing for the electoral campaign of FdI in Milan, and of performing the Roman salute (Cangemi 2022). According to Albertazzi, FdI now seems the natural choice for those people who nurture neo-fascist sympathies, which they encounter in a party well established in the political arena (2022). However, fascist residues also lie in the Lega, which emerged as a regionalist party, opposed to a centralised state, a key feature of fascism (Campani and Lazaridis 2017). Hence, the fascist legacy inherent in the current Lega further bears witness to the shift that the party underwent from a regionalist party advocating the independence of the imagined community of *Padania,* to a nationalist party appealing to both north and south of the Italian peninsula. This shows that the fascist legacy can be inherited not only by the Italian populist radical right, such as FdI as heir to the MSI. Fascist traits can also arise during the evolution of parties, such as the Lega. Moreover, this proves the populist radical right's dynamism, which varies according to different contexts: as federalist demands proved unfeasible and immigration was increasing, the Lega thought it would be advantageous to give immigration greater prominence in its agenda, while dropping, to a large extent, its regionalist stance.

Despite the presence of these opportunity structures, legal constraints have posed an obstacle to the Italian populist radical right, which has nevertheless been able to overcome them. Given the ardent condemnation of fascism by the newly-born Italian Republic, the 1952 Scelba Law banned the "reorganisation of any form of the dissolved fascist party" (Article 1) and instituted the crime of apology of fascism (Article 4) (Caiani, Della Porta, and Wagemann 2012: 37), encompassing the instigation and reiteration of fascist regimes, thus resulting in the criminalisation and ostracisation of neo-fascist parties. Indeed, for all its lifespan the MSI oscillated between accentuating its fascist legacy and de-emphasising it, in the attempt to overcome its isolation as a political pariah (Newell 2000: 270–271). The 1993 Mancino Law introduced punishment for any discrimination in terms of ethnicity, religion, and race (Caiani, Della Porta, and Wagemann 2012: 37). Nevertheless, the populist radical right has often by-passed these legal constraints, FdI remains determinedly ambiguous about its fascist legacy, and, generally, the Italian populist radical right is not immune to racism.

Racism, as illustrated from a theoretical perspective in Chapter 2 and from an empirical viewpoint in Chapters 5 and 6, often conjures up colonial fascist representations of the colonised Other. The connection made by the Italian populist radical right between immigrants and disease is suggestive of the fascist colonial belief in the biological difference between the healthy Italian Self and the sick colonised Other. The spiritual strand of fascist racism advocated by Evola,[2] who had an influence on the French movement Nouvelle Droite and, in turn, on the Italian populist radical right (as explained in Chapter 5), comes through in the Italian populist radical right's focus on the distinction between different cultures, which is apparent in particular in the category of inferiorisation of immigration (Meotti 2017). Notwithstanding the sporadic presence of fascist residues in the populist radical right, it is necessary to note that the Italian populist radical right's racism revealed by the interviews is by far distant from the fascist biological and spiritual racism, because it avoids references to biological differences and does not believe in the division between the body, the soul, and the spirit.

8.3 Selective Fascist Memory: What Causes Discomfort and What Is Forgotten

Selective memory in the Italian populist radical right is not limited to colonialism but also extends to fascism: indeed, fascism represented the acme of Italian colonialism in terms of extension and magnitude of racism towards the colonised Other. The Lega and FdI appear restless and resentful when they hear talk about fascism in conjunction with colonialism and immigration. An FdI representative's bitter criticism that "it makes no sense to talk about immigration and fascism in the same interview" (C20180109G) is a case in point. Such resentment, in the interviews, is rooted in the belief that Italy should have the courage to consign fascism to history (F20170408T), which does not amount to a critical appraisal of fascism, but to the forgetting of its most negative aspects. Therefore, predictably, the proposal[3] drafted by Emanuele Fiano, a PD Member of Parliament (Skytg24 2018), for a law that would punish with jail sentences those distributing fascist propaganda, especially on the internet, and fascist memorabilia, found staunch opposition by the Italian populist radical right. In the words of an FdI representative, "The Fiano law proposal is crazy, this country has to face its past in a positive sense, even if there have been some negative elements" (F20180104F). Also, the Lega, in its interviews, expresses its scepticism over the Fiano law proposal, as it believes that "it is senseless to erase the traces of the past. (…) How can we file a legal case against a 70-year-old person that has a lighter representing Mussolini?" (G20180105M).

Therefore, the Italian populist radical right's aversion to the Fiano law proposal is undergirded by a selective memory of fascism, obliterating its most negative aspects, which also underlies these parties' hostility towards the Scelba (1952) and Mancino (1993) Laws, respectively forbidding the revival of fascist organisations, and racist and neo-fascist violence and discrimination. Against the backdrop of the spike in racist violence in Italy in summer 2018, in August 2018 the Lega Minister for the Family Lorenzo Fontana suggested abolishing the Mancino Law, echoing the Lega's 2014 proposal of a referendum on its abolition (Repubblica 2018). Fontana's suggestion was grounded in the belief that the Mancino Law buttresses anti-Italian racism, and found support in the Lega's leader Salvini, who, in 2014, campaigned for the Mancino Law's abolition (Repubblica 2018). Therefore, it is clear that the Lega does not interpret the objective rise in racist violence as a worrying return of neo-fascist ideas, thus demonstrating that it has selectively forgotten fascist wrongdoings. While the Scelba and Mancino Laws have not been repealed yet, the Fiano law proposal stalled in the Senate after being approved by the Chamber of Deputies, and is still lying dormant there, since the Lega took power in March 2018 in a coalition government with the M5S. In January 2022 Fiano submitted again a more thorough proposal, including further details,[4] to the Chamber of Deputies, but the proposal has not been approved yet.

In fact, as the interviews suggest, the Italian populist radical right does largely ignore fascist brutalities, including not only massacres, but also the suppression of liberties and the virulent racism against the Other. The latter included the colonised, but also the Jews, homosexuals, Slavs, and the Roma, to name but a few. Similar to the Italian populist radical right's behaviour concerning the memory of colonial crimes, the Lega and FdI tend to relegate most of the negative aspects of fascist memory to oblivion and highlight its positive aspects.

8.4 Selective Fascist Memory: What Is Celebrated and What Is Remembered

The restlessness encountered when dealing with negative aspects of the fascist past leaves room to pride in fascist achievements. An FdI representative firmly claimed that "honestly, fascism remains unparalleled for its achievements, social justice, honesty, national pride, and social prestige" (G20180109C). This view is widely shared among the Italian populist radical right, which emphasises the positive aspects of fascism, such as the spirit of national cohesion (C20180109G, F20170111S, L20180105S, S20180103B), land reclamation programmes (see, for instance, C20170106V, F20180104F, F20170111S, L20180105S), social justice (C20180109G), architectural design (F20170111S, F20180104F, G20170111R, L20170410P, R20180104M), rationalism and the concept of modernity (G20170111R), maternity benefits (F20170111S, G20170111R), pensions (F20170111S, M201701113R), benefits for the sick (G20170111R, P20161219B), and child education (G201701112G, G20170111R).

Curiously, when prompted to comment on the fascist belief that the colonised were inferior to Italians, one Lega representative shifted the focus onto Mussolini's protection of Muslims, by specifying that "Mussolini was the first to brandish the sword of Islam. He wanted Italians to believe that [the colonised] were inferior, but he knew they were not" (M20170104G), as Mussolini was the first leader to symbolically declare himself as the protector of Islam, in Tripoli in 1937, to express his sympathy towards colonised Muslims (Wright 2005). Similarly, the same Lega representative, contrary to the long-established scholarly view of fascism as relentlessly championing the superiority of Italian national and racial identity over the alleged inferiority of Africans, applauded fascism as the epitome of multiculturalism: "*Faccetta nera* [a fascist racist song demeaning the African colonised] was a song expressing unmatched appreciation for multiculturalism, as it promised to bring colonised Africans to Rome and grant them rights" (M20170104G).

The positive appraisal of fascism by the Italian populist radical right is also clear when party representatives were prompted to comment on Mussolini's preoccupation that "the entire white race would be submerged by races of colour" (cited in Ben-Ghiat 2006: 384). In fact, in the interviews, the Lega and FdI tend to consider Mussolini far-sighted and Mussolini's statement as founded, since they interpret it in the light of the conflict of civilisations brought about by immigration (see, for instance, C20170106V, F20170110F, G20170112G, G20170111R). As a Lega representative noticed, "demographic data prove that Mussolini was right: in Europe the child/woman ratio is 2:1, in Africa it is 3:1" (G20170112G), which recalls the demographic threat posed by immigration that emerged in the criminalising discourse of the Italian populist radical right described in Chapter 6. Mussolini's statement leads Lega representatives to make a connection with the so-called Kalergi plan (F20170104M, M20170104G), i.e., the conspiracy theory dear to the Italian populist radical right, believing that immigration is a scheme devised by elites in order to allow different races to mix, thus making them easier to control (Il Post 2018). However, it is important to note that, in the interviews, Italian populist radical right representatives clearly specified that they do not like talking about race (see, for instance, C20170106V, L20170104N, N20180108C, P2170404L, S2018010F), and that within the Italian populist radical right there are some representatives rejecting Mussolini's claim, while expressing doubt about the fact that the "black races would prevail over the white race" (see, for instance, F2060905L, G20170109D, L20170410P, L20180105S).

Although a basically positive assessment of fascism materialises in the discourse of the Italian populist radical right in the interviews, the Lega and FdI are not completely oblivious to the negative traits of fascism. In the words of an FdI representative, "fascism was a dictatorship, abolished democracy, committed cruelties, and introduced racial laws" (M20180105M). In fact, the Italian populist radical right does firmly condemn some negative aspects of fascism, such as the racial laws (see, for instance, C20180109G, C20170106V, F20170111S, M20180105M), the engagement in the Second World War (C20180109G, F20160905L, P20161219B), the limitations on freedom (C20180109G, M2017004F, P20170404L), and the rapprochement with Hitler (C20170106V, C20180109G, F20160905L). Criticism of fascist colonial policies emerges when, if prompted to comment on the fascist colonial policy to separate colonised children from Italian children in schools (Rodogno 2006), the Italian populist radical right unforgivingly declared that this measure did not make any sense (G20170112G). Furthermore, Lega representatives from south Tyrol expressed resentment at Mussolini's treatment of their own region (C20170106V), which was indeed forcefully Italianised. The goal of Italianisation aimed at obliterating the identity of the German-speaking ethnicity residing there. The protection of local identity against forceful Italianisation resonates with the Lega's origin as a regionalist party, geared towards the defence of the identity of *Padania* against the allegedly rapacious Roman central governance (see, for instance, Passarelli 2013).

With regards to the negative elements of fascism pointed out by the Italian populist radical right, it is essential to note that conflating the degeneration of fascism with Mussolini's rapprochement with Hitler risks discounting the scale of fascist cruelty, by transferring blame from the fascist to the Nazi leader. Similarly, in the interviews, while recognising the brutality of fascism, an FdI representative underlined that "for sure fascism was not a dictatorship as brutal as the Stalinist or the Nazi one, or even the modern dictatorship of Kim Jong-un" (E20170404C). The emphasis on the cruelty of communism is widespread within FdI and the Lega (see, for instance, E20170404C, L20170104N, P2161219B, S20180103F), in order to emphasise the fact that fascism was not the only dictatorship in Europe, thus defusing criticism of it. Therefore, redirecting blame from fascism onto Nazism or communism is a frequent discursive strategy observed in the Italian populist radical right: through blame reversal, the populist radical right redeems fascism and makes other totalitarian regimes look worse in comparison.

8.5 Of Mixed Assessments of Fascism

The tendency to emphasise the positive undertakings of fascism, mixed with the denunciation of the negative aspects of the fascist regime, often discounted in light of reportedly worse communist and Nazi crimes, leads to mixed results when the Italian populist radical right is asked to assess fascism. The task proposed was

132 *Memory and Forgetting*

to give a mark to fascism ranging from one, corresponding to "the best system at that time," to five, corresponding to "a brutal dictatorship."[5] While some Italian populist radical right representatives preferred not to give a mark, but to offer rich evaluations of fascism, the rest gave a wide variety of marks, roughly equally distributed in the range from two to four. Therefore, the Lega, FdI, and populist radical right intellectuals tend to avoid the extremes one and five, apart from one Lega representative, who claimed that fascism started as the best system conceivable at that time and ended as a brutal dictatorship (F20160905L). Interestingly, an FdI representative candidly admitted that if posed this question during a party assembly, his party fellows would all give one to fascism, corresponding to "the best system conceivable at that time" (S2080103F). Therefore, when analysing the scores emerged from the interviews, it is necessary to keep in mind the moderating impact the interview context may have on the interviewees, who may feel cautious about voicing extreme opinions. Hence, it is difficult to confidently conclude whether the Italian populist radical right has yet cut its ties with fascism or not.

8.6 Reasons for Selective Memory

This section will suggest possible reasons behind the selective memory of colonialism and fascism. While analysing interviews about colonial memory in Chapter 7, possible justifications for selective memory were proposed. Given the similarity between the explanations for selective memory of colonialism and selective memory of fascism, this section will offer a comprehensive and succinct examination of reasons for selective memory applying both to the colonial and the fascist past.

The interviews with the Italian populist radical right reveal different motivations underpinning the way the Lega and FdI shape their memory of colonialism and fascism. In the interviews, the Italian inferiority complex of being Europe's internal Other is reflected not only in the criticism of short-lived and unsuccessful colonialism that has been discussed earlier, but also in the implicit emphasis on the fact that Italy retreated from its colonies dramatically, since fascism had lost the Second World War; this is unlike France and the UK, who emerged from the war as victorious. This bitterness about the abrupt end of the Italian fascist and colonial experience recalls Caramani and Manucci's (2019) and Manucci's (2020) argument about the victimisation affecting Italy's memory of its fascist past, where Italy portrayed itself as a victim of European major powers, and, in doing so, it detached itself from any feeling of culpability and guilt over fascism. Moreover, in the interviews, the Italian populist radical right claims that colonialism is associated with fascism (R20180104M, S20180103F), thus "destined to *damnatio memoriae*" (S20180103F), i.e., condemned in its memory, hence forgotten. This view clearly transpires from the words of a Lega representative, who, interestingly, concurrently demonstrates interest towards the colonial past, thus deviating from the colonial indifference examined in Chapter 7: "Colonialism is little studied and should be object of school curricula (…) It is linked to a dark page of Italian history, because it happened during fascism" (E20210506P). These opinions resonate with Pinkus's argument that Italian colonialism was uncritically demonised as a fascist enterprise, thus "bracketed off from the national psyche as an anomaly" and "exorcised" (2003: 300; 302). As a result, colonialism and fascism are considered as a painful parenthesis in Italian history and selectively forgotten.

Yet, the self-redemptory myth of *Italiani brava gente* seems the most plausible reason why the Italian populist radical right's selective forgetting has invested Italy's colonial and fascist history. Indeed, as mentioned above, when tackling the Italian populist radical right's belief in the difference between Italian colonisers and other more cruel European colonial powers, in their interviews the Lega, FdI, and populist radical right intellectuals express their firm conviction that Italian colonisers were good people, bringing roads, schools, and houses to the colonies (A20180103DC), along with food and sympathy (M20170104G), and never engaging in exploitation (E20170404C, G20170407P, G20180105M, R20180108D). Moreover, an FdI representative proudly added that "Italian colonisers are remembered fondly in former colonies" (F20170111S), thanks to the above-cited good deeds that they bestowed upon the Italian *Oltremare*; another FdI representative claimed that "Italians are still welcome in their former colonies" (F20170408T). In the interviews, the myth of *Italiani brava gente* seems rooted in Catholicism, a religion allegedly spreading love and making Italian colonisers more lenient. This myth was crafted to portray Italian soldiers as chivalric and polite, and civilians as tolerant and pleasant (Del Boca 1992: 113). As Del Boca points out, the Italians' emphasis on the myth of *Italiani brava gente* finds its roots in fascist propaganda, mystifying Italian colonialism under fascism, and in the nostalgic personal convictions of Italians who experienced the colonial adventure as a "beautiful, long holiday" (1992: x). Therefore, selective colonial forgetting is deeply seated in the Italians' biased self-representation as fair, benign, and courteous, which results in the erasure of colonial and fascist violence.

A cause of fascist selective memory is rooted in the lack of a thorough appraisal of fascism in the post-war period. After the fall of fascism in July 1943, Italy embarked on a process of "defascistisation," including the removal of fascist monuments, buildings, murals, and symbols such as the *fasci*, and the change of fascist topographical names, to erase the memory of fascism (Foot 2009: 66). In post-war Italy, the left prioritised the memory of the Resistance and was critical of fascism, but the violence of fascism was not emphasised, in order to minimise the civil war aspects of the Resistance, which involved a struggle between Italians (Foot 2009: 64). The right removed fascist violence and buried it in the name of the civil war (Traverso 2017). When in the early 1990s, what Foot calls the "neo-fascist right," namely AN, entered mainstream politics, it imposed its own fascist memories, by triggering debates over fascist street names, buildings, and symbols (2009: 70). In the scholarly debate, the recent revisionist rehabilitation of fascism has countered the trend of extolling the Resistance while denouncing fascism. Nevertheless, revisionism has avoided a critical examination of fascist violence, which is still consigned to a "collective amnesia" (Mammone 2006: 213). The

134 *Memory and Forgetting*

forgetting of the fascist past is related to the mourning of it (or lack thereof). Historian Nicola Tranfaglia's book eloquently titled *An Uncomfortable Past* mentions the bereavement engendered by the end of Mussolini's dictatorship, coupled with the bereavement caused by the loss of the colonies (1996: 33). Bereavement expressed itself through melancholia. According to Tranfaglia's argument, Italy was so destabilised because of the end of fascism and Italian national pride was so shattered, that the memory of fascism was even erased (1996: 90).

The forgetting of fascism is also evident in education, which is managed by the state and, therefore, embodies the messages the latter intends to deliver to younger generations. Indeed, textbooks and school curricula are representative of the way the state intends to mould students' opinions and, consequently, public opinion (Labanca 2003: 10), since textbooks become a medium to propagate national narratives (Procacci 2003) and ideological values (Jacob 1988). The Italian educational system did not help the process of recovery of fascist memory, as secondary schools have not accurately transmitted the history of the twentieth century to the youth, who may be misled by simplistic mystifications of historical events represented in the newspapers and on TV (Tranfaglia 1996: 104).

8.7 The Politics of Memory: Bringing Together the Strands of the Argument

To sum up the core arguments constructed in Chapters 7 and 8, in the interviews with the Italian populist radical right, the *damnatio memoriae* (Pinkus 2003), the perception of being Europe's internal Other (Allen and Russo 1997), and the narrative of *Italiani brava gente* (Del Boca 2005) affect both the memory of Italian colonialism and the memory of Italian fascism. Their most unsettling events undergo selective forgetting. Indeed, colonialism is *tout court* associated with fascism, which boosted and expanded the colonial enterprise through a racist ideology. Hence, since they were linked to fascism, colonial crimes also drifted out of the national psyche (Pinkus 2003), leaving an eloquent silence in education and political debate. This silence was exacerbated by the fact that Italy saw itself as unjustly inferior to the European Great Powers (Allen and Russo 1997), which unfairly dismissed fascism and deprived Italy of its colonies after the Second World War. Moreover, the fable of *Italiani brava gente* (Del Boca 2005) portraying Italians as incapable of wrongdoings similarly affects both colonial and fascist memory through the selective forgetting of atrocities.

The populist radical right never mentions or implicitly expresses melancholia for fascism: this is undisputable. On the contrary, while the Italian populist radical right does not nurture an explicit postcolonial melancholic longing for the return of colonialism, chiefly viewed as short-lived and unsuccessful, the colonial and the fascist past are selectively celebrated. This selective memory determined by selective colonial forgetting is evident in the Italian populist radical right's general emphasis on the positive aspects of colonialism and fascism, which allegedly brought infrastructure, civilisation, modernity, and rational architecture to the colonies. In fact, in the interviews, the Italian colonial and fascist crimes that did undeniably occur are largely downplayed in comparison with the seemingly more brutal crimes committed by major European powers and with the allegedly more gruelling Nazi and communist totalitarian regimes. In such a way, the Italian populist radical right depicts Mussolini's colonial enterprise as purely symptomatic of the age of the scramble for colonies, thus exonerating fascist Italy from its responsibility for colonial wrongdoings.

Selective colonial memory distorted by the forgetting of uncomfortable events becomes clear when the Italian populist radical right predominantly rejects the necessity to apologise to Italy's former colonies for colonial crimes, thus being oblivious to them; or clarifies that Italy should apologise to its former colonies only if it has committed crimes, thus being vague about whether they happened or not. Additionally, while a few Italian populist radical right representatives acknowledged the moral responsibility to aid former Italian colonies, selective colonial forgetting is manifest when the Italian populist radical right largely sanctions the diplomatic indifference Italy displayed towards its former colonies when they were swept through by wars and dictatorships. In such a way, these parties reject any moral responsibility towards the formerly exploited and mistreated overseas territories. This is symptomatic of the politics of memory in which the populist radical right engages: colonial and fascist memory become politicised and used for the political goal of constructing a sanitised and cohesive national memory of the colonial and fascist past. The politics of memory emerges undoubtedly in the service of the political goal of pursuing Italy's strategic interests, even the weaving of diplomatic relationships with dictators, while retreating from the diplomatic sphere when former colonies were most in need of help. Another revealing example of the politics of memory permeating the populist radical right is the Friendship Treaty signed by Berlusconi and Gaddafi in 2008, which was conceived as purely strategic, unconnected to any moral obligation to apologise to Libya for colonial brutality, and merely targeted at stopping migration inflows from Libya into Italy.

These memories of colonialism and fascism, purified from uncomfortable events result in the selective forgetting of colonial and fascist past atrocities, with significant political consequences. Indeed, the Italian populist radical right's selective forgetting of fascism and colonialism, following Andall and Duncan's (2005), Labanca's (2002), Chambers's (2008), De Cesari's (2012), Galeazzo's (1994), and Ponzanesi's (2005) arguments on the link between attitudes towards colonial memory and attitudes towards immigration in wider Italian society, affects the heirs of the colonised, i.e., the immigrants. They are not welcome and become the victims of colonial rhetoric, racism, and even human rights violations. This behaviour evidently emerges in the interviews with the Italian populist radical right analysed in Chapters 5 and 6, and in the Lega-M5S government, which, under Salvini's vice-premiership, forbade immigrants from disembarking into Italy, thus keeping them at sea and infringing their right to claim asylum. Salvini's restrictive immigration strategy, therefore, shows that the Italian populist radical right is not prepared to encounter the immigrant Other, onto which it expresses deep-seated racism drenched in colonial rhetoric, and against which it violates

136 *Memory and Forgetting*

basic human rights. Hence, the politics of memory, rooted in selective memory, has obvious ramifications on today's Other: the immigrant.

Therefore, the Mediterranean in the Italian populist radical right's imaginary has ceased to be a desirable space for colonial expansion, the fascist *Mare Nostrum*, and has been replaced by the view of the Mediterranean as what I define as a "Mare Vostrum." The latter is a threatening space, a source of immigration, and a space across which colonial violence did occur, but the responsibility for it is denied by the Italian populist radical right, as this party family provides a memory of colonialism and fascism that does not recognise the destructive impact of colonialism, downplays the negative aspects of colonialism and fascism, and precludes the possibility of offering apologies to former colonies or taking moral responsibility for their suffering after the demise of Italian colonialism. Nevertheless, this shift in the perception of the Mediterranean from a treasured *Mare Nostrum* to what I identify as a distant "Mare Vostrum" is not purely confined to the Italian populist radical right.

Lastly, it is important to remember that the Italian populist radical right's selective forgetting of colonialism and fascism is not exclusive to this party family, as it is also reflected in Italian politics and society at large. However, this commonality does not undermine the originality and significance of the investigation of the relationship between the Italian populist radical right's racism and colonial and fascist memory. First, the studies exploring colonial fascist memory in Italian society and politics do not deal precisely with the Italian populist radical right. Second, the presence of a selective memory of colonialism and fascism in Italian politics and society does not preclude the fact that this memory can also be traced among Italian populist radical right parties. In fact, also nativism, formed by racism and ethno-cultural nationalism, as elucidated in Chapter 2, goes beyond the confines of the Italian populist radical right.

Therefore, this project argues that the Italian populist radical right displays both a selective memory of Italian colonialism and fascism, and racism. Indeed, it seems that the Italian populist radical right's positions on colonial and fascist memory and racism reflect wider Italian society's selective colonial and fascist memory, and anti-immigrant racism. In fact, the Italian populist radical right may engage in the politics of memory, in order to capitalise on an underlying sentiment widely shared among the Italian population, in order to improve its electoral gains. In the case of racism, the Italian populist right makes the issue particularly salient, to electorally profit from it, while in the case of selective colonial and fascist memory, it may simply mirror the views of significant sections of wider society to appeal to a larger electorate.

8.8 Conclusion

In August of 2018, amidst the political turmoil surrounding Salvini's ban on immigrant ships docking in Italian ports, Giuliana De Medici, the daughter of Giorgio Almirante (the defunct MSI leader), praised Salvini's enthusiasm and courage, claiming he reminded her of her late father (Romano 2018). It is inaccurate to define the current Italian populist radical right as completely neo-fascist, because it does formally eschew violence and fascist symbolism, despite not yet having broken the umbilical cord with the fascist matrix (Traverso 2017). Yet, the mere fact that the daughter of a clearly neo-fascist party leader traces a resemblance between her father and Salvini provides an interesting hint prompting reflection on the Italian populist radical right's ambiguous stance on fascism and its implications for the Italian populist radical right's anti-immigrant racism.

In fact, despite being shrouded under a mantle of civic values, the Italian populist radical right's racism contains echoes of colonial rhetoric, and colonial racism is intertwined with fascism. Additionally, the Italian populist radical right is largely oblivious to fascist and colonial brutalities. Regarding fascist memory, which is the focus of this chapter, on the one hand, according to the interviews, a sizeable portion of the Italian populist radical right does condemn fascist brutalities such as the racial laws, the lack of freedom, the involvement in the Second World War, and the rapprochement with Hitler. Nevertheless, the criticism of fascism is often mitigated by the claim, widespread in the Italian populist radical right, that fascism was far less brutal compared to other contemporary totalitarian regimes, such as communism and Nazism. On the other hand, a part of the Italian populist radical right offers a positive appraisal of fascism, clearly grounded in a kind of memory that is not mindful of fascist wrongdoings. Indeed, the praise for national cohesion, fascist architecture, rationality and modernity, land reclamation works, social security, and child education tends to obscure fascist brutalities.

The willingness to consign fascist brutalities to oblivion is evident in the Italian populist radical right's resentment at hearing questions on fascism in the interviews and in their staunch opposition to the existing laws and proposed legal measures punishing racial discrimination, fascist propaganda, and fascist organisations. It is a case in point that the Lega Minister for the Family Fontana proposed to repeal the Scelba and Mancino Laws, which, along with the Fiano law proposal, aroused bitter feelings in the Italian populist radical right interviewees. Selective fascist forgetting also affects Italian society and politics beyond the populist radical right: the memory of fascist crimes was suppressed, and the narrative of the Resistance predominated, by downplaying the civil war elements of it, including fascist crimes (Foot 2009).

The feeling of being Europe's internal Other (Allen and Russo 1997), the *damnatio memoriae* of fascism (Pinkus 2003) and the myth of *Italiani brava gente* (Del Boca 1992) occasionally resurface in the discourse of the Italian populist radical right, as revealed by the interviews. The Italian populist radical right's memory of fascism is deeply affected by the selective forgetting of uncomfortable events, and is predicated on the *damnatio memoriae* that fascism is condemned to, whereby fascist painful memories are denounced and deleted from the Italian national psyche; and on Italy's feeling of being Europe's internal Other, stripped of its colonies by the iniquitous post-war settlement. Another reason explaining why portions of fascist memory are swept away on the Italian populist radical right is to be found in the self-absolving myth of *Italiani brava gente*, developed

138 *Memory and Forgetting*

by Del Boca (2005) but not applied by the author to the Italian populist radical right.

Notes

1 Literally, "Black lobby."
2 For a thorough analysis of Evola's thought, see Ferraresi (1987).
3 For the full text of the 2017 Fiano law proposal, consult the following webpage: www.senato.it/service/PDF/PDFServer/BGT/01043956.pdf.
4 For the full text of the 2022 Fiano law proposal, consult the following webpage: http://documenti.camera.it/leg18/pdl/pdf/leg.18.pdl.camera.3443.18PDL0176210.pdf.
5 Ignazi himself posed the same question to representatives participating at a congress of AN (2005).

References

Albertazzi, D. (2022) "Daniele Albertazzi on the radical and extreme right in Italy and Switzerland", *Illiberalism*. Available: https://www.illiberalism.org/daniele-albertazzi-on-the-radical-and-extreme-right-in-italy-and-switzerland/ [12 January 2022].
Allen, B. & Russo, M.J. (eds) (1997) *Revisioning Italy: National Identity and Global Culture*, Minneapolis: University of Minnesota Press.
Andall, J. & Duncan, D. (eds) (2005) *Italian Colonialism: Legacy and Memory*, Oxford, Bern: Peter Lang.
Ben-Ghiat, R. (2006) "Modernity is just over there: Colonialism and Italian national identity", *Interventions; International Journal of Postcolonial Studies*, vol. 8, no. 3, pp. 380–393.
Caiani, M., Della Porta, D. & Wagemann, C. (2012) *Mobilizing on the Extreme Right Germany, Italy, and the United States*, Oxford: Oxford University Press.
Campani, G. & Lazaridis G. (eds), (2017) *Understanding the Populist Shift: Othering in a Europe in Crisis*, New York: Routledge.
Cangemi, A. (2022) "Lobby nera, dopo l'inchiesta di Fanpage.it indagati anche Ciocca, Bastoni e Valcepina", *Fanpage*. 21 June 2022. Available: https://www.fanpage.it/politica/lobby-nera-dopo-linchiesta-di-fanpage-it-indagato-anche-ciocca-bastoni-e-valcepina/ [22 August 2022].
Caramani, D. & Manucci, L. (2019) "National past and populism: The reelaboration of fascism and its impact on right-wing populism in Western Europe", *West European Politics*, vol. 42, no. 6, pp. 1159–1187.
Chambers, I. (2008) *Mediterranean Crossings: The Politics of an Interrupted Modernity*, Durham, NC: Duke University Press.
Cremonesi, M. (2018) "'La razza bianca rischia di scomparire' Fontana sotto accusa per la frase choc", *Corriere della Sera*. 15 January 2018. Available: https://www.corriere.it/politica/18_gennaio_16/elezioni-2018-attilio-fontana-lega-lombardia-razza-bianca-rischia-sparire-06f0ced2-fa33-11e7-b7a0-515b75eef21a_preview.shtml?reason=unauthenticated&cat=1&cid=id06TH2_&pids=FR&origin=http%3A%2F%2Fwww.corriere.it%2Fpolitica%2F18_gennaio_16%2Felezioni-2018-attilio-fontana-lega-lombardia-razza-bianca-rischia-sparire-06f0ced2-fa33-11e7-b7a0-515b75eef21a.shtml [21 May 2018].
De Cesari, C. (2012) "The paradoxes of colonial reparation: Foreclosing memory and the 2008 Italy–Libya Friendship Treaty", *Memory Studies*, vol. 5, no. 3, pp. 316–326.

Del Boca, A. (1992) *L'Africa nella coscienza degli Italiani: Miti, memorie, errori, sconfitte*, Rome: Laterza.
Del Boca, A. (2005) *Italiani, brava gente?: Un mito duro a morire*, Vicenza: N. Pozza.
Ferraresi, F. (1987) "Julius Evola: Tradition, reaction, and the radical right", *European Journal of Sociology*, vol. 28, no. 1, pp. 107–151.
Foot, J. (2009) *Italy's Divided Memory*, New York: Palgrave Macmillan.
Galeazzo, P. (1994) "La nuova immigrazione a Milano. Il caso dell'Eritrea", in *Tra due rive. La nuova immigrazione a Milano*, Barile, G., Dal Lago, A., Marchetti, A. & Galeazzo, P. (eds), Milan: Franco Angeli, pp. 367–412.
Ignazi, P. (2005) "Legitimation and evolution on the Italian right wing: Social and ideological repositioning of Alleanza Nazionale and the Lega Nord", *South European Society & Politics*, vol. 10, no. 2, pp. 333–349.
Il Post Redazione (2018) "L'aggressione a Daisy Osakue", *Il Post*. 30 July 2018. Available: https://www.ilpost.it/2018/07/30/aggressione-daisy-osakue/ [21 November 2018].
Labanca, N. (2002) "Le passé colonial et le présent de l'immigration dans l'Italie contemporaine", *Migrations Société*, vol. 14, no. 81–2, pp. 97–106.
Labanca, N. (2003a) "Studies and research on fascist colonialism, 1922–1935", in *A Place in the Sun: Africa in Italian Colonial Culture from Post-unification to the Present*, Palumbo, P. (ed.), Berkeley: University of California Press, pp. 37–61.
Labanca, N. (2003b) *La Libia nei manuali scolastici italiani: 1911–2001*, Rome: ISIAO.
Mammone, A. (2006) "A daily revision of the past: Fascism, anti-fascism, and memory in contemporary Italy", *Modern Italy*, vol. 11, no. 2, pp. 211–226.
Mammone, A. (2018) "È tempo di patrioti", in *Destra*, Fumagalli, C. & Puttini, S. (eds), Milan: Feltrinelli.
Manucci, L. (2020) *Populism and Collective Memory. Comparing Fascist Legacies in Western Europe*. London: Routledge.
Meotti, G. (2017) "La truffa del nuovo Olocausto", *Il Foglio*. 11 August 2017. Available: https://www.ilfoglio.it/cronache/2017/08/11/news/la-truffa-del-nuovo-olocausto-148502/ [1 April 2020].
Newell, J.L. (2000) "Coming in from the cold: The extreme right in Italy", *Parliamentary Affairs*, vol. 53, no. 3, pp. 369–485.
Passarelli, G. (2013) "Extreme right parties in Western Europe: The case of the Italian Northern League", *Journal of Modern Italian Studies*, vol. 18, no. 1, pp. 53–71.
Pinkus, K. (2003) "Empty spaces: Decolonization in Italy", in *A Place in the Sun: Africa in Italian Colonial Culture from Post-unification to the Present*, Palumbo, P. (ed.), Berkeley: University of California Press, pp. 299–320.
Ponzanesi, S. (2005) "Beyond the Black Venus: Colonial sexual politics and contemporary visual practices", in *Italian Colonialism: Legacy and Memory*, Andall, J. & Duncan, D. (eds), Oxford, Bern: Peter Lang, pp. 165–190.
Procacci, G. (2003) *La Memoria controversa. Revisionismi, nazionalismi e fondamentalismi nei manuali di storia*, Cagliari: AM&D Edizioni.
Repubblica Redazione (2018a) "Legge Mancino, ecco cosa prevedono le norme approvate nel 1993", *Repubblica*. 3 August 2018. Available: https://www.repubblica.it/politica/2018/08/03/news/legge_mancino_razzismo_fascismo-203295702/?refresh_ce [21 November 2018].
Repubblica Redazione (2018b) "Legge Mancino, scontro nel governo. Fontana: 'Abroghiamola'. Salvini: 'Sono d'accordo'. Ma arriva lo stop di Di Maio e Conte", *Repubblica*. 3 August 2018. Available: https://www.repubblica.it/politica/2018/08/03

/news/razzismo_fontana_legge_mancino-203291231/?ref=RHPPLF-BH-I0-C8-P1-S1.8-T1 [21 November 2018].

Romano, L. (2018) "La figlia di Almirante: 'In Salvini rivedo l'entusiasmo di papà'", *Il Giornale*. 23 August 2018. Available: http://www.ilgiornale.it/news/politica/figlia-almirante-salvini-rivedo-lentusiasmo-pap-1567394.html [21 November 2018].

Skytg24 (2018) *Apologia del fascismo: Cosa è, quando e come viene punita.* 7 June 2018. Available: https://tg24.sky.it/cronaca/2018/06/07/apologia-fascismo-cosa-e.html [21 November 2018].

Stefanoni, F. (2017) "Berlusconi: 'Se nessuno vince avanti con Gentiloni. Mussolini? Non era proprio un dittatore' 'Lo strappo di Salvini? Solo capricci'", *Corriere della Sera*. 14 December 2017. Available: https://www.corriere.it/video-articoli/2017/12/13/berlusconi-legge-fornero-tema-cui-non-mi-sono-mai-applicato/2f41d7ac-e02d-11e7-b8cc-37049f602793.shtml [21 May 2018].

Tranfaglia, N. (1996) *Un Passato scomodo: Fascismo e postfascismo*, Rome: Laterza.

Traverso, E. (2017) *Mutations of fascism: An interview with Enzo Traverso*. Available: https://www.versobooks.com/blogs/3112-mutations-of-fascism-an-interview-with-enzo-traverso [28 February 2017].

Wright, J.L. (2005) "Mussolini, Libya, and the sword of Islam", in *Italian Colonialism*, Fuller, M. & Ben-Ghiat, R. (eds), New York; Houndmills: Palgrave Macmillan, pp. 121–130.

Conclusion

In the Italian populist radical right, the Mediterranean is seen now as the place through which problematic, different, criminal, inferior, and abject immigrants arrive in Italy. The Mediterranean is now considered as a *Mare Vostrum*, i.e., an apparently dangerous place that washes up immigrants onto Italian shores. Such a depiction of the Mediterranean recalls the image of the colonised Other, living in the lands across the treasured *Mare Nostrum*, the term designating the Mediterranean in colonial times. However, in the contemporary Italian populist radical right, the Mediterranean has shifted from a *Mare Nostrum*, a treasured space of colonisation, to a *Mare Vostrum*, removed from the Italian populist radical right's memory of colonialism, which obscures the difficult elements of the colonial past while praising the positive elements. Considerations on the connections between anti-immigrant discourse and selective colonial memory can be expanded to the wider European context where several postcolonial countries have been dealing for decades with anti-immigrant sentiment as well as with the complex elaboration of the memory of their colonial past (see, for instance, Gilroy 2004; Mols and Jetten 2014; Ponzanesi 2012).

Contemporary Significance of the Research and Research Puzzle

Italy's fraught relationship with its colonial, and, by extension fascist past, and its nativism, specifically its racist component, have been brought to the fore in the aftermath of the killing of George Floyd, when anti-racist protests swiftly crossed the Atlantic and the Channel, and enthused thousands of people in Italian squares calling for the end of racial discrimination. In Italy anti-racists infused their protests with calls for increased migrants' rights in Italy and for a change in Italian law from *jus sanguinis*, namely citizenship acquired by descent, to *jus soli*, namely citizenship acquired by birthplace (Lupia 2020). Anti-racism flowed into the domain of public history, when activists demanded the removal of the statue dedicated to the famed Italian journalist and writer Indro Montanelli (Il Post 2020), who admitted to having bought a 12-year-old Eritrean wife while he led Italian colonial troops in the Italian occupation of Ethiopia in 1935. A few days later the statue was splashed with red paint and the words "razzista stupratore"

DOI: 10.4324/9781003252597-10

(i.e., racist rapist) were scribbled on the base of the statue. In 2019 the statue had already been targeted by feminist activists, when the group *Non Una di Meno* splashed pink paint over it in order to avenge Montanelli's Eritrean spouse and challenge the idea of colonial racist masculinity such statue represents (Mazza 2019).

The controversy surrounding Montanelli's statue did not just elicit a heated political debate around whether the statue should be kept intact, removed, contextualised, or complemented with additions and alterations to give justice to the suffering inflicted by colonialism. The debate threw Italy's racism and its connections with Italian colonialism, and fascism, into sharp relief. Indeed, Italy has not yet grappled with its colonial past, which has been sequestered on the fringes of memory but potently resurfaced in reaction to Floyd's killing and the ensuing global anti-racist protests. Postcolonialism (the analytical framework highlighting the colonial legacy in the present) becomes a useful prism through which to analyse the Italian populist radical right's tense relationship with its colonial past and its nativism, composed of nationalism and racism.

Driven by the urgency to uncover the complex relationship between nativism and colonial (including fascist) memory in the party family that owns the issue of nativism, this book has answered the following question: "*What is the relationship between the populist radical right and Italian colonial (and fascist) memory?*" This research puzzle has been investigated within the Italian context. More specific sub-questions that have been tackled in this work are:

i. *How does the populist radical right articulate the nation (which is key to understanding their nativism)? Is this articulation of the nation rooted in the colonial and fascist past?*
ii. *How does the populist radical right articulate race (which is key to understanding their nativism)? Is this articulation of race rooted in the colonial and fascist past?*
iii. *To what extent does the populist radical right hold a critical and balanced view of the national colonial (and fascist) past?*

The Argument of the Book

The argument put forward is, thus, constituted by multiple and intricate strands. This conclusion aims at untangling this complex web. First, the racialised construction of the colonial Other was instrumental to the creation of the Italian race and nation (see, for instance, Giuliani 2018). In fascist times the colonial Other became co-constitutive of the Italian Self. With the abrupt end of Italian colonialism in the Second World War and with the incipient immigration flows into Italy from former European colonies starting from the 1970s, the colonial Other turned into the immigrant Other. Especially since the 1990s, when immigration began to gain salience in political and public debates, the colonial past, tainted by racism and carried by the immigrant Other, has been increasingly visible, but, paradoxically, unseen at the same time.

Second, the visibility of the colonial past is evident in the framing of immigrants as problematic, different, criminal, inferior, and dirty and ill. The nativist discourse of the Italian populist radical right echoes a typically colonial rhetoric, whereby the colonised was Othered, criminalised, inferiorised, and abjectified by the colonising Self. These discursive representations of immigrants are not the exclusive reserve of the populist radical right and, at the same time, they are not generalisable to the whole Italian society. Certainly, the populist radical right reiterates colonial discursive tropes in their discourse on immigration, which is reminiscent of the colonial articulation of the colonised Other as inherently different, inferior, mentally and physically unfit, and bent to crime. These stereotypes drenched in simplifications and generalisations are spread in Italian society by uncritical media, a deficient education system, and right-wing political parties.

Third, the reiteration of colonial rhetoric is underpinned by the invisibilisation of a nuanced colonial memory, lacking a critical appraisal of the colonial past. Hence, the Italian populist radical right engages in the politics of memory, by portraying a version of the colonial past that emphasises the positive elements of colonialism and expunges colonial violence. This is geared towards the piecing together of a cohesive and glorious narrative of the national past. This is also suggestive of a subtle postcolonial melancholia: while the Italian populist radical right does not advocate the return of the colonies, it does indulge in the idealisation of the colonial past as a golden age. A similar selective memory affects the fascist past, which emphasises apparently positive aspects of fascism, while decreasing the magnitude of fascist atrocities when contextualised within the historical period characterised by totalitarianisms.

Contribution to the Literature

The innovation inherent to the strands of argument unfolding in this book is to shine light on an underappreciated topic, which has so far been neglected in the academic literature. This neglect is regrettable, given the urgency to uncover thoroughly and critically the discourse of the populist radical right, which is set to win the 2022 national elections. In what follows, the literature on which this book is based will be summed up, in parallel with the highlighting of the major nodes of the argument proposed in this book.

Starting with conceptual debates, a vast literature has examined the Italian populist radical right's definition, terminology, and taxonomy. While clarity and consensus around the definition, terminology, and taxonomy of the Italian populist radical right are affected by academic disagreements, this book established clear parameters to define, label and identify the parties to be analysed. Among the plethora of definitions of Italian populist radical right, this book adopts a revised version of Mudde's 2007 concise definition of populist radical right, including the call for a strong state,[1] populism, and nativism (composed of nationalism and racism). Therefore, according to this definition, the Italian populist radical right demands a strong state, against the perceived imminent political and social decay. The Italian populist radical right calls for a strong state to counter immigration, through authoritative security forces and firm laws, such as the reform of the so-called Law of Legitimate Defence. However, the respect of law and order on which a strong state is predicated is scarcely mentioned with regards to Italians. The Italian populist radical right also adopts a populist ideology pitting the pure people against the corrupt elites, as well as against the immigrant out-group. From an ideological point of view, the Italian populist radical right's populism is patent when the parties analysed project themselves as the representatives of the pure people opposed to the corrupt elites and the national out-group.

The corrupt elites are exemplified by the state, the government, competing political parties, as well as supranational actors, such as the EU. Populism is articulated against the elites, mainly in conjunction with their management of immigration. The government is criticised for succumbing to the "Germanocentric" EU's desires, and for uprooting the identity of the Italian people through a shameful management of immigration. Competing parties, such as the left and the M5S are blamed for their leniency towards immigration. The nemesis of the Italian populist radical right, i.e., the EU, is blamed for taking advantage of immigration to dump immigrants onto Italy. This Italian populist radical right's perception of being the victim of the EU reflects the deep-seated Italian feeling of being Europe's internal Other, which is grounded in a late nation-building process (compared to other European countries), in the economic and social fragmentation between the north and south, in a short-lived and unsuccessful colonialism, and in the scarring experience of fascism.

This anti-elite populism is articulated in conjunction with excluding populism, which delineates the borders of the people along ethno-cultural lines excluding immigrants. In such a way, ordinary people are defined on two axes: a vertical axis pitting the pure and ordinary people against the elites, and a horizontal one pitting the people against the out-group (De Cleen and Stavrakakis 2017). The Italian populist radical right's anti-elite and excluding populism is asserted against the background of a perceived decline investing the state, the government, politicians, society, especially its demography, and the economy. The Italian populist radical right, therefore, comes to the rescue as the saviour of the people from decline.

The immigrant out-group is, more specifically, the focus of a further ideological feature of the populist radical right: nativism, which this book distils into nationalism and racism. The Italian populist radical right espouses a predominantly ethno-cultural nationalism, safeguarding the purity and homogeneity of the ethno-cultural nation defined by history, culture, language, and myths. This ethno-cultural nationalism needs to be problematised in the case of the early Lega, which first adopted regionalist claims. Predominantly, ethno-cultural nationalism is coupled with reactionary values evoking a romanticised past marked by the prominence of a homogenous ethno-cultural national community, standing against a gloomy multicultural present.

The parties classified within the Italian populist radical right and studied in this project are the Lega and FdI. While FdI emerged in 2012 from the ashes of AN, the latter and the Lega surfaced in the early 1990s, projecting themselves as untainted parties amidst the political corruption scandal of *Tangentopoli* hitting mainstream parties, despite the Lega being involved in the scandal. Voting based on opinion rather than on clientelist ties, the salience of issues such as immigration, and a new mixed majoritarian and proportional electoral system allowed the rise of new parties, especially those mobilising an anti-immigrant platform, and made pre-electoral coalitions necessary to gain seats in Parliament.

Terminological debates over the use of *populist radical right* or *neo-fascism* as a label for the parties examined in this book, inevitably invoke the discussion over the relationship between these parties and fascism. This relationship, studied through the concept of memory, is explored in depth in later chapters. In Chapter 1, on a purely terminological and definitional level, the book made the terminological choice of defining the Lega and FdI as *populist radical right*, instead of *neo-fascist*. Even if FdI, through its predecessor AN, genealogically derives from the post-war neo-fascist party MSI, and both the Lega and FdI share with fascism ethno-cultural nationalism and racism, the Italian populist radical right is not neo-fascist. Undoubtedly, its definition, based on key ideology features, does not include the myth of the palingenesis, the widespread use of violence, and the authoritarianism characterising fascism. The term *populist radical right* is more apt to capture unambiguously the ideology held by the parties examined in this book, which are not anti-democratic, but operate within a democratic system, at least formally, since individual rights and liberties are applied in a way that excludes the out-group. Moreover, although ethno-cultural nationalism and racism against the formerly colonised Other evoke fascist colonial racism, ethno-cultural nationalism and racism are now toned down in the Italian populist radical right. Indeed, ethno-cultural nationalism is mixed with civic undertones, and racism against immigrants is no longer expressed in biological terms, but mainly in ethnic and cultural terms. Nationalism and racism intertwine to form nativism, which is one of the pillars of the populist radical right's ideology, along with the call for a strong state and populism against elites and immigrants.

Notwithstanding the continuity in essence, although not in intensity and quality, of racism and nationalism between colonialism, especially in its fascist stage, and the contemporary populist radical right, the conception of the Mediterranean in colonial, and fascist, times signals rupture. In fact, the Italian populist radical right's nativism excludes and attacks the immigrant Other who comes to Italy through the Mediterranean, which used to be a treasured space of colonisation especially under fascism. It is, in fact, under fascism that colonialism took on its most marked racist connotations against the colonised Other. Despite these continuities and ruptures between colonialism, and fascism, and the populist radical right's attitude towards immigration, to date little attention has been paid to the topic in academic literature. Surely, there is a glaring omission in the literature on a systematic analysis of the colonial, and fascist, memory nurtured by populist radical right, and the populist radical right's nativism. As Chapter 1 suggests, postcolonialism becomes a valuable analytical framework to remedy the above mentioned scholarly omission, by focusing on the political and instrumental use of colonial, and fascist, memory in the Italian populist radical right's nativism.

146 Conclusion

The populist radical right has claimed issue ownership of nativism, but this sentiment is not circumscribed to the confines of the Lega and FdI. In fact, nativism is also fomented and spread by mainstream parties co-opting populist radical right ideology, by the media, including social media, which often uncritically propagate a threatening representation of the immigrant, and by the educational system, which largely represents immigration in a simplistic and uncritical way. The Italian populist radical right, therefore, exploits latent nativism, making immigration a salient issue, in order to increase its electoral gains.

The theoretical foundations of nativism are explored in Chapter 2 through a historical perspective considering the Italian colonial and fascist era. Fascism boosted and developed Italian colonialism, and constructed the Italian national and racial identity against the colonised Other. Indeed, even though it already emerged during the liberal era, racism was the hallmark of colonialism under fascism. It is under fascism that Italy stretched its colonial expansion, underpinned by a firm belief in the racial superiority of Italians vis-à-vis the colonised Other, and by racist violence. The construction of the Italian self, vis-à-vis the colonised Other, has a two-pronged implication. First, it implied the shaping of racism against inhabitants of territories across the Mediterranean, which evokes the racist attitudes exercised now against the immigrant Other, arriving in Italy through the Mediterranean. Second, the dichotomy between Italian Self and colonised Other implied a shift in the Italian national and racial identity from being built on the rift between northern Italians, corresponding to the Self, and the southern Other, envisaged as backward, inclined to criminality, and mentally and physically unfit. In a curious twist of fate, the Italian south became conceived as the cradle of Italianness, embodied by the fascist values of rurality, virility, and loyalty to the church, the state, and the nation. The projection of the lack of civilisation abroad was instrumental in allowing Italy to strengthen its national and racial identity, and to soften the divisive perception of southern Italians as the nation's Other. In such a way, fascism enabled the strengthening of Italian nationalism through a racist construction of the colonised Other, in a clear nativist mix. After the abrupt demise of fascism, Italy lost its colonies to the Allies. Racism contrasting the Italian Self against the colonised Other was not buried with the Italian colonial venture, but resurfaced in the discourse articulated against the heirs of the colonised Other, i.e., the immigrant, which was explored at length in Chapters 5 and 6.

After having laid solid theoretical foundations for the empirical part of the book, the book proceeds with an explanation of the methodology in Chapter 3. In order to investigate the relationship between the Italian populist radical right's colonial and fascist memory, and nativism, this project deployed qualitative methods to analyse the rich, nuanced, and complex data gathered through semi-structured interviews and manifesto analysis. As explained in the methodological chapter, semi-structured interviews allow a certain degree of flexibility in selecting the questions to ask, in order to follow interesting leads and capture detailed information. At the same time, a set of standardised questions maximises data validity. The rationale behind interview questions is explicated in Appendix 1. Concerning the risk of scarce representativeness inherent in interviews, this methodological downside has been overcome by selecting a heterogeneous sample, cutting across different geographical areas, ages, and levels of involvement within the parties chosen. Unfortunately, gender balance was impossible to attain.

While the interviews generated the majority of the data, they were complemented by party manifestos dating to 2013 and 2018, when the last national elections were contested. At the time of writing, new national elections have been called for 25 September 2022, where FdI is on course to winning a sizeable victory, which makes this critical book even more topical. The limitation intrinsic to manifestos is that they project to the public the external image of the party, sometimes a more moderate and palatable one, and they represent a monolithic ideological position, concealing the ideological heterogeneity of the party. These disadvantages are overcome by using the interviews to probe the latent and heterogeneous ideology of the party, constituted by a multiplicity of party representatives operating at local, regional, and national level, from the north, centre, and south of the peninsula, and from young to more senior individuals. Both interviews and manifestos are coded through a dynamic process: first codes drawn from categories existing in the literature are deployed, then new codes are generated during the analysis of the texts.

To analyse the text from interviews and manifestos, this project deployed Critical Discourse Analysis (CDA). CDA maintains that discourse reproduces and resists social power abuse and inequality, as reflects social relations. CDA is multidisciplinary and focuses on social and political issues. Therefore, starting from CDA methodological underpinnings, this book argues that the Italian populist radical right's discourse is a social action reproducing social inequalities, and enmeshed in the social, economic, and historical context of Italy, marked by the influx of immigrants, and the legacy of colonialism and fascism. Interesting discursive elements inherent to political discourse are binary conceptualisations that highlight the contrast between the Self and the Other; metaphors, such as "invasion" and "slaves" used to negatively connote the immigrant Other; first person possessives indicating the collectivity of the Italian nation against the Other; negative vocabulary delegitimising the Other; hyperbole to exaggerate the negative impact of the phenomenon of immigration; the semantic reversal of blame to shift criticism from fascism to Nazism and communism; the topos of threat to induce fear of the Other; the strategy of denial to reject accusations of racism before slipping into racist statements; the fallacy of sameness and of difference, to depict the in-group as homogeneous and different from the out-group; and legitimation through authorisation, to buttress arguments against the Other, by resorting to data or to apparently authoritative data sources. To avert the danger of bias and subjectivity inherent to interviews, party manifesto analysis, and CDA, this book has striven to achieve neutrality and objectivity in the interpretation of texts, triangulating the data from the interviews and the manifestos with the existing literature.

Chapter 4 delved into the analysis of the interviews and the manifestos, by analysing the first ideological components of the Italian populist radical right's nativism: nationalism. The Italian populist radical right is undeniably nationalist, although it displays a curious blend of ethno-cultural nationalism, characterised by culture, identity, forefathers, history, traditions, art, language, community, character, ethnicity, heirs, national symbols, and religion, with sporadic civic undertones, such as the right to work, progress, values, and territory. The reactionary face of the Italian populist radical right is manifest, in the realm of the analysis of nationalism, in these parties' aversion to multiculturalism, which would allegedly lead to anarchy and to deplorable cultural hybridisation.

The Italian populist radical right's emphasis on nationalism must be considered against the backdrop of the traditional view of Italy's weak sense of national identity, which has even been described as a sort of "inverted patriotism" (Dickie 2001: 26), due to the late nation-building process, compared to other countries such as France and the UK; the fragmentation of Italy into different regions, and a fault line between the north and south. The clear nationalist character of the Italian populist radical right is interesting because the Lega originated as a regionalist party calling for the secession of the imaginary nation of the *Padania*, corresponding to northern Italy, from the rest of the country, before turning into an Italian nationalist party. However, the belief in the difference between the north and the south has not completely faded away in the Lega, as some of its representatives still called into question the unity of the nation, to which they prefer local identity.

The primarily ethno-cultural nationalism cropping up in the interviews with populist radical right representatives and intellectuals is challenged when the Italian populist radical right, while being firmly opposed to the introduction of the *jus soli* granting Italian citizenship to immigrants living in Italy, symbolically opens up the borders of the nation to regular immigrants. Indeed, the majority of the Italian populist radical right claims that regular immigrants can become part of Italy. This is meant to re-instate the dichotomy between regular and irregular immigrants, who are thus further scapegoated, and to make the Italian populist radical right appear more moderate, according to the civic turn of the populist radical right displayed across Europe. In such a way, the Italian populist radical right can attract a larger electorate, thus maximising its chances to access government, or maintain its position in government.

Racism conceptually flows from the predominantly ethno-cultural nationalism of the Italian populist radical right. Given the demise of biological racism, contemporary racism derives from the perception of the ethno-cultural difference between the Italian in-group and the immigrant out-group, and manifests itself through the belittling, discrimination, exclusion, and stigmatisation of those perceived as different, hence as Others. Inspired by Hall's (1997) definition of racism as discursive and contextual, Chapters 5 and 6 uncovered the Italian populist radical right's racist discourse, analysing it against the background of the Italian history of colonialism and fascism. Despite Italy's self-absolving myth of immunity to racism, it is clear that Italian national and racial identity is deeply grounded in a racist articulation of the Other, which has been reconfigured in different forms over time, but has always been a necessary component of the Italian national and racial identity. In the 1990s, when immigration began to be profiled as an issue Italian society and politics had to face, racism against the previously colonised Other resurged under the guise of racism against immigrants.

Although this would go beyond the scope of this book, it is necessary to clarify that, since the post-war period, racism has not retreated before suddenly re-emerging in the 1990s, but has been deeply ingrained in the neo-fascist MSI. The MSI strived, for the whole duration of its political life, to strike a difficult balance between being an extremist party, thus a political pariah, and operating within the democratic system. In terms of immigration policy, the MSI adopted an ambivalent posture: it favoured international cooperation with the immigrants' countries of origin, while engaging in violence against immigrants, proposing their expulsion, and being fundamentally racist. Importantly, racism is not a purely political phenomenon, but rather is well entrenched in Italian society at large beyond the confines of the MSI, its heir AN, FdI, and the Lega. School textbooks, which are key to shape young minds, contribute to either the neglect of the topic of immigration, or to a simplistic representation of the immigrant Other as a victim or a danger. This racism, seeping in at the popular level, is capitalised on and in turn fuelled by the media and by political parties, including the populist radical right and mainstream parties, that strategically make immigration a salient issue to attract voters. This became evident in the March 2018 Italian elections, when the Italian populist radical right party the Lega became a coalition government partner scoring 17% of the votes, and in eight months it almost doubled its supporters (Benedetto 2018). The popularity of the populist radical right is not declining: at the time of writing, FdI is leading the opinion polls ahead of the September 2022 national elections.

Going back to the analysis of the empirical examples of the racist component of nativism, in the interest of clarity, Chapters 5 and 6 broke down the Italian populist radical right's racism into six categories. First, through the problematisation of immigration, the Italian populist radical right portrays immigration as an uncontainable problem, in social and economic terms, thus espousing the logic of emergency and exceptionality, which considers immigration as an abnormal and unpredictable phenomenon requiring emergency measures. This logic of emergency and exceptionality is evident in the 2017 Minniti-Orlando Decree against NGOs reportedly cooperating with migrant smugglers while rescuing immigrants. Such logic also implied the extension of detention centres and cooperation with northern African countries with dubious human rights records. The problematisation frame of immigration resonates with the socio-demographic and economic causes of racism explored in various studies. According to some deterministic socio-demographic explanations, racism arises due to *anomie*, a sense of alienation and isolation driven by the social change brought about by immigration. Immigrants are, thus, perceived as strangers invading familiar spaces and turning them into alien and distant places. A concurrent explanation for votes for the populist radical right is similarly socio-demographic in essence. Indeed, according to the notorious cultural backlash theory, the racist turn now is motivated by a reaction against post-modern values diffused in the 1970s, of which multiculturalism is an example. These socio-demographic arguments explaining racism are challenged by competing evidence that immigration generates closer contact and appreciation between the in-group and the out-group, and by arguments questioning the view that it is the older generations that mainly vote for the populist radical right.

Populist radical right's racism is rooted not only in socio-demographic change, but also in unfavourable economic situations, characterised by economic crisis and unemployment, which lead the in-group to fear the competition with the out-group in the job market. Nevertheless, even this deterministic explanation founders, when considering that immigrants may take up unskilled jobs scorned by the in-group. In this case, immigrant workers have an impact on less-educated Italian workers, but not on more-educated ones. Additionally, the economic justification for racism fails to account for the fact that historically not all countries that underwent economic crises witnessed the rise of populist radical right's racism and not all countries with populist radical right racist parties experienced economic crises. For instance, Spain and Portugal were badly hit by the 2008 recession, but did not see populist radical right racist parties thrive until recently in the guise of VOX in Spain (founded in 2013) and of Chega in Portugal (founded in 2019). Furthermore, the Swiss People's Party (SVP) and the Austrian Freedom Party (FPO) flourished in Switzerland and Austria, respectively, although these countries were not debtors, but creditors in the 2008 recession.

Scholarly research has merged socio-demographic with economic explanations for racism giving them a psychological grounding. Indeed, ethnic competition theory holds that individuals are naturally prone to identifying themselves positively with their in-group and oppose themselves to the out-group. At times of economic scarcity, this leads to competition for resources with the out-group. Nonetheless, it is important to add that this does not necessarily lead to racism; in fact, if one assumed that the representation of the out-group in opposition to the in-group intrinsically causes racism, then racism would be deterministically considered as a normal human condition. Therefore, no single explanation for the success of the populist radical right motivated by racism appears satisfactory. Instead, a comprehensive evaluation of different explanations, enriched by a nuanced and critical assessment, is a valuable tool to understand the discourse of the populist radical right on immigration.

Second, through the differentiation of immigration, the Italian populist radical right distinguishes between deserving refugees, who are welcome, and undeserving economic migrants, who are rejected. This Manichean dichotomy between deserving refugees and undeserving economic migrants is mapped onto the dichotomy between welcome and worthy regular immigrants, and criminal irregular ones. Inconsistent statistical data is deployed to consolidate the suspicion that only a tiny minority of immigrants applying for refugee status are actually refugees.

Third, the Othering of immigration, grounded in the Italian populist radical right's conception of the immigrant as inherently Other, is evident in the Italian populist radical right's sweeping claim that immigrants threaten national identity and social cohesion, create discrimination at the expense of Italians in the welfare system and in the job market, and trigger alienation and decadence. Therefore, the Italian populist radical right champions a policy of "Italians First" prioritising

Conclusion 151

the in-group in the welfare system and the job market. The explanations of racism outlined above are a useful prism through which to make sense of the Othering of immigration.

Fourth, through the criminalisation of immigration, the Italian populist radical right frames immigrants as intrinsically criminal Others. The Lega and FdI buttress their claims, by resorting to statistical data showing the reportedly high percentage of immigrants among the perpetrators of crimes. A criminalising metaphor frequently deployed to describe immigration is invasion, along with the criminalising view of irregular immigrants, and with the association of immigrants to crime. Indeed, immigrants' crimes become hypervisibilised and are represented as more serious than the crimes committed by the in-group, because of the immigrant status of the perpetrators. Hence, the criminalisation of immigrants is demarcated along ethnic or religious lines, whereby certain ethnicities seem to be more disposed to crime.

Muslims, indeed, appear to be the main enemy of the Italian populist radical right: they are almost unanimously associated by the latter to terrorism and to a holy war waged by Islam against the West. Mosques, predictably, attract the rage and criticism of the Italian populist radical right, which proposes to close them down or strictly control them. The Islamophobia the Italian populist radical right taps into is rife in Italy, where knowledge of Islam is superficial, but hatred of Muslims is widespread, and popularised by writer Fallaci, who has been a source of inspiration and admiration for the Italian populist radical right, and beyond. The centrality of Islamophobia in the Italian populist radical right's discourse and its traction in wider Italian society is rooted in its ability to fuse different strands of thought widespread in the West after the demise of communism. First, Islam supplanted communism as the enemy of the West, and such inimical framing has been exacerbated since 9/11 and the ensuing "war on terror," which fuelled anti-Muslim hatred. The fear of a Muslim political occupation of Europe combated through the "war on terror" has also been grounded in Eurabianists' assumptions about the union of the two shores of the Mediterranean to form a Eurabian entity dominated by Muslims. According to the racist conspiracy theory propagated by writer Ye'or, the decline in Christianity and in the demographic strength of Europe has paved the way to its cultural and political takeover by Arab countries, after they entered into closer cooperation with Europe in the 1970s, against the US (2005).

While these strands of thought find wide resonance in Italian society, the Italian populist radical right in particular uses them to justify its securitisation policies envisaged within the call for the strong state, including expulsion of irregular immigrants, their punishment with reclusion or the payment of a fine, and their vehement request of a reform of the Law of Legitimate Defence.

Furthermore, through the inferiorisation of immigration, the Italian populist radical right depicts the Other as essentially inferior. Immigrants, thus, become represented as lazy, beasts, and even slaves. Muslims are the principal target of the inferiorisation of immigrants, since they are disdained for their alleged lack of respect for women's rights, for the principle of reciprocity between different religions, and for human rights in general. Finally, through the abjectification of immigration, the Italian populist radical right represents the Other as intrinsically connected to dirt and disease. The ostensible lack of hygiene of immigrants and their supposed spread of once eradicated illnesses are frequently mentioned by the Italian populist radical right. The abjectification of immigrants became evident during the COVID-19 pandemic, when immigrants were seen as a danger to public health.

Therefore, as revealed by these categories, the Mediterranean on the Italian populist radical right becomes reframed from a *Mare Nostrum*, i.e., a desired space of colonisation under fascism in order to signal Italian geopolitical prestige, to spread the ideology of the new man, to revive the Roman grandeurs, and to demonstrate demographic power, to what I define as a "Mare Vostrum," i.e., a space not claimed any more by the Italian populist radical right, distanced as much as possible from these parties, and a source of a problem of uncontrollable proportions plotted by a majority of dishonest economic migrants who precipitate Italy into sharp decline, pose social and economic threats, bring crime and terrorism, are lazy, do not respect human rights, and carry illnesses and dirt. The main threat coming through the Mediterranean is represented by Muslims, who seemingly wage a holy war against the West, trigger a clash of civilisations, and do not guarantee women's rights, the right of reciprocity between religions, and human rights in general.

It is important to note that the analysis of the above categories shed light onto two intertwined discursive phenomena: the reiteration of colonial rhetoric and the civic turn of the populist radical right. Nonetheless, it is clear that the colonial rhetoric emerging in the Italian populist radical right's racist discourse is underpinned by a selective positive memory of Italian colonialism and the lack of a critical appraisal of it, which may discourage the Italian populist radical right from the re-iteration of colonial rhetoric. Indeed, the Othering, criminalisation, inferiorisation, and abjectification of the immigrant Other recall the same processes enacted against the colonised Other. As Cassata (2008), Conelli (2014), Fanon (1963), Galeotti (2000), Giuliani (2018), Matard-Bonucci (2008), Said (1978), and Todorov (1984) argue, the colonised Other was framed as essentially different from the colonising Self, prone to violence and criminality, depraved, inferior, and linked to contagion and pollution.

Furthermore, inferiorisation of immigration becomes intersected with religion and gender. Indeed, the Italian populist radical right's attack on immigrant prostitutes and on Muslim men's lack of respect for women's rights provides a revealing example of the colonial rhetoric of the Italian populist radical right, which hypersexualises the female bodies of the immigrant Other, while contradictorily projecting itself as the protector of Muslim women from Muslim men, recalling Spivak's (1988) colonial trope of white men defending brown women from brown men, to further reinforce the inferiority of the colonised female Other.

The second discursive process at work in the Italian populist radical right's discourse is the civic turn of the populist radical right, by which these parties project themselves as legitimate and credible, to attract a larger share of voters, by toning down their racism and appearing more civic. The civic turn of the populist radical right also relates to the mainstreaming of this party family, which has been accepted into the domain of government. Indeed, the civic turn is patent when the Italian populist radical right claims that it generally accepts immigration, but it rejects this specific kind of immigration on not clearly specified humanitarian grounds; when it demonstrates sympathy towards refugees; when it projects itself as the defender of national security, of women's rights, of the right of reciprocity, and of human rights in general, as well as in numerous other instances, when a minority of Italian populist radical right representatives rejected the racist trend of Othering, criminalising, inferiorising, and abjectifying immigrants. Indeed, comparatively few Italian populist radical right representatives contended that immigration does not pose a social or economic threat, that it is not connected to a holy war waged by Islam against the West, and that it is not related to the risk of disease and dirt.

To sum up the core argument conveyed in Chapters 5 and 6, the Italian populist radical right's perception of the Mediterranean, once a treasured space through which Italian fascist colonialism extended its power, has turned into what I define as a "Mare Vostrum," i.e., carrier of undesirable immigrants and removed from the Italian populist radical right's consciousness. Through interviews with Italian populist radical right representatives and intellectuals, and Italian populist radical right manifesto analysis, this project argued that the Mediterranean in the FdI's and in the Lega's discourse is represented as a threatening space of immigration, which carries immigrants that are inherently problematic, different from Italians, criminals, inferior, and abject, and that pose an economic and social problem of uncontrollable magnitude to Italy, plunging it into decline. Immigrants, in the Italian populist radical right's discourse, are also excluded from the predominantly ethno-cultural definition of the nation, although regular immigrants are given the possibility of belonging to it, and from the excluding definition of the people. Underpinning these representations of immigrants are two crucial strategies: the reutilisation of colonial rhetoric whose object has been transposed from the colonised Other to the immigrant Other; and the civic mantle used to cover otherwise utterly racist concepts, in the populist radical right parties' quest for acceptance and legitimacy in the political arena.

After examining the colonial rhetoric in the Italian populist radical right's discourse, Chapter 7 explored additional ways in which the selective colonial memory this party family harbours becomes evident. Drawing on studies developed for different geographical contexts, the chapter analysed whether the arguments on the melancholia towards an idealised past, on postcolonial melancholia, and on the lack of elaboration of in-group violence are applicable to the Italian populist radical right. Chapter 7 also drew on the few arguments on the selective forgetting affecting the populist radical right.

A colonial memory affected by a selective forgetting of colonial violence is not the preserve of the Italian populist radical right, but applies to wider Italian politics and society. For instance, Italian parties across the political spectrum between the end of the Second World War and the early 1990s did not offer an apology to Italy's former colonies. However, what is distinctive about the Italian populist radical right, as demonstrated through the interviews with Italian populist radical right representatives and intellectuals, is that even at present this party family does not acknowledge the need to apologise to the colonies that were once part of the Italian *Oltremare*. Importantly, this does not diminish the importance and effectiveness of the argument articulated about the correlation between anti-immigrant racism and a selective colonial memory in the Italian populist radical right. Instead, the affinity between selective colonial memory in the populist radical right on the one hand, and in Italian politics and society at large on the other hand, suggests that this kind of colonial memory is not exclusive to the Italian populist radical right, which taps into the framing of colonial memory widespread among the Italian population, also through the educational system. Contrary to the case of racism, though, selective forgetting may not be strategic to attract voters, as the Italian populist radical right does not make colonial memory a salient issue in its discursive repertoire.

A selective colonial memory purged of its most violent aspects, such as the colonial crimes that were intrinsic to colonialism in Libya, Ethiopia, Eritrea, and Somalia, emerges in the Italian populist radical right's refusal to acknowledge the link between the destructive impact of colonialism and the economic and political instability working as push factor for immigration; in its idealisation of the colonial past with an overwhelming emphasis on the positive elements of colonialism; in its downplaying of colonial crimes; in its refusal to apologise for colonial crimes to the former colonies, and in its rejection of the moral responsibility to intervene in the former colonies while they were swept through by civil war and dictatorships.

Italian colonialism was bolstered by fascism, and it is indeed fascism that constructed the Italian national and racial identity in opposition to the colonial Other, as was discussed in Chapter 2. Therefore, the analysis of colonial memory is not complete without a complementary analysis of fascist memory, which is the focus of Chapter 8. In fact, it is clear that this party family harbours a memory of fascism often affected by the forgetting of its violent elements. A selective memory of fascism is broadly purified of its most negative aspects, which are acknowledged by comparatively few Italian populist radical right representatives. Instead, the Italian populist radical right does not refrain from shedding a positive light on the fascist past. When it recognises the negative aspects of fascism, a non-negligible portion of the Lega and FdI blurs the acknowledgment of fascist brutalities through a comparison with the allegedly more brutal former European colonial powers. Additionally, the Italian populist radical right's ambiguity towards fascism is apparent in its unease when talking about fascism in the interviews and in their mixed grades given to fascism.

Individual memory and collective memory are inherently biased, as an individual and a group choose which aspects of the past to recollect. While there cannot be one objective memory, the Italian populist radical right's memory of colonialism and fascism could be more comprehensive and critical if it carefully considered both the positive and negative elements of the colonial and fascist past.

Instead, the Italian populist radical right does not construct its memory of colonialism and fascism in a balanced way. As Giuliani asserts,

> The public memory of the colonial and fascist past was purged of its legacy of racism and violence, and a sugar-coated version of events that could be palatable to a reconciled country was put forward. An official account of history that could keep a lid on the contradictions of its violent colonial domination and long-lasting, deep-rooted racism was seen as indispensable, and it needed to offer a new image of the post-fascist country that could be shared by Catholic conservatives, neo-fascists, and communists alike.
> (2018: 111)

The colonial and fascist memory, plagued by selective forgetting, is to be interpreted against the background of the Italian post-war experience, characterised by equating colonialism with fascism, which hindered a critical appraisal of both colonial and fascist history. Moreover, the myth of *Italiani brava gente* (Del Boca 1992), idealising Italians as inherently good and incapable of negative actions, has further obscured the memory of colonial and fascist violence. Additionally, Italy's perception of being Europe's internal Other meant that critical evaluations of the colonial and fascist past were deemed as dangerous to Italian prestige. This critical historical assessment was additionally impeded by the narrative of the Resistance that assimilated the victims of fascism to the myth of the Resistance against fascism. The resurgence of fascism under the guise of the neo-fascist MSI, to which AN was the heir, further contributed to the lack of a framing of an accurate fascist memory.

The Lega's proposal to abolish the Scelba and the Mancino Laws, which were designed to stave off the resurgence of fascism and racism (Repubblica 2018), is a case in point demonstrating the Italian populist radical right's opacity towards its fascist legacy. The fact that the Lega proposed the repeal of the Scelba and the Mancino Laws presages the risk of the normalisation of fascism in the Italian political and social realm. In addition to this, at the time of writing, in the opinion polls the leadership of FdI portends the danger of the acceptance among the Italian electorate of the fascist vestiges that are intrinsic to the party, despite Meloni's attempts at portraying it as mainstream to voters. With Meloni's entry into government as Prime Minister, the populist radical right would be ushered into power once again.

The attempt at mainstreaming through the use of civic discourse, or through the moderation of extremist edges, punctuates the interviews. The populist radical right, in fact, faces the dilemma between vote-seeking and office-seeking. Maximising votes among the populist radical right's core supporters implies loyalty to the populist radical right's original ideology, while seeking office entails appealing to the median voter and concentrating on delivering goods, by toning down its original ideology. As a consequence, the Lega and FdI have developed a shrewd strategy to moderate themselves in order to gain votes and, once in power, they feel free to experiment with more radical stances. Simultaneously, the

Key Takeaways from the Book

As a consequence, in the Italian populist radical right's discourse, the Mediterranean has shifted from a desired space of colonisation under fascism, i.e., a *Mare Nostrum*, to what I identify as a "Mare Vostrum," i.e., an apparently dangerous place that washes up immigrants onto Italian shores and that is removed from the Italian populist radical right's memory of colonialism and fascism. The Mediterranean does not serve any more to revive the splendours of the Roman Empire (Ben-Ghiat 2006: 382), or to project Italian power, the ideology of the new man (De Grand 2004), or demographic potency abroad (Taddia 2005: 213), as it used to do under fascist colonialism. On the other hand, the Mediterranean is now reframed as the place crossed by problematic, different, criminal, inferior, and abject immigrants on their way to Italy. Paradoxically, the Mediterranean is today marginalised in the Italian populist radical right's colonial and fascist memory, which obscures colonial and fascist violence while praising the positive elements of colonialism and fascism. This results in a subtle postcolonial melancholia idealising the colonial and fascist past as golden ages, and in the Italian populist radical right's refusal to offer either apologies for colonial brutalities or aid to its former colonies when they were destroyed by war. The marginalisation of a critical and thorough appraisal of colonial, and fascist, memory in the Lega and FdI stands in stark contrast with the solid roots the notions of nation and race lay in the fascist and colonial past. Ultimately, the fascist and colonial past serves not only as roots but also resurfaces in the guise of colonial echoes in the nativist discourse of the Italian populist radical right.

Note

1 In 2007 Mudde terms it *authoritarianism*, but *call for a strong state* is more appropriate to the Italian populist radical right. The Lega and FdI have shed authoritarian ambitions, including the introduction of the death penalty, and have operated, at least outwardly, within a democratic system. They have even vehemently opposed the Conte II unelected government for its seemingly undemocratic management of the pandemic. The Lega and FdI have been championing free and fair elections, a system of checks and balances, and the protection of individual freedoms, such as freedom of movement.

References

Ben-Ghiat, R. (2006) "Modernity is just over there: Colonialism and Italian national identity", *Interventions; International Journal of Postcolonial Studies*, vol. 8, no. 3, pp. 380–393.

Benedetto, R. (2018) "Il boom della Lega: è al 48% nel Nord-Est e supera il 22% al Sud", *Corriere della Sera*. 8 October 2018. Available: https://www.corriere.it/politica/18_ottobre_08/sondaggio-0c7498c2-cb3c-11e8-9a02-946640b28e26.shtml [21 November 2018].

Cassata, F. (2008) *La Difesa della razza: Politica, ideologia e immagine del razzismo fascista*, G. Turin: Einaudi.
Conelli, C. (2014) "Razza, colonialità, nazione", in *Quel che resta dell'impero: la cultura coloniale degli italiani*, Deplano, V. & Pes, A. (eds), Milan: Mimesis, pp. 149–168.
De Cleen, B. & Stavrakakis, Y. (2017) "Distinctions and articulations: A discourse theoretical framework for the study of populism and nationalism", *Javnost - The Public*, vol. 24, no. 4, pp. 301–319.
De Grand, A. (2004) "Mussolini's follies: Fascism in its imperial and racist phase, 1935–1940", *Contemporary European History*, vol. 13, no. 2, pp. 127–147.
Del Boca, A. (1992) *L'Africa nella coscienza degli Italiani: Miti, memorie, errori, sconfitte*, Rome: Laterza.
Dickie, J. (2001) "The notion of Italy", in *The Cambridge Companion to Modern Italian Culture*, Barański, Z.G. & West, R.J. (eds), Cambridge, UK: Cambridge University Press, pp. 17–34.
Fanon, F. (1963) *The Wretched of the Earth*, Paris: Presence Africaine.
Galeotti, C. (2000) *Mussolini ha sempre ragione: I decaloghi del fascismo*, Milan: Garzanti.
Giuliani, G. (2018) *Race, Nation and Gender in Modern Italy: Intersectional Representations in Visual Culture*, London: Palgrave Macmillan.
Hall, S. (1997) "Race, the floating signifier featuring Stuart Hall transcript", The Media Education Foundation. Available: https://www.mediaed.org/transcripts/Stuart-Hall-Race-the-Floating-Signifier-Transcript.pdf.
Il Post Redazione (2020) "La statua di Indro Montanelli a Milano è stata nuovamente imbrattata", *Il Post*. 14 June 2020. Available: https://www.ilpost.it/2020/06/14/statua-montanelli-imbrattata/ [21 September 2022].
Lupia, V. (2020) "Roma: Piazza del Popolo in ginocchio per George Floyd", *Repubblica*. 07 June 2020. Available: https://roma.repubblica.it/cronaca/2020/06/07/news/_i_can_t_breathe_manifestazione_a_roma_piazza_del_popolo_in_ginocchio_per_george_floyd-258640371/ [21 September 2022].
Matard-Bonucci, M. (2008) "D'une persécution l'autre: Racisme colonial et antisémitisme dans l'Italie fasciste", *Revue d'histoire moderne et contemporaine (1954-)*, vol. 55, no. 3, pp. 116–137.
Mazza, M.P. (2019) "Non una di meno: 'Imbrattare la statua di Indro Montanelli non è vandalismo, è riscatto'", *Open*. 9 March 2019. Available: https://www.open.online/2019/03/09/non-una-di-meno-imbrattare-la-statua-di-indro-montanelli-non-e-vandalismo-e-riscatto/ [21 September 2022].
Mudde, C. (2007) *Populist Radical Right Parties in Europe*, Cambridge, UK: Cambridge University Press.
Repubblica Redazione (2018) "Legge Mancino, ecco cosa prevedono le norme approvate nel 1993", *Repubblica*. 3 August 2018. Available: https://www.repubblica.it/politica/2018/08/03/news/legge_mancino_razzismo_fascismo-203295702/?refresh_ce [21 November 2018].
Said, E. (1978) *Orientalism*, London: Penguin.
Spivak, G.C. (1988) "Can the subaltern speak?", in *Colonial Discourse and Post-colonial Theory*, Williams, P. & Chrisman, L. (eds), New York: Columbia University Press, pp. 21–78.
Taddia, I. (2005) "Italian memories/African memories of colonialism", in *Italian Colonialism*, Fuller, M. & Ben-Ghiat, R. (eds), New York: Palgrave, pp. 209–219.
Ye'or, B. (2005) "Eurabia - Europe's Future?", Middle East Forum. Available: https://www.meforum.org/696/eurabia-europes-future.

Postscript

I finalised this manuscript in the summer of 2022, which was an eventful time for Italian politics. A few days later, the September 2022 general elections shook up the Italian political scene with FdI making its electoral breakthrough and scoring a resounding victory. These events made this book even more relevant to understand the style, ideology, historical background, and memory of FdI as displayed on the occasion of the September 2022 elections. This electoral victory, as well as the feverish electoral campaign preceding it, and the tumultuous government formation following it shone an incredible amount of light on FdI and its leader, Giorgia Meloni. Political developments, therefore, made it necessary and urgent to write up a postscript to my manuscript. In this space, I will trace the persistent and consistent ascent of FdI, compared to its ally/competitor Lega, headed by Matteo Salvini, before going into an in-depth analysis of the current FdI. Salvini and Meloni are not new characters recently appeared on the political scene, as they have featured extensively throughout this manuscript. What is new and noteworthy is the inversion of electoral fortunes brought to light in the 2022 elections, the changed party competition dynamics, and the reproduction and enhancement of the populist radical right ideology during the 2022 electoral campaign, elections, and ensuing government formation. Italian politics never fails to provide intellectual fodder for scholars of Politics, and Italy itself has been characterised as the "promised land" of populism (Tarchi 2015). While acknowledging the enormous amount of material deserving coverage, in the interest of space, this postscript will cover the 2022 events from the electoral campaign to the instalment of the new government, thus leaving the Meloni's agenda and the first government policies up for new research.

"The Politics of Memory in the Italian Populist Radical Right: From Mare Nostrum to Mare Vostrum" is the result of a six-year research capturing the features, variety, and evolution of the populist radical right in Italy, with a premium focus on its intricate, yet unescapable, politicisation of colonial and fascist memory. Since the start of the research in 2015, Italy has changed five governments, and witnessed the relentless ascent of the Lega and FdI at the helm of the populist radical right. The Lega reached the pinnacle of voters' support at the 2018 general elections, when it scored 17% of votes, and formed a government coalition with the catch-all populist party M5S. During its fourth experience in government, and the first experience in a wholly populist government formed by a populist radical right and a catch-all populist party, the Lega radicalised immigration policies. However, it steered away from thorny public discussions over the colonial and fascist past of Italy. Noteworthy and thought-provoking details about their politicisation of memory emerged during the interviews conducted for this manuscript and are amply analysed in the book. Meanwhile, FdI was, and had always been, in opposition until 2022. FdI, the party belonging to the lineage of the first Italian neo-fascist party, the post-war party MSI, embarked on a progressive and constant rise in polls. These data are a case in point: in the 2013 general elections FdI polled at 1.94% (Greco 2013); five years later, it polled at 4.3% (Diamanti 2018); in 2022, it gathered an extortionate share of votes, polling at 26%.

Let's rewind to July 2022. Italy is not new to political turbulence. Since 2016, Italy saw the rise and fall of five Prime Ministers. Yet, the government crisis of July 2022 threw Italy into the throes of epochal political change and trepidation, both abroad and at home. Mario Draghi, Italy's then Prime Minister and well-reputed figure at international level, thanks to his previous role as European Central Bank President, stepped down. He had ushered Italy out of the economic and healthcare crisis caused by the pandemic, and into an era of international credibility and relative economic stability. The wholly populist Conte I government and the centre-left plus populist Conte II government had rested on fragile alliances and compromises. The initial cracks widened irremediably, until Draghi was entrusted, as a technician, by the President of the Republic Sergio Mattarella to herald Italy into an era of stability through a technocratic government supported by a broad coalition including the Lega, the M5S, and the PD. FdI still clutched its role as bulwark of the opposition. This outwardly idyllic political situation, seeing Italy winning international credibility and seizing a considerable tranche of the much-desired Next Generation EU funds, was underpinned by precarious compromises between ideologically disparate political forces. This unstable equilibrium fell apart, when Draghi faced a confidence vote in Parliament and, despite winning it numerically, he lost the support of the parliamentary majority. Therefore, in the interest of moral integrity and of political stability, he tendered his resignations to Mattarella, who reluctantly accepted them on 21 July 2022.

Draghi's resignation kicked off an unusual summer electoral campaign, with a view to holding elections on 25 September 2022. The left suffered from splintering rivalries, with the major left-wing political party the PD losing a non-negligible chunk of its electorate, which moved to the so-called Third Pole made up of a rivalrous alliance between the former PD representatives Matteo Renzi (now leader of Italia Viva), and Carlo Calenda (now leader of Azione). The ideological coherence propping up the PD faltered, with the party struggling to form its new identity and to put forward credible and substantial proposals. The M5S saw the exit of its then-leader Luigi Di Maio, who founded Impegno Civico. The M5S tried to differentiate itself from the PD by insisting on the preservation of universal basic income, and the introduction of the minimum wage.

As this book is devoted to the study of right-wing parties, this postscript zooms onto them. Indeed, the right-wing panorama is not homogeneous, and its variegated composition did not bode well: the Lega, FI, and FdI joined forces on paper, forming the so-called centre-right coalition. Behind the officiality of this coalition created for strategic electoral purposes, these parties were treading separate paths. FI was shaken by factions during the electoral campaign, which resulted into some of FI's most powerful representatives, including FI's former Minister of Education Mariastella Gelmini and FI's former Ministry of Public Administration Renato Brunetta, transfer to the so-called Third Pole. Berlusconi tried to regain the political spotlight, which resulted into gross blunders, especially regarding a possible pro-Putin stance.

Salvini constructed his campaign as differentiated from Meloni's. Despite the underlying shared ideology made up of the three populist radical right pillars that run throughout the book (nativism, anti-system populism, and the call for a strong state), Salvini distinguished the Lega from Meloni's FdI on two counts: first, he unwaveringly supported the so-called PNRR (Piano Nazionale di Ripresa e Resilienza), translated in English as the National Recovery and Resilience Plan; second, his stance on the Russia-Ukraine war was fickle, given his strong personal ties with Russia's President Vladimir Putin. Salvini's flickering stance on this matter resulted into notorious and infamous blunders. On one instance, he flew to the Polish town of Przemyśl, on the border with Ukraine, and, while expressing the town mayor his support for Poland and the recognition of its tremendous efforts to host Ukrainian refugees, he was confronted by the mayor with a t-shirt carrying Putin's image, similar to t-shirts sported in the past by Salvini in his shows of friendship with Putin.

On the contrary, Meloni built her political campaign on her pledges of Atlanticism and support for Ukraine against the Russian invader. Her support for the PNRR, though, was more ambiguous, since she aimed at renegotiating its terms with the EU. These two main distinctive points setting Salvini's and Meloni's campaigns apart, demonstrate that the anti-system populist ideology they paraded during the time of the research for this book, then took on different forms. The anti-EU hostility became dormant in Salvini's electoral campaign, while it was tamed, but still not non-existent in Meloni's campaign, as evidenced by her attempt at reassuring the EU about FdI's respect for it, while putting up a sceptical stance about the allegedly unfair terms of the PNRR. As anti-system populism takes on myriad connotations, as explained in the book, the electoral campaign was testimony to it. Setting the EU aside, Salvini's unsteady stance towards Putin's invasion of Ukraine challenged the support for the US and Atlanticism, which, instead, emerged in the interviews conducted for this book. Meloni's staunch Atlanticism, on the contrary, confirmed the interviews results.

The Lega and FdI electoral campaigned are worthy of attention, since they embody the stylistic traits of the populist radical right as discussed in the book, such as a direct and emotional style. Anecdotes peppered Salvini's campaign, which was fought on the social media battleground, with teenagers hooked on Salvini's TikTok midnight live streaming sessions, and the older potential electorates seduced by Salvini's humorous Twitter posts ridiculing the PD by inviting them to relieve their caustic criticisms of the right wing by swallowing down a famous anti-acid medication. A direct appeal to the people as the righteous custodians of popular will was a leitmotif of both parties' electoral campaigns. Emotions differed. FdI's campaign comparatively steered further away from humour, and centred on the arousal of popular anger and on aggressiveness. FdI's communications manager, Tommaso Longobardi, orchestrated a strategic campaign on social media, trying to tailor messages to different social media platforms, such as Facebook, Twitter, and the youth social media channel TikTok. Meloni did not refrain from aggressive tones in addressing crowds at political rallies. She self-consciously joked about the fact that some media were remarking the swelling up of her neck veins as a sign of her aggressive discursive style (Corriere 2022). After stepping into her Prime Minister role, Meloni has considerably tamed her aggressive communication style.

Certainly, Meloni softened the most radical tones of FdI's ideology through an appeal to her ordinariness, and an ideological moderation. As pointed out in this book, one of the targets of populist appeal is the ordinary people. Meloni's self-representation as an underdog, fighting her way from a marginalised neighbourhood in Rome to Prime Minister, is in line with the conceptualisation of the people as the ordinary women and men struggling with their daily lives. Concerning ideology, Meloni adopted the "civic discourse" I analysed in the book. The civicness imbuing her discourse is evident, for instance, in her emphasis on national identity and conservative traits, which may be a cosmetic veneer concealing nativist and reactionary policies. Meloni has embarked on the complicated path of conjuring up an image of political and economic stability, and of sanitising her image at home and abroad. In the realm of fiscal policy, she blunted the edges of Salvini's overly ambitious proposal of a flat tax fixed at 15% for the self-employed and the employees, by proposing the increase of the self-employed income ceiling (to which the current 15% flat tax is applied) from €65,000 to €100,000, and by suggesting an incremental flat tax set at 15% and paid on incremental income. Meloni has also picked the EU for her first overseas visit, which is a powerful statement of her playing down the traditional FdI's Euroscepticism. The purification of FdI's image can occur only by taking distance from allegations of authoritarianism and neo-fascism. It is a case in point that Meloni relentlessly proclaimed FdI's pledge to liberty and democracy. In Meloni's maiden speech in Parliament, she denied any sympathy for anti-democratic regimes, fascism included; she denounced the 1938 racial laws as shameful, and vowed to combat racism and anti-Semitism.

This moderation trajectory confirms the populist radical right trend towards outward moderation identified in this book. However, FdI remains at the core a populist radical right party characterised by the ideological features outlined in this book. Meloni translated nationalism into nativism, and conservatism into a discriminatory and reactionary emphasis on religion and motherhood. On the nativist front, Meloni confirms the findings of this book: the championing of the nation above any partisan interest, as declared in her maiden speech in Parliament, transmutes into the championing of the so-called Western civilisation, grounded in the Judeo-Christian tradition, and allegedly based on the principles of liberty, equality, and democracy. Even if Meloni explicitly eschews racism, the identification of the West as the cradle of liberal democracy acts as a civic mantle to hide otherwise racist implications of such an identification of the immigrant Other as alien to democracy and other Western values. The repercussions on immigration policy are not hard to imagine: FdI proposes a naval blockade to prevent migrants from setting out on their Mediterranean crossing; in her maiden speech in Parliament, Meloni mentioned the government's mission to stop human trafficking in the Mediterranean, while not questioning the right of asylum for those fleeing war and persecution. This aligns with the differentiation of immigration constructed by the populist radical right and analysed in this book, which goes hand in hand with the criminalisation of irregular migrants.

On the gender issue, Meloni prides herself of being the first Italian female Prime Minister, who managed to break the glass ceiling of male-dominated politics. However, the ambiguity regarding gender underlined in the book resurfaces in the current government. First, Meloni did not hide her admiration for family policies enforced in Orban's Hungary, discriminating against the LGBTQ+ community, and offering tax benefits based on the number of children a family has. Second, the "prevention of abortion" inscribed in the centre-right coalition manifesto stirred up a storm of criticism. The ambiguous phrasing and the lack of specificity allowed the centre-right coalition to walk on a tightrope between adhering to conservative values giving women the opportunity to refuse abortion (which is anyway already enshrined in Italian law), and the moderate values keeping the right to abortion untouched. Second, on the prickly issue of abortion rights, Meloni's appointment of Eugenia Maria Roccella as Minister of Natality, Family, and Public Opportunities is a testimony to the possible drift towards radical threats to abortion and LGBTQ+ rights. While in the interviews used in this book the right to abortion was not touched upon, it fits well within the argument made herein concerning the ambiguous gender policies of the populist radical right, sceptical of the vaguely defined "gender theory," corresponding to awareness of LGBTQ+ rights, and bound to the dated view of women as intrinsically tied to motherhood. As Roccella publicly stated, a woman can realise her liberty only through motherhood. Another noteworthy point is that pro-liberty beliefs, such as the protection of the supposedly "traditional family" and of women's motherhood, are oddly conjoined with liberticide beliefs, such as the infringement on women's reproductive rights and on LGBTQ+ rights. This juxtaposition echoes the point made in this book about populist radical right's attitude to submit Italian women to traditional roles, while trying to project itself as the protectors of the liberty of Muslim women against allegedly oppressive Muslim men. Judging by the ministerial picks, the government is leaning towards a harsh rejection of the so-called "womb for rent," i.e., surrogacy, but, especially, of the right of adoption for civil partnerships, which in Italy lack legal equivalence to civil or religious marriage.

The topicality of this book is not limited to the treatment of the question of gender and of nativism in the current FdI ideology. The central argument articulated by the book is the reiteration of colonial discourse in the populist radical right, as well as the ghost of a selective colonial and fascist memory haunting these parties. In Meloni's speech to Parliament, the Prime Minister addressed the black activist and trade unionist Aboubakar Soumahoro using the Italian informal way, i.e., "tu." While this may have gone unnoticed to many, some more critical listeners have spotted the colonial echoes intrinsic to addressing the Other with the informal "tu." MP Soumahoro himself denounced, through a Twitter post, Meloni's reproduction of the colonial rhetoric inferiorising the Other by paternalistically addressing them in the informal way.

This regrettable episode aside, colonial traits have been dormant at the moment in this new government, but the fascist past is the terrain where the politics of memory battles have been fought. It is this terrain that is worth keeping an eye on. The swinging victory scored by FdI has inevitably conjured up images of the fascist past, given the genealogical connection between FdI and the post-fascist MSI. However, since the start of the latest political campaign, Meloni has acted as the moderate frontwoman of an otherwise not so moderate party. As mentioned above, in her maiden speech in Parliament, she very sternly dissipated doubts about possible fascist legacies. Time will tell whether this civic turn of FdI under Meloni's leadership is merely a strategic and cosmetic change to boost popularity in polls, bolster international credibility, and please the EU, which is due to disburse €21 billion as the second tranche of the PNRR. What is at stake is democracy, liberty for individuals regardless of their gender, race, and religion, as well as equality. The very values proclaimed by Meloni and, at the same time, already appearing under threat in the first days of the new government. To put Italy's standing on firm ground, the reckoning of the disastrous fascist and colonial past is needed to promote the above-mentioned values proclaimed by Meloni.

References

Corriere Redazione (2022) "Giorgia Meloni: «Io ci provo ad essere più pacata", *Corriere della Sera*. 30 August 2022. Available: https://www.youtube.com/watch?v=EZ4mEq3x6wY [10 November 2022].

Diamanti, G. (2018) "Il posizionamento di Fratelli d'Italia", *YouTrend*. Available: https://www.youtrend.it/2018/05/26/blog-il-posizionamento-di-fratelli-d-italia-giorgia-meloni/ [10 November 2022].

Greco, F. (2013) "Fratelli d'Italia, un trend in crescita", *YouTrend*. Available: ttps://www.youtrend.it/2013/07/10/fratelli-ditalia-trend-crescita/ [10 November 2022].

Tarchi, M. (2015) "Italy: The promised land of populism?", *Contemporary Italian Politics*, vol. 7, no. 3, pp. 273–285.

Primary Sources

Interviews round 1 (2016–2018)
Interview with A20180103D, 3 January 2018.
Interview with A20180103LC, 3 January 2018.
Interview with C20180109G, 9 January 2018.
Interview with C20170106V, 6 January 2017.
Interview with E20170404C, 4 April 2017.
Interview with E20180103G, 3 January 2018.
Interview with F20170110F, 10 January 2017.
Interview with F20180104F, 4 January 2018.
Interview with F20160905L, 5 September 2016.
Interview with F20170104M, 4 January 2017.
Interview with F20170111S, 11 January 2017.
Interview with F20170408T, 8 April 2017.
Interview with G20170405C, 5 April 2017.
Interview with G20170411C, 11 April 2017.
Interview with G20180109C, 9 January 2018.
Interview with G20170109D, 9 January 2017.
Interview with G20170112G, 12 January 2017.
Interview with G20180105M, 5 January 2018.
Interview with G20170407P, 7 April 2017.
Interview with G20170111R, 11 January 2017.
Interview with G20180110S, 10 January 2018.
Interview with G20170407SR, 7 April 2017.
Interview with L20170406C, 6 April 2017.
Interview with L20170104N, 4 January 2017.
Interview with L20170410P, 10 April 2017.
Interview with L20180105S, 5 January 2018.
Interview with M20170404F, 4 January 2017.
Interview with M20170104G, 4 January 2017.
Interview with M20180105M, 5 January 2018.
Interview with M20170113R, 13 January 2017.
Interview with N20180108C, 8 January 2018.
Interview with P20161219B, 19 December 2016.
Interview with R20180108D, 8 January 2018.
Interview with R20180104M, 4 January 2018.
Interview with R20180110PM, 10 January 2018.

Interview with S20180103F, 3 January 2018.
Interview with S20180108S, 8 January 2018.
Interviews round 2 (2021)
Interview with B20210517M, 17 May 2021.
Interview with C20210603C, 3 June 2021.
Interview with D20210329S, 29 March 2021.
Interview with E20210504P, 4 May 2021.
Interview with P20210422B, 22 April 2021.
Interview with P20210409M, 9 April 2021.
Interview with R20210426S, 26 April 2021.
Interview with T20210405S, 5 April 2021.
Interview with W20210422G, 22 April 2021.
Manifestos
FdI 2013, Manifesto.
FdI 2018, Manifesto.
Lega 2013, Manifesto.
Lega 2018, Manifesto.

Appendix 1 Rationale for Interview Questions

Two rounds of interviews were conducted. The interview questions were grounded in the theoretical and empirical literature on the populist radical right,[1] on racism, on colonialism, and on fascism. The choice of including questions on fascism is motivated by the fact that Italian colonialism prospered under fascism, and it was under fascism that Italian colonialism became markedly racist against the colonial Other. Academic literature has been complemented by relevant contemporary news concerning current affairs. Using contemporary news as interview prompts has the two-fold advantage of offering the interviewees up-to-date points for reflection resonating with their experience and knowledge, and of allowing the researcher to glean the desired insights based on the research aim that drives the investigation unfolding in this book. Interview questions were also tailored to the historical juncture in which they took place: in the 2016–2018 round, interviews were centred more conspicuously on the so-called immigration crisis, on colonial echoes and the spectre of racism surfacing in the discourse of the parties studied, and on the sporadic discussions over their relationship with fascism; in the 2021 round, interviews shifted focus from the so-called immigration crisis, to the COVID-19 pandemic, which had a terrible impact on Italian politics, economy, and society.

Given their semi-structured nature, the interviews are composed of essential questions, optional questions, and follow-up questions. The benefit afforded by semi-structured interview is, indeed, to have the liberty to deviate from a rigid script, and to follow interesting leads emerging from the conversation through additional questions beyond the script. Therefore, questions that are not foreseen and included in the list of essential, optional, and follow up questions are not only allowed, but also yield valuable material.

Essential questions were asked to all interviewees, except for a few cases where the interviewees were restless and uncomfortable with the topic, or had very little time available for the interview. The order of the questions was flexible, in order to adapt the sequence of the interview questions to the flow of the conversation. In general, a tripartite structure was maintained: the interview was opened with a discussion of contemporary matters, to get the respondent engaged and interested in the interview, before delving into the matters of nationalism and racism, which might have sounded to the interviewees as more abstract and distant. Finally, views on Italy's colonial past, and, incidentally, fascist past were elicited. Interviews were conducted in Italian and the wording of the questions was adapted to each interviewee, to ensure their understanding of the question.

What follows is a non-prescriptive list of possible interview questions, supported by the rationale underpinning their formulation. The interview usually started with an introductory question about the history of the interviewee within the party, which is a useful prompt to gain a broader picture about the timing of political affiliation to the party, and about the political career of the interviewee. Socio-demographic attributes, such as the interviewee's age, level of education, and occupation were asked in follow-up questions, emerged spontaneously, or were gathered from online resources if time was tight. Then, the interview tackled theoretical questions, including the interviewee's classification of the party they belonged to, and the topic of nationalism. The latter is one of the two ideological pillars of nativism, along with racism. Potential follow-up questions asked the interviewee to further elaborate on the geographical extension of the notion of the *patria*, to test if the interviewees, principally from the Lega, agreed with the party's traditional conceptualisation of the nation as corresponding to local entities, or with Salvini's nationalisation of the party, whereby the nation corresponds to Italy as a whole. Another question related to nationalism probed not only the interviewees' view of the meaning of the *patria*, but also their opinion about who belongs to the *patria*. Following possible questions dealt with the notion of multiculturalism, and of decline, which serves as a justification for the populist radical right's claim to save the people and the nation. In the follow-up questions, interviewees had the opportunity to fully elaborate on the alleged Italian decline, talking about their opinion on the Italian state and the elites, especially the EU. Therefore, they revealed various aspects of the call for the strong state and populism, which are the two elements, together with nativism, that make up the ideology of the Italian populist radical right.

The second section delved in-depth into sentiments towards immigration. It included different aspects of attitudes towards immigration, and it captured the nuances inherent to the populist radical right's discourse. In particular, this section aimed at highlighting the entanglement of civic discourse with otherwise racist statements carrying colonial echoes. A typical question asked was about whether immigration in Italy is out of control or not. This question was specifically based on the largely dominant "emergential" view of immigration identified in the Italian populist radical right (Castelli Gattinara 2017). Then, interviewees might be asked to ponder whether immigration might be beneficial to Italy as a receiving country, in order to allow them to consider immigration under a positive light. Following questions assessed whether the interviewees held a different or similar conception of economic migrants and refugees, which is another centrepiece of the Italian populist radical right's ideology, whereby refugees are welcomed, but asylum seekers are considered undeserving economic migrants until their refugee status is eventually approved. This question in particular allowed the interviewees to articulate their humanitarian concerns towards immigrants. This question was underpinned, specifically, by Albahari's 2015 argument about the oxymoronic juxtaposition of racist claims with humanitarian concerns for the plight of immigrants. In the 2021 round of interviews, the current pandemic circumstances called for a focus on the role of immigration during the COVID-19 pandemic, on the salience of the issue of immigration during the pandemic, and on the relationship between the government's approach to immigration and its approach to the management of the COVID-19 pandemic.

The effects of immigration were later analysed by asking broad questions about the implications of immigration on society and the economy. Follow-up questions went more in depth into the social and economic consequences immigration has according to the Italian populist radical right, i.e., immigration allegedly poses a social and economic threat. The interviewees were free to dispute this view. Afterwards, the interview moved the focus onto the Italian populist radical right's claim that immigrants increase criminality and Muslim immigrants bring terrorism. In follow-up questions interviewees were asked to give their judgement on the contemporary debates on legitimate defence, and on mosques, which are a subject of heated debate in the Lega and FdI. Following questions revolved around the compatibility between Muslim immigrants' traditions and Italian ones. Interviewees had then the chance to elaborate on the topic. Final questions within the second section explored the Italian populist radical right's belief that there is a connection between immigration and illnesses, as claimed several times by these parties, particularly during pandemic times.

The third section examined the Italian populist radical right's colonial and fascist memory. The essential question asked interviewees to express their judgment on Italian colonialism. Follow-up questions used some prompts, such as Fini's claim that former Italian colonies fared better under the fascist colonial empire (Casadio 2006), Mussolini's statement that the African race would have replaced the white one (cited in Ben-Ghiat 2006: 384), and examples of fascist colonial beliefs and policies, such as the fascist colonial conviction that Africans were inferior to Italians (De Grand 2004) and the separation of the colonised children in schools (Rodogno 2006), to investigate the interviewees' opinion on colonialism. Postcolonial melancholia was examined through follow-up questions in the case the interviewee expressed positive views of colonialism. Further questions probed into the interviewees' view on the apologies to former colonies, on diplomatic aid to the latter, and on Berlusconi-Qaddafi's 2008 Friendship Treaty. Follow-up questions revolved around views on the atrocities committed against the colonised, on the friendly relations between Italy and dictators governing the former colonies, and on *Mare Nostrum*. This term could conjure up images of the Roman and fascist colonial past, or the search and rescue operation in the Mediterranean guided by Italy between 2013 and 2014. Final reflections were prompted on whether Italian colonialism has been forgotten, and on possible causes of colonial forgetting. These include the myth of *Italiani brava gente*, the demonising equation of colonialism with fascism, and the inferiority complex affecting Italy, seen as Europe's internal Other, treated with superiority and paternalism within Europe, despite its belonging to Europe.

Since it is difficult to extricate the complex bundle of colonialism and fascism in relation to discussions over race, it is clear that questions concerning colonial memory inevitably triggered thoughts of the fascist past. The final interview question touched upon a thorny issue, and was asked only if interviewees did not express discomfort with the topic of the fascist past resurfacing in questions over the colonial past. Interviewees were asked to give a mark to fascism from one (the best system possible at the time) to five (a completely brutal regime), drawing on Ignazi's (2005) survey conducted at an AN congress. Interviewees, subsequently, had the chance to elaborate on both the positive and negative aspects of fascism freely and fully.

Note

1 For an in-depth literature review, see Chapters 1 and 2. In this Appendix explaining the interview rationale, the academic sources used are referenced only if they provide the basis for specific interview questions.

Index

abortion rights 163
Afewerki, Isaias 118
Africa 77–78, 82–83
Akkerman, T. 99
Albahari, M. 55, 58
Albania, and migration to Italy 10, 53, 78–79
Albertazzi, D. 14, 127
Alfano, Angelino 80
"Alfano bonus" 80
Algerian War 114
Allam, Magdi 85
Alleanza Nazionale (AN) 2, 13–15, 18, 51, 110, 133, 145
Almirante, Giorgio 136
Andall, J. 16, 18, 116, 135
animal/beast metaphors 90
anti-elite populism 51–53, 62, 77, 95, 144; *see also* elites
anti-EU sentiments 12, 25, 53, 112–113, 144, 161
anti-immigrant sentiments 2, 136–137, 141, 168; and crime 78–80; mainstream nature of 99–100; and the media 3, 28; and nationalism 47; and nostalgic narratives 17
anti-racist protests 116–117, 141
Antonsich, M. 40, 46
asylum seekers 58, 60–61, 80, 168
Austria 4, 50, 67, 150
authoritarian countries 77, 118
authoritarianism 12, 156n1, 162

Bachelet, Michelle 96–97
Balibar, E. 97
Barré, Said 117
Bergman, E. 87
Berlusconi, Silvio 14–15, 50–51, 119–120, 127, 135, 161

Berti, C. 35, 90
Black Lives Matter 116–117
Bossi, Umberto 76
Bossi-Fini Law (2002) 80–81
Britain 4, 17–18, 88, 93, 108–109, 111, 132
British Empire 17, 111
Brunetta, Renato 161

Calenda, Carlo 160
Calhoun, C. 55
Canovan, M. 52
Caramani, D. 126, 132
Caravita, S. 30
Carvalho, J. 14–15
Cassata, F. 152
Castellani, T. 30
Castelli Gattinara, P. 55
Cavalieri, A. 11, 35
Cecile 100
center-right parties 127
Centri di Identificazione ed Espulsione (CIE) 58
Chambers, I. 16, 135
Chilton, P. A. 69
churches 84, 92
citizenship 46–47, 48n3, 63, 95, 141, 148
civic nationalism 24–25, 56; *see also* nationalism
clash of civilisations argument 86
coalition governments 14–15, 18–19, 50, 160–161; 2001–2006 Berlusconi-led 80–81; 2008–2011 Berlusconi-led 80; 2018 election 69; Lega-M5S 69, 96–97, 99, 129, 135, 149; and mainstreaming 50; and radicalisation 50–51, 99
colonial memory 2, 5, 16–17, 36, 107, 109–111, 113–121, 126, 132–135,

141, 153–156, 164, 169–170; *see also* postcolonial melancholia
colonial rhetoric 106, 108, 116, 143, 152, 164
colonialism 100n5, 106; British 17–18, 108–109; and criminalisation 76; and the education system 3, 134; and fascism 4–5, 26–27, 107, 126, 132–133, 136, 146, 155; French 108–109; and gender 81–82; and immigration 15–16, 89, 107–109, 114; and inferiorisation 130; Italian 18, 109, 142; and the Italian populist radical right 2, 15–18, 107, 136, 152; and nativism 4; neo-colonialism 108; and *othering* 26–27, 64, 95, 98, 128, 142–143, 145, 152; and reproduction rates 78; Said on 51, 61, 64; studies of 61, 75, 107, 116; and violence 27, 113–115, 154
concentration camps 113–114
Conelli, C. 152
The Conquest of America (Todorov) 61
Conte I government 58, 160
Conte II government 55–56, 156n1, 160
co-optation 14–15
Corcione, Domenico 115
Cordero, G. 66–67
Corriere della Sera 29
Couperus, S. 107, 110
COVID-19 pandemic 55, 59, 64, 80, 96, 169
crimes 76, 78–80, 99
crimes of peace 55
Critical Discourse Analysis (CDA) 4, 35, 37, 41, 60, 68–69, 94, 147
Cronache di Ordinario Razzismo 29
cultural assimilation 28, 46, 68
cultural backlashes 65
cultural differences 64
"cultural hybridisation" 44
culture 40–41, 98

D'Alema, Massimo 115
Dal Lago, A. 78–79
damnatio memoriae 132, 134, 137
De Cesari, C. 16, 119–120, 135
De Donno, F. 15
De Gasperi, Alcide 112
De Medici, Giuliana 136–137
death penalty 12
Del Boca, A. 138
Democrazia Cristiana (DC) 14, 19n1, 112
Di Maio, Luigi 99, 160
Dickie, J. 25

dictatorships 118, 120
diplomatic indifference 117–120
Draghi, Mario 160
Duncan, D. 16, 18, 116, 135
Dutch Pim Fortuyn List (LPF) 57, 93

Eatwell, R. 87
economic competition 66–67, 70
economic crises 3–4, 64, 66–67, 111, 150
economic migrants 57–58, 60–62, 70, 150
educational system 3, 29–30, 44, 99, 134, 149
elites 12, 47, 51, 53, 144; *see also* anti-elite populism
Erdogan, Recep Tayyip 87
Eritrea 1, 16, 60, 109, 113, 117, 154
Eritrean immigrants 16, 60, 108
Ethiopia 16, 109–110, 113, 115–117, 141, 154
ethnic competition theory 4, 150
ethnic conflicts 66
ethno-cultural nationalism 24–25, 39–40, 42, 45–48, 97–98, 144–145, 147–148, 153; *see also* nationalism
"Eurabianist" conspirationist arguments 13, 87, 151
European Union (EU) 53, 112–113, 144, 162; sentiments against 12, 25, 53, 112–113, 144, 161
Evola, J. 128

Fallaci, Oriana 85–87, 94
fallacy of sameness/difference 69, 89
Faloppa, F. 50
Fanon, F. 61, 89, 152
fascism 170; and center-right parties 127; and colonialism 4–5, 26–27, 107, 126, 132–133, 136, 146, 155; criminalisation of 128–129; and fear of invasion 77–78; and the Italian populist radical right 2, 127–132, 131–132, 145; and Italy's national identity 26, 31; and multiculturalism 130; and nativism 4; and racism 126, 128, 146; studies of 116, 126
fascist memory 2, 5, 36, 126, 128–134, 136–137, 143, 154–156, 164, 169–170
Fassin, D. 58
Fella, S. 35
femonationalism 91
Fiano, Emanuele 129, 137
Fidanza, Carlo 127
Figo, Bello 91, 100
Fini, Gianfranco 110

First World War 27
Floyd, George 116, 141–142
Fogu, C. 16
Fontana, Attilio 127
Fontana, Lorenzo 129
Foot, J. 133
forgetting 106–107
Forza Italia (FI) 3, 14, 18–19, 51, 99, 127, 161
France 50, 57, 91, 108–109, 114, 132
Fratelli d'Italia (FdI) 1, 48, 87, 132, 144–145, 147, 149, 159–162, 164; on citizenship 47; civic elements of 69; in coalition governments 18–19, 161; on colonialism 107–111, 113–114, 133; and diplomatic indifference 117–120; and ethno-cultural nationalism 24, 45–47; on the EU 77; and fascism 127–131, 155; founding of 2–3, 13–14, 18, 110; on immigrants 95; on immigration 12, 54–55, 62, 108; and the Law of Legitimate Defence 81; manifestos of 37; on multiculturalism 43–45; and national identity 40; and the *patria* 41, 43; on refugees 57, 60; slogans of 39, 47, 63; on terrorism 77; on veils 91
Freedom Party of Austria (FPO) 50
Froio, C. 11, 35
Front National (FN, France) 57, 71n5

Gaddafi, Muammar 118–120, 135
Galeazzo, P. 16, 135, 152
Galli della Loggia, Ernesto 86, 116
Gandesha, S. 94
Gelmini, Mariastella 161
gender 81–82, 93, 163; *see also* women
Gentiloni, Paolo 119
Germany 17
Gilroy, P. 4, 17–18, 111
Giuliani, G. 2, 76, 91, 152, 155
Gomez-Reino Cachafeiro, M. 24, 39
Goodwin, M. 87
governments, populist radical right criticisms of 51–52, 144
Griffini, M. 121
group conflict theory 66
Guibernau, M. 67

Halikiopoulou, D. 56–57
Hall, S. 26, 28, 30, 97
human rights 92–93
human trafficking 88, 90
humanitarianism 56, 58, 69–70, 88, 152–153, 168–169

Huntington, S. P. 86
hypersexualisation 78, 80, 82, 152
hypervisualisation 76, 99–100

identity 40; *see also* national identity
Ignazi, P. 170
immigrants 16; associated with illness 75, 95–96, 99, 143, 152, 169; and belonging 45–47; criminalisation of 45, 75–89, 99, 143; fertility rates of 78, 87; Lega on 76, 89–90; *othering* of 13, 16, 28, 42, 56, 61–62, 65, 69–70, 94, 98, 135–136, 142, 146, 150–151; as out-group 26, 39, 153; perceptions of 45, 94; regular 40, 46, 48, 59, 61, 63–64, 148; resentment of 62; and terrorism 83; wages of 68; *see also* Islamophobia; *specific immigrant types*
immigration 168–169; abjectification of 94–96, 152; from Albania 10, 53, 78–79; blamed on the EU 53, 77, 112–113, 144; and colonialism 15–16, 89, 107–109, 114, 116; criminalisation of 54, 75–89, 130, 143, 151; as economic threat 63, 65–67, 70; in the educational system 149; and elites 12; ethno-cultural aspects of 42; framed as an emergency 55, 77, 149, 168; high levels of 65–66; as human trafficking 88, 90; inferiorisation of 89–94, 128, 143, 151–152; and the Italian populist radical right 13, 53, 97–98, 109–110, 153; lack of school study of 30; politicisation of 2; populist arguments against 4; problematisation of 51–57, 70, 77, 143, 149; socio-demographic arguments against 63–66; stereotypes of 28; and support for the populist radical right 65–66; and terrorism 76–77, 83, 88; threatening the national identity 62; trans-Mediterranean 4
immigration policy 14–15, 51, 53–54, 80–81, 149, 159–160, 163
immigration-related laws 77, 80
"I'm not racist, but" expression 50
individual security 81
Inglehart, R. 65
in-groups 4, 16–18, 25, 37, 39, 52, 63, 69, 76, 89, 113–114
International Labour Organisation 67–68
international politics 27–28
inter-racial marriages 95
interviews 36–37, 106, 126, 132, 146–147, 167–170

Index

invasion metaphors 77–78, 84, 147, 151
irregular immigrants 40, 148; and the 2009 Security Package 81; as criminals 78, 80, 163; economic migrants as 60–61; exclusion of 46, 48, 70; Lega/FdI definitions of 59; statistics about 80
Islam 29, 51, 83–84, 86, 91
Islamophobia 13, 29, 83–87, 90–91, 151; *see also* mosques; Muslim immigrants
Italian colonies, immigration from 108
Italian Constitution 43
Italian radical right 12, 19, 39, 47, 57–61, 63; *see also* populist radical right
Italiani brava gente 107, 133–134, 137–138, 155
Italians First policy 39, 47, 58, 63, 150–151
Italo-Libyan Commission 118–119
Italy 159–160; and belonging 45–47; changing electoral systems/voting patterns of 3, 14, 18, 145; decolonisation of 18, 109, 111, 121, 137, 146; "defascistisation" of 133; immigrant populations in 10, 16, 45, 108; inferiority complex of 132, 134, 137, 144; legal system of 77, 80; north-south divide 25–26, 31, 40, 131, 146; regionalism in 39; *see also* national identity

Jetten, J. 4, 16, 18, 109–111
jus sanguinis 46, 48, 141
jus scholae 46–47
jus soli 46–47, 141, 148

King, R. 67
Knigge, P. 65
Kristeva, J. 94

La Padania 85
La rabbia e l'orgoglio (Fallaci) 85
la Repubblica 1
Labanca, N. 16, 116, 135
labour standards 63
"law and order" platform 6, 76–77, 79, 87, 144; *see also* "strong state" calls
Law of Legitimate Defence 81, 144
Le Pen, Marine 50
Lega 87, 144–145, 159; on the 2008 Berlusconi-Gaddafi Friendship Treaty 120; and the 2018 election 69, 159–160; on citizenship 47; civic elements of 24, 69, 99; in coalition goverments 12, 14–15, 18–19, 50–51, 58, 69, 96–97, 99, 129, 135, 149, 161; on colonialism 107–110, 112–114, 133; and diplomatic indifference 117–120; and ethno-cultural nationalism 45–48, 144; on the EU 53; and fascism 127, 129–132, 155; and Forza Italia (FI) 14; on immigrants 76, 89–90, 95; on immigration 54, 62, 108; immigration policies of 12; and in-groups 39; on Islam 51; language use of 82, 109; and the Law of Legitimate Defence 81; manifestos of 37; on multiculturalism 43–45; and national identity 40; origins of 2–3, 14, 18, 39, 127–128; and the *patria* 41, 43; and racism 99; on refugees 57, 63; and *Tangentopoli* 14, 18, 19n1; on terrorism 76–77, 83, 85; on the UN 96
legitimation through authorisation 54–55, 60–61, 80, 84, 96
Lentin, A. 62
Leone, G. 18, 113
Lewis, Bernard 86
LGBTQ+ rights 93, 163
Libya 118–120
Lobby nera 127
Lombardi-Diop, C. 18, 112
Lombardy 44, 76
Longobardi, Tommaso 162
Lucano, Mimmo 58

Macron, Emmanuel 114
mainstream political parties 3, 12, 14, 28, 50, 80–81, 99–100, 127, 146, 155–156
Mancino Law (1993) 128–129, 137, 155
manifestos 147
Manucci, L. 126, 132
Mare Jonio 52
Mason, J. 36
Masslo, Jerry 10, 53
Mastrovito, T. 18, 113
Matard-Bonucci, M. 152
Mattarella, Sergio 15, 160
media 3, 28–29, 99
Mediterranea 52
Mediterranean Sea 1, 156; as *Mare Aliorum* 16; as *Mare Nostrum* 5, 16, 61, 97–98, 112–113, 136, 141, 152, 156, 169; as "Mare Vostrum" 5, 61, 98, 136, 141, 152–153, 156; and national identity 107
Meloni, Giorgia 1–2, 19, 47, 127, 159, 161–164

memory 106–107, 121, 145, 154–155; *see also* colonial memory; fascist memory; selective memory
Minniti, Marco 55
Mitscherlich, Alexander 17
Mitscherlich, Margarete 17
Mock, S. 56–57
Modood, T. 27, 108
Moffitt, B. 56
Mols, F. 4, 16, 18, 109–111
Montanelli, Indro 116–117, 141–142
Moscovici, Pierre 96–97
mosques 84–85, 87–88, 92, 151
mourning 17
Movimento Cinque Stelle (M5S) 3, 52; in coalition governments 12, 14, 50, 58, 69, 96–97, 99, 129, 135, 159–160; immigration policies of 12; language use of 82; populist radical right criticisms of 52, 144
Movimento Sociale Italiano (MSI) 14, 98, 127–128, 145, 149, 160
Mudde, C. 65, 143, 156n1
multiculturalism 27–28, 43–44, 79, 130, 149
Muslim immigrants 13, 64, 82–84, 86–88, 90–94, 151–152, 169; *see also* Islamophobia
Muslims 29, 90–92, 130, 151, 163
Mussolini, Benito 78, 95, 127, 130–131, 135
Mutz, D. C. 67

national identity 25–27, 30, 40, 44, 62, 95, 97–98, 144, 146, 148
nationalism 5, 23–25, 30–31, 41, 47, 116, 147–148, 168; *see also* civic nationalism; ethno-cultural nationalism
nations 23–24, 40
nativism 2–6, 16, 29–30, 144, 168; and the Italian populist radical right 2, 13, 26, 143–144, 146; and mainstream political parties 3, 146; and nationalism 5, 23–24, 98; and racism 23, 97
Nencini, Riccardo 86
neo-colonial sexism 92
neo-colonialism 108
neo-fascism 19, 137, 145, 162
neo-fascist right 11
neoliberalism 62
Norris, P. 65
nostalgic narratives 16–18, 109
Nouvelle Droite 61–62, 98, 128

Ogorchukwu, Alika 97
"online partisan crowds" 28
Operation *Mare Nostrum* 1
"ordinary people" 52, 144, 162
Orientalism (Said) 61
Osakue, Daisy 97
othering 61, 97; abjectification as 75, 94–95; and colonialism 26–27, 64, 95, 98, 128, 142–143, 145, 152; criminalisation as 75; and "domestication" 83; of immigrants 13, 16, 28, 42, 56, 61–62, 65, 69–70, 77, 94, 98, 135–136, 142, 146, 150–151; inferiorisation as 75, 89; internal 26–27; of Muslims 29; by the populist radical right 37, 98; and race 82, 148; vocabulary of 68–69; women 94

Padania 38, 127, 131, 148
Partito Comunista Italiano (PCI) 14, 112
Partito Democratico (PD) 3, 52, 55, 81, 99, 129, 160
Partito Nazionale Monarchico (PNM) 112
Partito Repubblicano Italiano (PRI) 19n1
Partito Socialista Democratico Italiano (PSDI) 19n1
Partito Socialista Italiano (PSI) 14, 19n1
Party for Freedom (PVV) 57
party manifestos 36–37
patria 40–41, 43, 45–47, 168
Pelinka, A. 68
Perrineau, P. 66
Perrino, S. 36
Pinkus, K. 18, 112, 133
political correctness 52
politics, distrust of 65
politics of memory 6, 135–136, 143, 160, 164; *see also* colonial memory; fascist memory; selective memory
Ponzanesi, S. 16, 116, 135
populism 11–12, 41, 65, 68, 144, 159
populist political parties 35, 42, 82, 147
populist radical right 5, 19, 145, 161; and civic nationalism 24; "civic turn" of 13, 56–57, 68–69, 79, 81, 88, 90, 93–94, 98–99, 152–153; on colonialism 133; defining 11; and ethno-cultural nationalism 25; fears about immigration 97–98; ideologies of 36–37, 155, 168; intergenerational support for 65; language use of 42, 82, 109, 147; mainstreaming of 50, 56–57, 93, 99; moderation of 5–6, 36–37, 40, 46, 48,

50–51, 56–57, 68, 78, 88, 99, 155–156, 162; and neoliberalism 62; nostalgic narratives of 16–17, 109; *othering* by 37, 56; and racism 28, 50, 57–58, 149–150; radicalisation of 127; studies of 143–156; and unemployment 66
Portugal 3, 67, 150
postcolonial melancholia 4, 17, 109, 111–113, 156, 169; *see also* colonial memory
postcolonialism 16, 100n5, 120–121, 142, 145
poverty 65
power dynamics 37
Proglio, G. 107
Putin, Vladimir 161

qualitative studies 35–36

racism 26, 30, 99, 148–150, 168; and colonial memory 5, 17, 116, 142; denials of 60; and the educational system 3, 99; and fascism 126, 128, 146; and fascist memory 5; growth of 96–97; "I'm not racist, but" expression 50; and the Italian populist radical right 2, 50, 69, 94, 128, 136; legitimation of 66; and mainstream political parties 28, 99; and the media 3; and the MSI 98; and national identity 44; and nationalism 25; and nativism 23, 97; and security 79; as taboo question 26, 50; and violence 97, 129
racist stereotypes 3, 29–30
Rackete, Carola 59
Ramirez, A. 92
realistic group conflict theory 66–67
reconciliation 17–18
refugees 57–61, 63, 69–70, 150, 168
Renzi, Matteo 160
Riace 58, 99
Roccella, Eugenia Maria 163
Roma 13, 29
Romano, Sergio 85–86
Rooduijn, M. 99
Russia-Ukraine war 161
Rutelli, Francesco 86
Ruzza, C. 35

Said, E. 61, 64, 89–90, 152
Salvini, Matteo 2, 35, 39, 52, 58–59, 69, 81, 90–91, 96, 99–100, 107, 127, 129, 135, 159, 161–162

Sarkozy, Nicholas 50, 114
al-Sarraj, Fayez 119
Sartori, Giovanni 29, 86
Scalfaro, Oscar Luigi 115
Scelba Law (1952) 128–129, 137, 155
Schäfer, A. 65
Schubel, T. 52
Sea-Watch 3 case 35, 59, 90
Second World War 18, 111, 131–132, 134, 137
selective memory 2, 6, 106–110, 120–121, 128–129, 132–134, 136, 143, 153–154; *see also* colonial memory; fascist memory
Serracchiani, Debora 76
Siddi, M. 107, 121
slave metaphors 90, 147
social media 29, 162; *see also* Twitter
Somalia 111, 117
Soumahoro, Aboubakar 164
Spain 3, 67, 150
Spivak, G. C. 92, 152
Srivastava, N. 15
statues 116–117, 133, 141–142
strategic compassion 58
"strong state" calls 11–12, 19, 29, 76, 80, 143–144, 156n1; *see also* "law and order" platform
Swiss People's Party (SVP) 50, 57, 87–88, 93, 150
Switzerland 4, 50, 67, 87–88, 93

Tangentopoli corruption scandal 14, 18, 19n1, 144–145; *see also* corruption
terrorism 76–77, 83–85, 88
Third Pole 160–161
3 October 2013 shipwreck 1, 112
Todorov, T. 61, 152
Tortola, P. D. 107, 110
"traditional families" 93–94
Tranfaglia, Nicola 134
Traverso, E. 2, 127
Triulzi, A. 18, 112
Tunisian immigrants 16
Twitter 28–29; *see also* social media
2001–2006 Berlusconi-led coalition government 80–81
2008–2011 Berlusconi-led coalition government 80
2008 recession 4, 67, 150
2008 Treaty on Friendship, Partnership, and Cooperation 119–120, 135, 151, 169
2009 Security Package 80–81

2017 Memorandum of Understanding 119
2017 Minniti-Orlando Decree against
  NGOs 149
2018 election 69, 81, 129, 149,
  159–160
2020 Zan Law Proposal 93

An Uncomfortable Past (Tranfaglia) 134
unemployment 66
United Kingdom 4, 17–18, 88, 93,
  108–109, 111, 132
United Nations 96
United States 116–117

Valente, A. 30
Vampa, D. 14
Van Dijk, T. A. 57–58
Vasilopoulou, S. 56–57
Vatican 93

veils 91
violence 27, 97, 113–115, 129, 154
Vlora incident 10, 53

war crimes 17–18, 113–114
War on Terror 86, 151
Werbner, P. 27, 108
White replacement theories 13, 83, 87,
  130–131, 151, 169
Wodak, R. 37, 69
women 82, 90–92, 94, 163; *see also*
  gender
The Wretched of the Earth (Fanon) 61

Ye'or, Bat 87, 151

Zan, Alessandro 93
Zaslove, A. 66
Ziller, C. 52

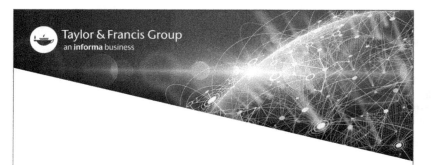

Printed in the USA
CPSIA information can be obtained
at www.ICGtesting.com
LVHW012011160324
774517LV00004B/625